LANGUAGE AND LITERACY SERIES
Dorothy S. Strickland and Celia Genishi
SERIES EDITORS

The Complete Theory-to-Practice Handbook of Adult Literacy:
Curriculum Design and Teaching Approaches
*Rena Soifer, Martha E. Irwin, Barbara M. Crumrine,
Emo Honzaki, Blair K. Simmons, and Deborah L. Young*

Literacy for a Diverse Society:
Perspectives, Practices, and Policies
Elfrieda H. Hiebert, Editor

The Child's Developing Sense of Theme:
Responses to Literature
Susan S. Lehr

The Triumph of Literature / The Fate of Literacy:
English in the Secondary School Curriculum
John Willinsky

The Child as Critic: Teaching Literature in
Elementary and Middle Schools, THIRD EDITION
Glenna Davis Sloan

Process Reading and Writing: A Literature-Based Approach
*Joan T. Feeley, Dorothy S. Strickland,
and Shelley B. Wepner, Editors*

Inside/Outside: Teacher Research and Knowledge
Marilyn Cochran-Smith and Susan L. Lytle

Literacy Events in a Community of Young Writers
Yetta M. Goodman and Sandra Wilde

The Politics of Workplace Literacy: A Case Study
Sheryl Greenwood Gowen

Whole Language Plus: Essays on Literacy
in the United States and New Zealand
Courtney B. Cazden

Whole Language *Plus*

◆◆◆◆◆◆◆◆◆◆◆◆◆

Essays on Literacy in the United States and New Zealand

Courtney B. Cazden
with
Patricia Cordeiro
Mary Ellen Giacobbe
Marie M. Clay
Dell Hymes

 Teachers College
Columbia University
New York and London

Published by Teachers College Press, 1234 Amsterdam Avenue
New York, NY 10027

Library of Congress Cataloging-in-Publication Data

Cazden, Courtney B.
     Whole language plus : essays on literacy in the United States and
New Zealand / Courtney B. Cazden with Patricia Cordeiro . . . [et
al.].
     p.   cm.—(Language and literacy series)
     Includes bibliographical references and index.
     ISBN 0-8077-3210-9 (alk. paper). — ISBN 0-8077-3209-5 (pbk:
alk. paper)
     1. Literacy—United States.   2. Literacy—New Zealand.   I. Title.
II. Series: Language and literacy series (New York, N.Y.)
LC151.C39   1992
302.2'244'0973—dc 20   92-17657

ISBN 0-8077-3210-9
ISBN 0-8077-3209-5 (pbk.)

Printed on acid-free paper

Manufactured in the United States of America

99 98 97 96 95 94 93 92   8 7 6 5 4 3 2 1

This book is dedicated to two special New Zealand teachers:
Marie Clay, professor emeritus at
the University of Auckland, and
James Laughton, principal of Richmond Road Primary
School, Auckland until his death in 1988.

Contents

Introduction

This book is a collection of essays on language learning in contexts where cultures are in contact and sometimes conflict, and literacies are also.

It is made up of chapters that were written at different times during the past 20 years. Connected here, they contribute to a single argument about literacy education: that immersion in rich literacy environments is necessary but not sufficient. The title of the book, *Whole Language Plus*, is a caption for that argument.

The argument has two themes. The first is that as people of any age learn to read and write, they need help in focusing attention on specific features of written language; they need deliberate, well-planned help in attending to parts as well as wholes. That part of the argument is previewed in Part I and discussed in detail through the chapters in Part II.

"But," some whole language teachers will say, "we do mini-lessons already, just as you suggest." For such teachers, I hope this book will support their work and perhaps suggest some new ideas to try. For others—both teachers and those who write and speak about literacy education—I hope it will stimulate more thinking about, and more visible and vocal attention to, such mini-lessons—or "instructional detours" as one metaphor calls them.

The second theme is that there are many ways to read and write, many literacies, in different cultural contexts, for different purposes, with varying degrees of social power. In our complex society, literacy learning doesn't stop with basic skills in school. People of all ages encounter new literacy demands that may conflict with more familiar ways of using language. In these situations, documented in the chapters in Part III, people need help in understanding texts in contexts: how literacies fit into today's social world. In other words, *Whole Language Plus* argues that readers and writers need sometimes to analyse text wholes down into parts or out into contexts.

Part IV is about literacy education in New Zealand. During the past 10 years, I've made seven trips there. The specific purposes have been new each time: visiting professorship, Fulbright research fellowship, interview research in one primary school, and several conferences.

Initially, having read several books by Sylvia Ashton-Warner, I was interested in early literacy. Once in New Zealand, I became just as interested in the valiant efforts in that small country—by Maori and Pakeha (white) alike—to create a truly bicultural society. I identified deeply with Pakeha New Zealanders, realizing that my own background was just like theirs—just the result of an earlier tide of British colonialism on another shore. These chapters contribute to the themes of the book as a whole by providing vivid and unfamiliar examples of some of our shared concerns.

In format, the book is somewhat unusual, even for a collection of essays. Each chapter has a Foreword and an Afterword that speak directly to this book's readers.

It is customary in books that include previously published articles to give details of each chapter's previous life only in unobtrusive type. This editorial convention assumes that the author's mental contexts of time, place, and audience at the time of writing have become irrelevant, and that the articles now have a timeless textual autonomy, even for readers who will surely apprehend them into very different contexts in their own minds. Some of the chapters argue against just such autonomy, and for the importance of "contexts in the mind" of both writers and readers. Therefore, a brief biography of each chapter is given in its Foreword.

Putting together any collection for public display brings new learnings to the collector. As I selected and re-edited these chapters—initially just to delete repetitions and update references—I saw new connections and understood new implications for today's issues. These have been added in the Afterwords.

I owe special thanks to the co-authors of three of these chapters: Marie Clay, Patricia Cordeiro, Mary Ellen Giacobbe, and Dell Hymes; and to the two New Zealand educators to whom the book is dedicated: Marie Clay and (in memoriam) James Laughton.

Part I

◆ ◆ ◆

Basic Perspectives

1

◆ ◆ ◆

Whole Language
as a Learning Environment

Foreword. *Chapter 1 was written as an invited "Commentary" for* Language Arts *in 1978 and reprinted in the same magazine in 1983 by editor Julie Jensen in her "patchwork" issue that chronicled "the journal, the profession and the times" on the occasion of* Language Arts*'s sixtieth anniversary. As a kind of Op-Ed piece, it sets forth a point of view without documentation.*

At the time of writing in the late 1970s, my concern was with the destructive fragmentation of language inherent in many of the outcomes of the back-to-basics movement. I don't know whether this is still "the most serious problem facing the language arts curriculum" some 13 years later; certainly the growth of the whole language movement in explicit contrast to that fragmentation has dramatically changed the national scene. But because a major theme of this book is the limitations of the whole language movement as it is sometimes conceptualized and realized in practice, I want to explain my commitment to some of its fundamental principles right at the start.

The most serious problem facing the language arts curriculum today is an imbalance between means and ends—an imbalance between too much attention to drill on the component skills of language and literacy and too little attention to their significant use. Responding to real or imagined community pressures, able and conscientious teachers all over the country are providing abundant practice in discrete basic skills; while classrooms where children are integrating those skills in the service of exciting speaking, listening, reading, and writing activities are becoming rare exceptions. Writing, particularly, is "an endangered species." Duplicating paper, used for short answers, is soaring in sales, while the use of lined composition paper is on the decline.

I am not suggesting that practice exercises in the details of grammar, spelling, or punctuation be eliminated. But an even more important responsibility now is to stimulate the integration of those language skills across the school day and across the school curriculum.

The need for such integration is not simply motivational; it comes from the very nature of skilled human action, whether driving a car, playing the piano, or reading and writing. In any such skills, there is an important distinction between two levels of awareness, which can be called focal attention and subsidiary attention. In driving a car, our focal attention is on the road some distance ahead; and, subject only to our subsidiary awareness, our hands exert pressure on the steering wheel when necessary to keep the car evenly in the lane. When playing music, our focal attention is on the notes we are reading or on a mental image of the sounds we want to re-create, and our fingers are pulled into place to play those scales and drills. In speaking or writing, our focal attention is on the idea, the meaning we wish to convey, and all of the means to that end—whether movements of our vocal cords or of our fingers—are run off automatically in the expression of that idea.

Acquisition of such skills requires two things: first, practice of the component skills so that subroutines are run off automatically and attention can be focused at higher cognitive levels; and second, the availability of opportunities for the integration of the component parts into larger, meaningful wholes. By the very nature of skilled human action, practice in driving a car, playing music, or writing a composition cannot be enough. There must also be frequent contexts that require the integration of those components into some larger act. And that larger act must have a personal purpose, an intentionality that alone provides the meaning that binds the parts into the whole.

Language arts must be integrated into all curriculum areas, and language must be meaningfully used throughout the school day. That does not mean that there cannot be times for practicing language skills. It does mean, however, that the purposeful use of those skills can be provided most powerfully outside the language arts and in the service of the subject areas of literature, science, social studies, and mathematics. Do children have an opportunity for discussions about the results of their science experiments? Do they ever interview people in their family or community to answer questions provoked by their social studies? Are they ever required to make up word problems in mathematics for their classmates, as well as to solve them?

The elementary school must retain its concept of the whole, unfragmented learner; it must keep intentional activity at the core of the process of education; and it must always remember that the language arts are the curriculum area that cannot stand alone. Only linguists have language as their subject matter. For the rest of us—especially children—language is learned not because we want to talk or read or write about language, but because we want to talk and read and write about the world.

Afterword. *As written, this chapter seems to pertain only to monolingual English language arts. But the danger of "reductionism"—fractionating complex tasks into component parts that, no matter how well practiced, can never reconstitute the complex whole—applies to all education today. And it must be of special concern where language learning is a significant educational goal, as it is in second-language learning and bilingual education.*

2

Whole Language Plus
Active Learners and Active Teachers

Foreword. *Here, in a writing style very different from Chapter 1, is one explanation of why an instructional focus only on "whole language" is not enough and why some "plus" is needed. It was written as a discussion of "contemporary issues and future directions" in the* Handbook of Research on Teaching the English Language Arts *(Flood, Jensen, Lapp, & Squire, 1991). What we know about active learners is contrasted with our professional indecision about how best to be an active teacher.*

Discussion of the important distinction between focal and subsidiary attention, mentioned in Chapter 1, is expanded here.

♦ ♦ ♦

The cognitive revolution of the last 25 years has dramatically changed our views of learning. Instead of inscription on an inert blank slate by means of the learner's practice and the culture's reinforcement, we now picture an active mind—from birth on—constructing knowledge through some internal integration of preconceptions and new information. In this psychological sea change, language acquisition has had pride of place as the most remarkable manifestation of human mental capacities (e.g., the work begun by Roger Brown [Kessel, 1988]). It has also been influential in arguments about language education.

Consider some examples of the complexity of the young language learner's task. Slobin (1982) illustrates this complexity by answers to the seemingly simple question, asked just after the action it refers to, "Who threw the ball?" Expressing the answer in English is such "first nature" to us that only a comparison of equivalent answers in other languages calls our attention to intrinsic complexities. In Figure 2.1 answers are shown in five languages. The three core semantic elements (agent, action, and object) are indicated in capitals, and obligatory grammatical features are in square brackets.

The point of listing all these details is to show the complex learning that has to be done, and is done, by young children: learning not only grammatical features of the language (including word order), but also those aspects of the event that must be attended to. The task is not simply to map verbal elements onto self-evident features of the nonverbal world, but also to learn which features of that world have to be encoded in language. In at least one of these non-English languages, children have to learn to attend to features that do not become "first

Figure 2.1 "Daddy threw the ball" in five languages (from Slobin, 1982, by permission)

English:	Daddy	threw	the	ball.
	AGENT	ACTION		OBJECT
	[focus]	[past]	[definite]	

German:	Vater	warf	den	Ball.
	AGENT	ACTION		OBJECT
	[focus]	[past]	[def.]	
		[3rd per.]	[sing.]	
		[sing.]	[masc.]	
			[object]	

Hebrew:	Aba	zarak	et	ha	kadur.
	AGENT	ACTION			OBJECT
	[focus]	[past]	[obj.	[def.]	
		[3rd per.]	particle]		
		[sing.]			
		[masc.]			

Turkish:	Top- u	baba-	m	at- ti	
	OBJECT	AGENT		ACTION	
	[def.]		[possessed	[past]	
	[obj.]		by	[3rd. per.]	
			speaker]	[sing.]	
				[witnessed by speaker]	

Kaluli:	Balow	do-	w	sanditabe.
(Papua	OBJECT	AGENT		ACTION
New		[possessed	[ergative	[recent past]
Guinea]		by speaker]	agent]	

nature" to us: the relation of the agent to the speaker (Turkish), whether the action was witnessed by the speaker (Turkish), the real-life gender of the agent (Hebrew) or the grammatical gender of the object (German), whether the past was recent or long ago (Kaluli), and whether the agent has made a transitive action and therefore must get a special 'ergative' marking (Kaluli). Yet all these features are learned by children, without direct tuition, sometime during their preschool years.

Research on the acquisition of one language not included in the above set, a Bantu language of southern Africa (Demuth, 1989), provides an even more surprising contrast to our familiar experience. Sesotho is the language spoken by the people of Lesotho, a small African nation surrounded by South Africa although politically independent of it. In that language, there is a functional restriction in the grammar such that new information cannot be placed in the subject position in a sentence. Therefore the question asking for information about who threw the ball would have to be asked in a passive construction, in English translation "The ball was thrown by whom?" And the corresponding answer would have to be, "The ball was thrown by Daddy."

Because of this functional restriction, passive constructions are much more common in everyday Sesotho conversation than in English, even in conversation with young children. And, presumably because of this greater frequency, children growing up in that language community learn to use passives productively—that is, without an immediate model—at much younger ages. That's the surprising fact: Whereas children learning English, German, and Hebrew do not control the comprehension and production of passive sentences until well into their elementary school years, children learning Sesotho do so before they are 3. Whatever the intrinsic cognitive complexity of passive constructions, frequency of experience—in hearing and trying to say—seems to override the cognitive problems. There could be no better example of what Rommetveit (1985) calls "the cultural development of attention" (p. 194).

How is such success achieved? There is not yet agreement on the set of children's nonconscious mental "operating principles" that best fits this cross-linguistic evidence. (Compare Slobin [1985] and Bowerman [1985] for detailed discussion.) For example, while children may search for consistent patterns, they do learn irregular items, such as the irregular English past tense verb *threw*; they may search first for meaningful features, but they do learn the arbitrary markings of gender obligatory in many languages (as in the article preceding the object *Ball* in German, in Figure 2.1); and while they may search first for forms that are functionally necessary, they do learn complex constructions for which simpler alternatives are available, such as English tag questions ("It's not hot, is it?" or "She can't go, can she?") for which "right?" would do just as well. No one language is harder or easier to learn overall; different languages, and the cultural patterns with which they are used, are just hard and easy in different ways.

For us as teachers, this descriptive research on first-language acquisition can be paralyzing or energizing. There is no question that young children's remarkable success contrasts dramatically with the considerably less universal success of much language learning—reading as well as writing—in school. As one response to this disheartening contrast, we can let exaltation of the power inherent in all children's minds divert our attention from problems in the schools.

In a content analysis of 50 years of one journal, the *Harvard Educational Review* (HER), which in 1954 published Brown and Bellugi's first article on the language acquisition of Adam and Eve (pseudonyms for the first two children they studied), a sociologist of communication (Schudson, 1981) suggested why "language became a central concern of HER in the 1970's":

> As educators have grown disheartened with the power of schools to affect students or change society, they have turned to a faith in the natural abilities of children to achieve for themselves. This emphasis is most evident in research on the child's capacity for learning language. . . .
>
> That study of language touched on universal themes, revealed common human elements, and illuminated the biological nature of learners and, perhaps, their divine spark as well, was symbolized in Brown and Bellugi's decision to provide the two children they studied with the names Adam and Eve. . . .
>
> An understanding of language, then, seemed to offer a way through social policy debacles and intellectual despair. A focus on language and the ability of the preschool child to show the most remarkable capacity for rule-governed behavior and the learning of exquisitely complex grammatical systems—regardless of genes, family background, or the quality of schooling—offered hope for the liberal position that the educational community had long tried to sustain. There was almost a new theology of education arising out of the study of language. (pp. 20-21)

A second reason for paralysis, in addition to the disheartening contrast between learning at home and at school, is the stance of cultural relativity underlying much of the descriptive language acquisition research. For example, during discussion at the interdisciplinary symposium that resulted in the book *Awakening to Literacy* (Goelman, Oberg, & Smith, 1984), researchers could not even agree on a view of the child as an active learner. Editor Goelman reports:

> Several speakers from the audience were eager to know if the participants could agree on a view of the child as an active learner. They referred to research findings presented at the symposium that supported this view and urged that if some sort of explicit, agreed-on statement to this effect could be produced, it would be of great benefit for those working directly with children. The participants were not able to produce such an unequivocal statement. Schieffelin [the anthropologist who studied children learning Kaluli in Papua New Guinea] commented that this view of the child as an active learner is not universal across cultures or, in a historic sense, across time in our own culture. Such an unqualified statement, Schieffelin believed, might not be helpful when working with some children from a culture in which this view is not accepted within a larger cultural framework. (p. 213)

If the researchers could not even agree on a view of the child as an active learner, they certainly could not agree on—and some were not even willing to discuss—implications for the role of the active teacher.

While such a cultural relativity stance is entirely appropriate for social science researchers, it is inherently impossible for teachers (Cazden, 1983a). Teaching is value-laden, interventionist work; and we have to answer the hard questions: What is wrong with school classrooms as environments for language learning? Why don't the language learning capacities that work so miraculously at home work the same magic in school? Why don't children who come to school speaking a nonstandard dialect of English acquire standard English? Why don't all children quickly pick up the ways of speaking expected in school (Cazden, 1988a)—in sharing time, or large-group lessons, or small-group discussions? How can we help more children repeat their oral language learning successes in reading and writing in school? In short, how can the active child best be helped by the active teacher?

THE ACTIVE TEACHER

The most obvious implication from what we know about environments for successful language learning is epitomized by the report from Lesotho: Children learn what they live, what they hear and try to speak, in a context of meaningful, functional use with people who care about them and have confidence that they will learn. This, I assume, is the core message of what has come to be called "the whole language movement." As researcher, former primary school teacher, parent, and now grandparent, I'm convinced it is an essential part of the foundation for our work. But it seems to be only a part of that foundation, absolutely necessary but not sufficient for all children in school.

More than 20 years ago, psycholinguist John B. Carroll (1966) suggested answers to the same question I have asked here:

> Might it not be possible for a child to learn to read [and, I would add, to write] in somewhat the same "natural" way that he learns his native language? Could reading perhaps be "acquired" through conditions and experiences analogous to those by which the child acquires his native language, rather than by the slow, careful teaching processes which we have thought necessary? (p. 577)

After a careful comparison, Carroll concludes that school literacy programs should become more like the successful environments for oral language acquisition in specific ways: (1) the provision of a rich language environment that includes the full complexities, "irregularities and all"; (2) writing and reading experienced as parallel and reciprocal processes, as speaking and comprehending speech are to the younger child; and (3) school reading and writing tasks "meaningful in the sense of having functional relations to [the child's] experiences, his desires, and his acts" (p. 579).

We get away without fully implementing Carroll's three requirements, yet without obvious failure, with those children whose out-of-school experiences provide them with "contexts-in-the-mind" (Chapter 4) for more decontextualized academic lessons. But for children without such experiences, Carroll's admonitions become more critical. And for all children, we still have a long way to go in providing the rich literacy environments he calls for. For example, we violate his second recommendation of reading and writing as parallel and reciprocal processes when we continue to provide fiction to read and yet assign expository texts to write. Children would not learn to speak a language they do not hear; how do we expect them to learn to write forms they do not read?

But no school provides a lifetime for immersion in all the new literacy forms. And so Carroll also suggests that in school, "there is a certain efficiency to be gained" by teacher-initiated supplements:

In effect one appeals to the attention of the child on a periodic basis. The proper strategy, from this analysis, is to present a rich diet of reading [and again, I would add, writing] materials at every stage, but as a parallel tactic also to call the child's attention to particular items or patterns, in a systematic way, so as to facilitate his own developmental progress through spiraling levels of complexity. (p. 581)

In the abstract, Carroll's recommendations may seem noncontroversial. But in specific cases, heated controversies continue more than 20 years later, seemingly unabated by needed research. The most obvious controversy is over the teaching of beginning reading, usually glossed as "phonics instruction" versus "whole language" programs—for instance, between the recommendations of *Becoming a Nation of Readers* (Anderson, Hiebert, Scott, and Wilkinson, 1985) and its critics in *Counterpoint and Beyond* (Davidson, 1988). Again and again, Davidson's authors argue against "contrived models of reading and writing experiences" (p. 18); they urge "focus on meaningful experiences and meaningful language rather than merely on isolated skill development" (p. 23); and they assert that "intensive formal instruction is totally inconsistent with the concept of emerging literacy" (p. 24). But there is still no research evidence that immersion in rich experience is sufficient for all children. And not all instruction is contrived, isolated, and inconsistent with development.

With respect to reading, Clay's research in New Zealand (1985a, 1991) is a case in point. Her work is cited frequently in *Counterpoint and Beyond* (Davidson, 1988) to support whole language programs. But Clay and Cazden argue (Chapter 9) that Reading Recovery, the daily individual tutorial program for children who have not caught on to reading after one year in school, differs from whole language as well as phonics in significant ways.

For example, during the writing segment of each daily tutorial, the teacher and child together transcribe a sentence that the child has composed. The teacher helps the child attend to the sounds in oral language by means of visual aids developed by Soviet psychologist Elkonin (1973). Then, once the sounds are figured out, and the letters written, the teacher asks the child to practice writing some of the words from visual memory. As the tutorial days and weeks go by, teacher help is reduced, and the child writes more and more alone.

In this program, children's sound awareness is developed in writing rather than reading because getting to sounds from oral language rather than from letters builds on the resources children bring to literacy tasks.

There are many assertions by Davidson's authors about the need to build on children's strengths. In the development of Reading Recovery, Clay and her colleagues have figured out how to do just that.

With respect to writing, three recent experiences may further explain my concern. First, language educators in both England and New Zealand have expressed ambivalence over the effect on classroom practice of descriptive U.S. research on children's invented spelling. Yes, they say, it is good to have this picture of young children's preinstruction, intuitive knowledge. But unaccompanied by research on how to help children build on that knowledge toward conventional spellings, the descriptive research seems to paralyze teachers and make them give up even reasonable and helpful aids.

Second, in two important articles, black language arts educator Delpit (1986, 1988) argues for the importance of deliberate teaching of the "culture of power" to black children:

> If you are not already a participant in the culture of power, being told explicitly the rules of that culture makes acquiring power easier. . . . Unless one has the leisure of a lifetime of immersion to learn them, explicit presentation makes learning immeasurably easier. (1986, p. 283)

Finally, teachers who do supplement rich immersion with minilessons may feel that the latter are old-fashioned and should not even be necessary in a perfect "whole language" world. For example, one first-grade teacher invited me to visit his classroom to see the writing program he was justifiably proud of. For more than an hour, the children wrote and then listened while many took turns reading aloud from "the author's chair." Only as I was leaving the room, with the teacher now engaged in shifting the class from writing to math, did I notice on the overhead projector a transparency with a child's story prepared for a class discussion of some editing conventions. Here was, in fact, a classroom with a rich main road to meaning *plus* what Clay and Cazden call an "instructional detour" to momentarily call the children's attention to matters of form. But that detour was not considered worthy of showing off, much as I would have valued it.

CONCLUDING COMMENTS

Delpit's phrase "explicit presentation" may be a critical point of controversy. In thinking about the implications of language acquisition research, philosopher Polanyi's (1964) distinction between focal and subsidiary awareness has been influential (Cazden, 1972). In one familiar example, when hammering in a nail, our focal attention is on the nail, with only subsidiary attention paid to the hammer. In early language acquisition, the child's focal attention is clearly on matters of intention and meaning; yet just as clearly, language structure—although attended to only subsidiarily—is acquired. So it is easy to conclude that focal attention to matters of language form should never be necessary; and that we can agree with the Dutchess who said to Alice in Wonderland, "and the moral of *that* is—'Take care of the sense, and the sounds will take care of themselves.'"

But even Polanyi, (1964), much as he emphasizes the importance of focal attention to meaning in all personal knowledge and skill, speaks also of the value of maxims, or "rules of art":

> Maxims are rules, the correct application of which is part of the art which they govern. The true maxims of golfing or of poetry increase our insight into golfing or poetry and may even give valuable guidance to golfers or poets; but these maxims would instantly condemn themselves to absurdity if they tried to replace the golfer's skill or the poet's art. Maxims cannot be understood, still less applied by anyone not already possessing a good practical knowledge of the art. . . . Once we have accepted our commitment to personal knowledge, we can also face up to the fact that there exist rules which are useful only within the operation of our personal knowing, and can realize also how useful they can be as part of such acts. (p. 31)

Vygotsky's (1962) discussion of the relationship between spontaneous and scientific concepts fits here, too. Scientific concepts (like Polanyi's maxims) can only be integrated into a foundation of spontaneous concepts (that develop in the course of practical experience); but once that foundation is in place, scientific concepts can stimulate further development.

As a way of summing up his recommendations for an optimal mix of rich environment plus periodic instruction in the details of text forms, Carroll (1966) suggests the metaphor of "parallel tracks." Clay and Cazden (Chapter 9) suggest, instead, the metaphor of "instructional detours." The idea of a detour preserves what I believe to be essential: the prior establishment of a main road of meaningful language use, to which the detour is a momentary diversion when needed.

Or, in still another metaphorical contrast, we need to provide vitamins as well as food—vitamins (not medicine) that are concentrated forms of essential ingredients for those who need more specific nutrition than that provided by a healthy diet alone.

To assert the need for such combined ingredients in an optimal environment for literacy learning in school does not tell us what to supply when, and how. But it does argue that this, rather than arguments between one extreme and the other, is where research and documentation—by teachers as well as researchers—needs to be done. I have mentioned one program, Reading Recovery, because it exemplifies the kind of mix that I believe we need in other areas of English language arts, a mix that builds on children's strengths in comparable ways and continues the "cultural development of attention" (Rommetveit, 1985, p. 194) started at birth. Wolf (1988) documents analogous practices with older learners. We now know much about the active child; but we still have much to learn about the active teacher.

Afterword. *Because the picture of how children learn their mother tongue has become such an important foundation for the philosophy of the whole language movement, and for the claim that written language can be learned in the same way, I want to explain two fundamental limitations of that usual picture.*

First, it is not possible to overcome the limitation recognized by Carroll 25 years ago: Classrooms cannot duplicate the conditions of oral language immersion in the home; they cannot infuse reading and writing with all the frequency, immediacy, and feelings of speech.

Margaret Donaldson, professor emeritus of developmental psychology at the University of Edinburgh and author of the widely read Children's Minds *(1978), has entered the controversy on this issue in Great Britain with a space-travel fantasy (n.d.). The beings on her planet have "mother brows" rather than "mother tongues":*

> *Let us imagine a planet inhabited by beings called Browfolk. The Browfolk are just like ourselves except that they have little windows set into their foreheads in which graphic symbols can appear, coming into view one at a time and moving across the forehead to disappear at the other. Forehead symbols accompany most of the social activities of these beings, contributing greatly to the success of their cooperative endeavors. Also the symbols may appear in different colours, expressive of states of feelings. . . .*

Sometimes a shutter closes over the window. But we are informed by returning space explorers that, behind the shutter, symbols are still regularly being produced for the private purposes of the individual concerned. Explorers also report that Browfolk children learn to produce and interpret the forehead symbols with precisely the same speed and ease as human children learn to manage the sounds of the mother tongue. . . . Written symbols are, so to speak, their mother brow.

Human beings, however, do not have a mother brow. We do not use written symbols for the spontaneous expression of thoughts and emotions in our direct 'face-to-face' dealings with one another. So for us the learning of these symbols—how to produce them, how to make sense of them—is a profoundly different enterprise from the learning of speech. (n.d., pp. 12–13)

Donaldson suggests four ways in which literacy learning can become closer to the learning of speech, all prominent in whole language classrooms: shared reading, helping children to produce written language from the beginning, use of print embedded in the environment, and the provision of books written in the patterns of children's speech. But, she argues, these "are only starting points. What is to follow is a whole new kind of enterprise" that requires "active, systematic teaching" (n.d., pp. 22, 31).

The second limitation is with the picture of oral language learning itself. What this chapter omits is the ways in which parents speaking with very young children do more than immerse children in the conversations of family life. In the course of that conversation—and, in some families, in the course of reading aloud—they also talk in ways that constitute just as powerful strategies for the "cultural development of attention" as those of the Reading Recovery teachers, even though parents may have absolutely no tutorial intention in mind.

One way of categorizing such strategies, whether conscious or not, is suggested in Chapter 8: "scaffolds, models, and direct instruction."

3

How Knowledge About Language Helps the Classroom Teacher —or Does It?
A Personal Account

Foreword. *This personal account was written back at Harvard soon after I spent the 1974–75 school year as a full-time classroom teacher in San Diego and published the next year in* The Urban Review. *Although it is more about oral language than literacy, it is included here as an introduction to the theme of languages, literacies, and cultures in contact, and also as an expression of my identification with classroom teachers. The San Diego context is explained more fully at the beginning of the chapter.*

♦ ♦ ♦

Two years ago, an exhibit of Native American children's art was shown around the country. Among the strikingly beautiful drawings and paintings, a few pieces of writing were also displayed. Two of those writings can speak for many children:

From a Navajo child in New Mexico:

Our teachers come to class,
And they talk and they talk,

Till their faces are like peaches.
We don't;
We just sit like cornstalks.

And from an Apache child in Arizona:

Have you ever hurt
    about baskets?
I have, seeing my grandmother weaving
    for a long time.
Have you ever hurt about work?
I have, because my father works too hard
    and he tells how he works.
Have you ever hurt about cattle?
I have, because my grandfather has been working
    on the cattle for a long time.
Have you ever hurt about school?
I have, because I learned a lot of words
    from school,
And they are not my words.

These are not new ideas; rather they are particularly effective expressions of ideas that are all too familiar. In a setting where we hope there can be important growth in children's use of language for learning and for life, teachers talk too much, and the words in the air are more ours than theirs.

When I took a leave from Harvard in the fall of 1974 to become, for one year, a fully certified and full-time public school teacher of young children, I was determined that my classroom would be different. After 13 years in a university, it was time to go back to children, to try to put into practice some of the ideas about child language and education that I had been teaching and writing about, and to rethink questions for future research. In this personal account, I will try to explain some of the reasons why it turned out to be so hard, and why those Native American children are so often right.

WHY IT WAS SO HARD

I taught in a section of San Diego that is one of the lowest in the city in income and school achievement, a community that is now about evenly divided between black and Chicano families. I had 25 children in a combined first, second, and third grade. From the very beginning there were objective problems, as anyone who knows urban schools could have predicted.

From September until Christmas, there was construction on the school site, construction that would have been finished by September in any middle-class area. As a result, the school was on double sessions, and a fifth-grade class of nearly 40 entered our room at noon as we left. Our room had to be filled with desks, all in rows, and none of our materials could be left out overnight.

Actually, in the fall we didn't have many materials. My room had been a library the year before and so was empty in September except for an oversupply of bulletin board decorations. The school's central storage area had been demolished during the summer, and so no surplus was available for me. Everything we eventually used had to be deliberately selected and then borrowed, bought, or made—in all ways very different from the well-stocked room of my last pre-Harvard teaching years.

After Christmas, the fifth grade could move out, and we were able to organize our own room. Then in the spring, construction started again, this time on a new lunchroom. We didn't go back on double sessions. But periodically it was too dangerous for children to go outside at all. Lunch was served in the classroom for the rest of the year. For a while, there was no recess and we all had to go to the outdoor bathrooms in lines and on schedule.

In such conditions, interest in the quantity and quality of children's language seemed a luxury in the extreme.

Subjective impediments were added to the objective conditions. People ask whether children had changed in 13 years. I don't know; but I'm sure I have changed. My subjective impediments are less generalizable to all teachers, but I suspect not unique to me either. Any colleagues going back to the classroom may have some of these reactions.

First was my rustiness as a teacher of children. Rustiness means that a repertoire of ideas isn't available on the tip of one's tongue and one's fingers. Not only my room was poorly prepared; my mind was too.

Second, there are the contrasts between teaching in a university and teaching in a public school. I had thought physical stamina would be a problem. It wasn't. But whereas in the university every day is different, in schedule and place, in a public school there are six or seven hours every day within the same four walls. And nothing in the university is like the crowded living during most of those hours, where one can never tune out the visual and auditory stimuli, and the demands for attention of 25 children.

As Jane Torrey wrote me from Connecticut College last year, "the problem is to think abstractly in the face of all that concrete reality." I lived in LaJolla, 17 freeway miles from the school, not so much because LaJolla was richer and prettier—which it is—but because it was where I could live a more familiar mental life for a few hours every afternoon. There, in an office at the University of California San Diego (UCSD), I could read and write and think different kinds of thoughts in the peace and quiet that became particularly blessed by contrast with the rest of the day.

Finally, there were my multiple, often conflicting ideas about the kind of teacher I wanted to be. Ideas from 13 years ago; from the classrooms I have visited since then in the United States and England; from more theoretical ideas about child language and multicultural education; from what I've read of national evaluations of Head Start and Follow Through; from prevailing practices heard or overheard in the teacher's lounge; and from my more immediate, less reflective responses to the level of children's voices and actions. I wanted to be firm and open, structured and authentic, and all the other good adjectives at the same time. I had been one kind of good teacher 13 years before. Having learned about alternative and not wholly compatible models, I seemed less able to be any one model really well.

Other people have described similar conflicts. David Reisman, talking last fall about experiments in college teaching, spoke of the "pedagogical despair" that results from too many incompatible goals (lecture, Harvard Graduate School of Education, September 18, 1975). And the philosopher and theologian Paul Tillich (1966) has the following paragraph at the beginning of his autobiographical book, *On the Boundary*:

> In the Introduction to my *Religious Realization* I wrote—"The boundary is the best place for acquiring knowledge." When I was asked to give an account of the way my ideas have developed from my life, I thought that the concept of the boundary might be the fitting symbol for the whole of my personal and intellectual development. At almost every point, I have had to stand between alternative possibilities of existence, to be completely at home in neither and to take no definite stand against either. Since thinking presupposes receptiveness to new possibilities, this position is fruitful for thought; but it is difficult and dangerous in life, which again and again demands decisions and thus the exclusion of alternatives. (p. 13)

When William Sloan Coffin announced his resignation as Yale's chaplain, he said that "Growth demands a willingness to relinquish one's proficiencies." (*New York Times*, February 20, 1975). I know what he meant. I nearly gave up more than once, and probably would have without warm and strong support from many people. First, from the school staff. That support was partly due to the way my year was arranged. Because I was not paid by the San Diego school system, I did not count in official calculations of the number of teachers at school. Therefore, my presence meant that the other five primary teachers each had about five fewer children than usual. So I was a help where it counts. More personally, the teachers all have to take courses at local colleges for salary increments and advanced degrees, and rightfully resent being told what to do by professors who have never been in a classroom. Knowing exactly who I was and why I was there, they were genuinely glad to watch, and even participate in, the continuing education of a professor who came to live her working life again, even if for only one year.

Other people helped, too, such as LaDonna Coles, who became my co-teacher when funds were cut and my aide was transferred. And finally there were Hugh (Bud) Mehan, director of the Teacher Education Program at UCSD, and two of his students (Sue Fisher and Nick Maroules), who spent hours every week talking over what I had done and they had seen.

THE CHILDREN

To give you a flavor of the children, here are some notes on their language—their talking and reading and writing:

First, their attitudes toward Spanish. In the beginning of the year, negative attitudes toward the Spanish language were very strong. The community had been largely black. With more and more Mexican-American families moving north from the border, the community is now balanced at about half-and-half and will probably become predominantly Chicano in future years. I am not bilingual, but my co-teacher LaDonna Coles is. In the fall, when she or the Chicano children talked Spanish, the black children literally put their hands over their ears.

To validate and enhance the status of Spanish in the classroom, we turned on *Villa Alegre*, as well as *The Electric Company*; made many bilingual word puzzles; tore out all the illustrations with bilingual captions from my year's accumulation of *Sesame Street Magazine*. And I took every opportunity to have the Chicano children teach me

Spanish. However limited the status of translation as a technique for second-language learning, all the children enjoyed these translation games. When two children arrived from Mexico after Christmas, translation became a necessity as well as a game. Rodolfo, one of those two, was very talkative and participated, in Spanish, in all discussions. Miguel, the third-grader least motivated and least successful in reading and math, was by far the most capable translator in both directions—into Spanish and into English—and achieved positive recognition in the classroom for the first time.

The attitudes of the black children did change, dramatically so. Greg, for example, who in the fall always put his hands over his ears, began to assert himself by saying *Callete* to a noisy neighbor. He would ask Rudolfo to teach him to count in Spanish. And he eagerly attended a Spanish class for bilingual education teachers who needed children to practice on.

Second, their comments on language. Everett, a tiny first-grader whose excess energy sometimes erupted in cartwheels across the room, sits quietly and reflects on words in a husky whisper. "*Little* is a big word and *big* is a little word." Then seeing *on* written on the blackboard, he said, "You take the *n* off *on* and put it in front and it'd be *no.*" Another time, while reading, he came to w-h-a-t and asked, "What's this word?" I told him *What* and he laughed—"When I asked you 'what's the word,' I said it myself!"

Third, their invented spellings. Alberto, another first grade boy, writing illustrated stories everyday on drawing paper at school or paper towels at home (Figures 3.1, 3.2, and 3.3), invented spelling to fit his Spanish accent:

> An tis coner is drragn. (In this corner is dragon.)
> I like to go to the scwl on the wek. (I like to go to school in the week.)
> I like fruwt to et on th morning. (I like fruit to eat in the morning.)
> Tis is the syde. (This is the city.)
> At tree I see Popy. (At three I see Popeye.)
> I like to ryd a bwk wet the tehr. (I like to read a book with the teacher.)

Fourth, their delight in reading nonsense material. Not just the easy-reading trade books by Dr. Seuss and others that have multi-

Figure 3.1   Alberto's drawings

plied since I taught before; but also the new *Monster* books from Bowmar Press, the *Spidey* comics jointly published by The Electric Company and Marvel Comics, and the zany sentences with jazzy musical punctuation on the 90-second Sound-Out films in Houghton Mifflin's Interaction program. Such material, plus good multiethnic realism, seems the best combined answer to the problem of "relevance."

Fifth, their attitudes toward sex roles.   One day, Alfredo projected his concept of male superiority onto an innocuous-looking Row-Peterson preprimer illustration of a boy and a girl in the water. Notic-

Figure 3.2   Alberto's drawings (*continued*)

ing that only the girl was on a rubber animal. Alfredo said, "The girl scared of the water. Her got that. The boy no got that. He no scared."

Last, their sense of humor.   When LaDonna, my co-teacher, was explaining to me that she was taking some of the children to her bilingual education class after school because "we need some real live children," Greg overheard her and quipped, "Ain't no one dead in here is there?" And at the end of another day, when I wished out loud during a spelling lesson for a key to turn Greg on and off, Wallace said, "Yeah, and you'd leave him off most of the time, wouldn't you!"

Figure 3.3 Alberto's drawings (*continued*)

But such anecdotes, lively as they may be, don't depend on special knowledge. I've tried hard—at moments of encounter with the children last year, during more reflective times for planning ahead and remembering later, and this year back at Harvard thinking retrospectively about the classroom experience—to consider how knowledge about language helps the classroom teacher.

In a recent review of six new educational psychology texts in *The Educational Psychologist*, A. J. H. Gaite wrote:

Educational psychologists or at least those who write textbooks have a love-hate or an approach-avoidance relationship with the topic of human development. Rarely can they leave it alone (or out) but rarely do they afford it anything like proper coverage. Further, many seem particularly blind to the importance of language development as a topic relevant to educational settings. (1975, p. 203)

I welcome Gaite's remarks. But as the title of this chapter suggests, I am less sure than I was two years ago about the points of relevance, and more aware of the limitations of what we now know. Admittedly, there probably were subtle but pervasive influences of knowledge on my teaching that I was not and still am not aware of. I can only recount the "aha" experiences, where an explicit connection was made between knowledge and classroom practice.

WHERE KNOWLEDGE HELPS

Three clear examples come to mind of children's language that I interpreted and responded to differently than I might otherwise have done. First, were the invented spellings exemplified so well by Alberto's captions for his pictures. I welcomed them as expressions of powerful and important cognitive activity and felt confident that they would gradually shift, as they did, toward conventional orthography without explicit correction.

Second, there was Black English, so omnipresent that I ceased to hear it and occasionally talked it myself. For instance, from Carolyn:

He on the wrong page.
There go Leona's (about a painting on the wall).

I knew that there was no evidence that sentences such as these are in any way cognitive liabilities for the children who speak or hear them. Carolyn's Black English features reflect cultural differences, not the developmental differences of invented spellings. But cognitively they belong in a single category: examples of powerful language-learning capacities at work, in children's minds at particular stages of development, and with particular models of language to learn from.

These two examples suggest that one important function of knowledge about language for teachers is to put the language forms used by children back where they belong, out of focal awareness. Normally, in out-of-school conversations, our focal attention as speakers and listeners is on the meaning, the intention, of what someone is trying to say. Language forms are themselves transparent; we hear through them to the meaning intended. But teachers, over the decades if not centuries, have somehow gotten into the habit of hearing with different ears once they go through the classroom doors. Language forms assume an opaque quality. We cannot hear through them; we hear only the errors to be corrected. One value of knowledge about language—its development and its culturally different forms—is not to make the language of our children more salient to our attention. Quite the opposite. That knowledge reassures, and it lets language forms recede into the transparency that they deserve, enabling us to talk and listen in the classroom as outside, focusing full attention on the children's thoughts and feelings that these forms express.

Shuy (1973) has discussed how the study of Black English has been a factor in educational change. His is the only attempt I know of to document such change from research on language. I hope he is right that progress exists and that the change is not only in curriculum materials, but also in our ears.

A third example from my experience came in interpreting test-induced distortions in children's speech. In response to requests from early childhood coordinators in several California school districts, I tried out the CIRCUS battery of tests of oral language put out by Educational Testing Service to see if it might be useful in fulfilling the requirement for oral language evaluation now mandated by California's early childhood education program. One of the subtests asked the children to complete such statements as *Here is a child. Here are two* _____. Eight of these items asked for such irregular forms, and the seven first- and second-graders in my class who were native speakers of English gave 35 overgeneralizations out of 56 possible responses— *childrens, feets, mines, morest, gooder,* etc.

Having spent months of my graduate student life coding transcripts of child speech for the presence of such overgeneralizations (Cazden, 1968), I felt sure I would have been sensitive to them if they had appeared with such relative frequency in the children's spontaneous conversation. I could not believe that the test responses reflected the children's more spontaneous speech. On the regular plural, possessive, and comparative items, the children got 74 out of 98 right. Something was strange about only the irregulars.

I could think of no way to obtain tokens of *mine, most, better* and *best* in a more casual and less contrived situation, but eliciting plurals seemed possible. From *Ebony* magazine (since all seven children were black), I cut pictures of a group of children and a group of men. For pictures of feet, I drew around my own. A few days after completing the tests, I found a moment to ask the seven children individually and as casually as possible, "What's that a picture of?" The overgeneralized plurals dropped from 15 to 6. (See Cazden, 1975a, for more extended discussion.)

My experience with these eight items is not intended at all as a general criticism of CIRCUS. That is an important effort to test productive oral language of young children, and the Spanish version now in preparation will be even more welcome. The point here is not criticism of the test, but rather a demonstration of how knowledge about situational influences on child language can give the classroom teacher a basis for interpreting and questioning the language elicited in tests, and even in some cases a basis for obtaining more representative samples of speech as a check on test validity.

WHERE KNOWLEDGE IS LIMITED

All three of these examples of relevant knowledge—about development, cultural differences, and situational influences on children's language—concern language form, not content; structure, not function. Despite the many times that I and others have written (e.g., Cazden, John, & Hymes, 1972) that it is the way language is used in the classroom that is important in influencing educational achievement—and I still believe that is true—it was knowledge about language structure that was in my head as I set out across the country from Harvard to San Diego.

In a symposium at which Follow Through sponsors discussed their work in progress on assessments of children's productive language (American Educational Research Association, San Francisco, April 20, 1976), Elizabeth Gilkeson of the Bank Street College of Education spoke of the significance of such assessments for staff development. In her words, what happens to teachers as they use particular evaluation instruments is "the internalization of an analysis sytem." I had internalized one such system—that handles structural features of language very well. But it was too narrow for classroom relevance, as those Follow Through sponsors (Bank Street, EDC, Far West Laboratory, High/Scope, and Tucson) know so well.

This focus on structure separate from use, on linguistic means separate from social and cognitive purposes, is not only where I had been, but where the language development field as a whole has been. The field is changing. The communicative aspects of competence are beginning to be studied as rigorously as linguistic competence, more narrowly defined, has been. But these beginnings are understandably

with the youngest children. It will be a while before these more functional developmental studies provide even suggestive extrapolations to
children in the elementary school years. It will be even longer before
we understand the relationship between the development of communicative competence and the development of cognition. In terms of
academic disciplines, the fields of sociolinguistics and cognitive psychology have to converge in an analysis of language as it is used with
others and to ourselves.

I'm not suggesting that teachers shouldn't listen more carefully to
what children say. But I am suggesting that it's not obvious what the
most productive focus for their attention should be. Further, I am
suggesting that the best focus is probably not what existing research
can say the most about.

Of course, research knowledge about language is not the only
basis for improved action. I think it's fair to say that there is a general
trans-Atlantic contrast at this point. Whereas Americans like me have
worked "down," trying to derive implications for education from theories about language and its development, colleagues in England have
worked "up" from instances of the best classroom practice. An excellent example of the English genre, perhaps the best there is, is *The
Language of Primary School Children* by Connie and Harold Rosen
(1973). It is one outcome of a project of the Schools Council in
England, designed to collect materials which would show the range of
language actually used by children in the 5-to-11 range and also
exemplify the best current practice in the schools. An assumption of
the opening chapter on "Context," as James Britton points out in his
Preface, is that "it is the particular kind of shared life created by all
those who work together in a school which determines how language
will be used by teachers and pupils (p. 12)." In the beginning of the
chapter on "Talking," the Rosens together ask "Can we be more specific
about both the kinds of experience of talking which a good school
should offer and the most propitious conditions in which to offer it?"
(p. 41). They answer that "we still lack the analytical tools for handling
taped talk. . . . But we cannot afford to wait and must do what we can"
(p. 42). At the end of the book are some 20 pages of "Notes" where
links to theory and practice are explored. These notes speak optimisti-
cally about what we will be able to learn from sociolinguistics about a
theory of context that "could perhaps lead teachers to decide more
precisely what features of the situation they wish to alter and in what
way so that children will speak more powerfully and act more effectively" (p. 260).

EXAMPLES OF POTENTIAL RESEARCH

It is not surprising that there should be a time lag between the development of a field, in this case sociolinguistics, and the application of its concepts and methodologies to a specific setting, the classroom. Work on this application is now in progress at four sites at least—the Center for Applied Linguistics (Roger Shuy and Peg Griffin), Rockefeller University (William Hall, Michael Cole, and Ray McDermott), UCSD (Hugh Mehan), and Harvard (with Frederick Erickson and Jeffrey Shultz). This work has two interrelated but separable foci: children's functional or communicative competence and socio-linguistic analyses of the language of teaching. I'll give an example of potential research in each category from my experience last year [1974-1975].

Children's Functional Competence

Giving instructions is one important functional competence. In any classroom, children often help each other with their academic work. Sometimes this is formalized by the teacher who specifically asks one child to help another. A multigrade classroom such as mine in San Diego was a particularly natural setting for this activity, and such tutoring very frequently took place.

Many reasons can be given why encouraging children to teach each other is a good thing: We all learn something best by having to teach it to another; self-confidence is built when a child can successfully fulfill such a leadership role; the community is strengthened when members understand that having particular knowledge or skill entails a responsibility to teach others who don't. But the value of peer teaching doesn't mean that it happens easily or always successfully. Surprisingly, in reports of children as tutors, only achievement gains are reported. Analyses of the actual teaching interaction are not given. (See Gumperz & Herasimchek [1973] for one rare analysis.)

When a wireless microphone became available to the Cazden/Mehan teacher-researcher team, we planned what we called an "instructional chain" for part of the hour in which a particular child wore the microphone. Instructional chains are an example of what I have called "concentrated encounters": naturally occurring interactions that are more carefully planned for language assessment or research. They contrast with the less natural "contrived encounters" of most tests, including the CIRCUS example above. (See Cazden, 1975b, for further discussion.) I taught the focal child a task; the child rehearsed back to me what he or she was going to do and say, and then that child became the tutor for other children. Naturally occurring groups, as for reading and spelling, were used. Tasks were selected so that the knowledge and skills required were within the capabilities of the peer group, but so that some essential information had to be taught by the child teacher; the tasks could not be self-evident from the materials alone or the tutor would have no essential work to do. For example, in a puzzle from *The Electric Company Activity Book*, a coded message is deciphered by crossing out letters that spell the opposite of a given word. The original directions that explained about crossing out opposites were deleted so that part of the instruction could only be learned by the children from their child tutor.

In some cases, child tutors and tutees were selected to make code-switching from English to Spanish likely. For example, I taught a bilingual first-grade girl two spelling tasks in English and then asked her to teach them to a bilingual boy. The child's rehearsal of the instructions in English were halting, brief, and incomplete. To her tutee, she rephrased the instructions in fluent Spanish, combined with crisp, exaggerated pronunciation of the English words her tutee had to spell.

Mehan has analyzed two instructional chains in which two black girls, Carolyn and Leola, each taught a task to the same reading group of five second- and third-graders. He shows how my verbal instructions were partially transformed into less verbal but functionally equivalent demonstrations by both child tutors (personal communication, 1975). A large body of research on children's referential communication strategies comes immediately to mind (e.g., Heider, Cazden, & Brown, 1969, and review by Glucksberg, Kraus, & Higgins, 1975). But more than referential communication is required in any teaching act—by children and adults alike. And we know far less about how children accomplish other interactive requirements of the teaching role.

Although Carolyn and Leola were alike in substituting more ostensive demonstrations for my verbal description of the tasks, the two tutoring sessions were also very different. There was much more off-task behavior when Carolyn was teaching, even though Leola had to teach a harder task. Many questions about functional language competence can be examined in this one speech event. For example:

How does the tutor try to get the attention of the tutees? Where does the tutor look while teaching, and how does she try to control the tutees' gaze? Can the tutor engage simultaneously in teaching and visual monitoring of her tutees?

How does the tutor cope with questions? With interruptions? Can she avoid getting sidetracked and successfully keep herself and tutees on task?

How do tutors cope with errors in the work, and with behavior problems during it?

Does the tutor try in any way to achieve a status difference between herself and her usual peers? Does she engage in noninstructional peer talk or not? Does she laugh or remain solemn? While the tutor has been so designated by the teacher, she must maintain that status relationship by her own interactional work. (Even adult teachers soon learn that ascribed status is not sufficient!) In some tapes of instructional chains being collected at the Center for Applied Linguistics, child tutors stand while the tutees sit, use a pen while tutees use pencils, and carefully guard a paper that the tutees can't see.

The Language of Teaching

Important influences on talk are the relationships of power and social and psychological distance that obtain among the speakers. Questions about power and distance are admittedly of special interest to me because I felt them both acutely last year. But I don't believe they were idiosyncratic phenomena. I think I just lived a more extreme version of widespread aspects of teacher–pupil relationships.

I had problems with power—or discipline, as it's usually called—partly from my ambivalence (or more accurately, multi-valence) about models of teaching that I mentioned earlier. And in social distance, I was—or at least I started out—at the extreme, too. Not just that I'm Anglo and all my children were black and Chicano; that, I knew, would be the case before I entered the classroom. But I hadn't thought about other ways in which that distance would be so extreme. I was from Boston and I was teaching in San Diego. I didn't know southern California, and when children talked to me about their lives, I didn't even know the places they were talking about. I came not only from a different cultural world, but also from a different physical, visual, geographical world. Finally, when I was teaching in the 1950s, my own two daughters were about the age of the children I was teaching. They were in the elementary grades at the same time, so that I was more a part of a children's culture. At least I listened to some of their television programs, and I saw some of their movies. Thirteen years in a university, and my daughters have grown up. I am now totally out of that children's world. I rarely watch television; I don't know one sports team from another. In all ways, not just the obvious cultural ones, I was about as far from those children as anyone could have been.

But there I was. What could be done to change that situation, to lessen the distance, to come closer to the shared life that nourishes talk in the ways Connie and Harold Rosen describe? Mehan and his students, who spent so many hours in my classroom, commented on how much I physically reached out to touch the children. I don't think that was true 13 years ago. I personally may have changed in the intervening years, and there is supposed to be generally more touching now than in the 1950s. But I think these general changes were accentuated in the classroom by an impulsive reaching out across the gap that seemed so enormous. Fortunately, we did more than touch.

In retrospect, attempts to decrease the distance fall into three categories. One was some overlapping of lives outside of school. In the fall, especially during the time when there was a double session and I had to stay on the school grounds a couple of hours after the children left but couldn't even get into my room, I took turns walking children home, seeing the important landmarks along the way—candy store or tavern, creek to cross or abandoned car to avoid, saying "hello" to their mothers if they wanted to come to the door. I sometimes carried a Polaroid camera with me and took a picture of the child and his or her bicycle, or of a clubhouse under the foundation of his or her house.

Then the children started asking me, "Where do *you* live?" Well, I lived 17 miles up the freeway across the street from the ocean in LaJolla. That's another kind of distance that is social as well as physical. Again, perhaps an extreme, as those who know LaJolla may think. But most teachers commute to the children's world from their own. And so we took the children to LaJolla, in small groups, in LaDonna's car and mine. Again, it was easier because of the double sessions in the fall. We had ice cream and cookies; they wandered around and marveled at the little two-room apartment I had all to myself. Then we walked across the street to swim and play on the beach. (I wasn't the only teacher in the school who took children to her home; at least one other had done it for years.)

A second way to build a shared life was the creation and use of memorable events within the classroom life itself. Visitors became important because there were a number of them. Some of them were visitors who came through the children. For one social studies unit we talked about where we and our families came from, and put this on a large map of North America: orange for us, green for parents, and so forth (an idea gleaned from David and Frances Hawkins's Mountain View Center in Boulder, Colorado, on my way west). As our map showed, I had come from a long way away; many of the Chicano children had come from Mexico; and the black children's parents had come from many different parts of the country (for reasons I still don't understand, an especially high proportion came from Arkansas). Mothers came in to share their experiences in growing up in another kind of place and their reasons for moving to San Diego.

Some of the visits were from my friends; one was a woman from Santa Fe who is a bilingual folk singer and sang with the children in both Spanish and English. A teacher on vacation from Boston spent a week in the classroom and did science. Another teacher from Berkeley stopped in for a day and brought some beautiful Chicano legends his group had published. Almost accidentally at first, and then deliberately, we started taking Polaroid pictures of these visitors, tape-recording on cassettes their songs and stories. These pictures and cassettes became treasured by all the children. They would say "Do you remember when . . ." and tell other people who came into the classroom about these special events. They would listen to the cassettes again and again; and with the science teacher they started a correspondence that lasted the rest of the year.

A third way to lessen distance is to avoid activities that increase it. We didn't pledge allegiance to the flag all year. The decision to omit it was triggered the very first morning. Before school officially started, a mother appeared with her daughter who would be in our class. She explained firmly that she was a Jehovah's Witness and Jeanie could not pledge allegiance or do any holiday activities. Almost without thinking, I told her we wouldn't be pledging allegiance and I wasn't big on holidays either. This was post-Watergate United States, in a city where one is rarely out of sight of reminders of the Air Force, Navy, or Marines. I had no inclination to pledge allegiance to them. But more important than Jeanie's religion or my politics was my sense that pledging allegiance was not an activity these children and I could meaningfully share. Robert Coles's (1975) quote from a white schoolteacher in Alabama confirmed my decision:

> I had a girl once, she was quite fresh; she told me she didn't believe a word of that salute to the flag, and she didn't believe a word of what I read to them about our history. I sent her to the principal. I was ready to have her expelled, for good. The principal said she was going to be a civil rights type one day, but by then I'd simmered down. "To tell the truth," I said, "I don't believe most of the colored

children think any different than her." The principal gave me a look and said, "Yes, I can see what you mean." A lot of times I skip the salute to the flag; the children start laughing, and they forget the words, and they become restless. It's not a good way to start the day. I'd have to threaten them, if I wanted them to behave while saluting. So, we go right into our arithmetic lesson. (pp. 13-14)

There are clear indications of these relationships of power and distance in the videotapes of my classroom. One way to deal with tensions about discipline is to talk. If silence seems potentially a dangerous vacuum, fill it; talk can maintain power as well as express it. People who have used various systems of classroom interaction analysis come up with a 66 percent rule. If you tally who talks by words, by lines in a transcript, or by moments of time, teachers talk about 66 percent of the time. Recently, some students in a Harvard seminar did such a tally on the discussion that I had with my children on Martin Luther King's birthday. It turned out that I talked 62 percent of the time, disastrously close to the 66 percent average. Those two Native American children, whose writing I quoted at the beginning of this paper, could have been writing about my classroom. (Mehan [1979] and Cazden [1988a] give further analyses of talk in this classroom.)

Other people have written of power and distance in ways that suggest hypotheses for further research. Waller, in his fine book on *The Sociology of Teaching* (1961), discusses them both. From recent work in sociolinguistics, we know something about the effects of power and distance, and its opposite, intimacy or solidarity, on language use. One of the earliest and most elegant sociolinguistic analyses is Brown and Gilman's (1972) historical and cross-language study of the distribution of second person pronouns: intimate T as in French *tu* versus formal V as in the French *vous*. I realized only in rereading their work recently that Brown and Gilman report how the choice of T or V does not always inhere in people and their static relationships, but can also express shifts in feelings of solidarity accompanying changes in the context of their activities. In their words,

We have a favorite example . . . given us indepenently by several French informants. It seems that mountaineers above a certain critical altitude shift to the mutual T. (p. 262)

Not only forms of address change along dimensions of power and solidarity; other aspects of that change seem to affect educationally important aspects of interaction. There is accumulating evidence that power relationships exert a constraining effect on the language of the less powerful person. Labov's (1970) contrast between the one-word responses of a black child to a white interviewer and his fluent and complex talk to black peers is a familiar example. Mishler (1975) finds in his analyses of natural conversations in first-grade classrooms that children's responses to other children's questions are more complex than their responses to adult's questions and suggests that "questions from persons with more power (that is, adults) tend to constrain a child's response so that it is less complex than if the questioner is more equal in power (that is, another child)" (p. 2).

Goody (1978) has made an ethnographic study of question-asking in Gonja which is particularly rich in hypotheses that should be tested in the United States. She focuses on a contrast between the information and command functions of questions. "Where is my dinner?" for example, may be either a request for information or an implicit command that the dinner be brought. She finds that children freely ask information questions of each other, but never of adults. She suggests as an explanation that "people ask information questions most readily of those in a similar status" (p. 36), and conversely "that it is very difficult for those in high-status roles to ask a question that is perceived as being *just* about information" (p. 38).

Because these generalizations do not fit close kin relationships, Goody suggests,

> a cross-cutting dimension which might be described as intimacy or privacy at one extreme with casual public relations at the other . . . [and which] seems to have a systematic effect of exaggerating or de-emphasizing the command channel. Within the family familiarity appears to cushion the effects of status imbalance to some extent. (p. 38)

Power tempered with intimacy may partly explain why parents can be such superb teachers of the truly remarkable learnings that happen in the preschool years. In a rare study, Hess, Dickson, Price, and Leong (n.d.) compared the ways mothers and teachers talk to 4-year-old children from varied socioeconomic backgrounds in the San Francisco area. In two tasks, both sets of adults were asked to play a communication game with the children and to teach them to sort blocks in particular ways. Overall, the children learned as well from their mothers as from their teachers. More interestingly, the mothers used a more direct style.

Examples of mothers' direct requests:
Tell me how these blocks are alike.
Now match the *O*'s. Match the letter there.
Tell me what it is as you do it.
Examples of teachers' indirect requests:
I wonder how these blocks are alike.
Where do you want to put that?
Can you show me where you would put that one?

Combined with these more direct requests, the mothers more often elicited elaborated answers from the children while teachers more often posed questions in a form that invited merely *yes* or *no*.

Personal intimacy seems to be replaceable, as a tempering influence on power, by strong cultural solidarity. To put it bluntly, discipline and order maintained by someone perceived as an insider to the community is psychologically very different from attempts at comparable discipline ("oppression") imposed from without. That contrast is probably the best way to distinguish "education" from "intervention," and may also explain at least part of the hoped for educational benefits of "community control." The combination of power and cultural solidarity occurs in some of the most effective schools we know of: the Jewish *heder* in Eastern Europe, Makarenko's residential youth community in post-revolutionary Soviet Union, Black Muslim schools in the United States, and classrooms in the People's Republic of China. According to McDermott (1977), the Amish schools in Pennsylvania fit this description also.

Given the problem of distance that many Anglo teachers like me have ("white liberals" in Piestrup's [1973] analysis), I suspect I am not alone in expressing an ambivalence about the exercise of power. It may be better for education, however, to retain that power firmly and consistently, as parents do, and temper it with whatever forms of solidarity or intimacy are individually available. I could never be a true insider to the children's community. But people like me can become, if we work at it, familiar, trusted, and therefore educationally effective adults. Social distance is a fact of life like age and caste; psychological distance is not an inevitable result.

Afterword.   *More and more teachers will be sharing my experience of feeling an outsider to their students' worlds. Demographic pro-*

jections are clear: a sharp increase in the percentage of minority children with a simultaneous decrease in the number of minority teachers. According to one typical estimate, there will be 40 percent minority students but only 5 percent minority teachers by the year 2000.

Of course, formal education has always and everywhere been education outside the family—education in which the child is given over to someone not of primary kith and kin. But the challenge of providing effective education increases when that someone is not even from the child's language and cultural community and is moreover a member, and representative, of a group with more status and political power in the surrounding society.

The challenge also increases as "effective education" means extending to more and more students the high literacy goals that were, until this century, expected only in academies for the social and intellectual elite (Resnick & Resnick, 1977).

But the metaphor of "teacher as stranger" has another, equally challenging and more positive, meaning. To philosopher Maxine Greene (1973) being a stranger affords a perspective that teachers must have:

> *To take a stranger's vantage point on everyday reality is to look inquiringly and wonderingly on the world in which one lives. . . . We do not ask that the teacher perceive his existence as absurd; nor do we demand that he estrange himself from his community. We simply suggest that he struggle against unthinking submergence in the social reality that prevails. . . . He must consciously engage in inquiry. (pp. 267, 269, 268)*

The two meanings are related: When the world seems unfamiliar, as it was for me in San Diego, inquiry is stimulated. Can we, as Greene suggests, look more inquiringly at our more familiar literacy teaching worlds?

Part II

Wholes and Parts

4

◆◆◆

Contexts for Literacy
In the Mind and in the Classroom

Foreword. *This chapter was given as a talk to the First South Pacific Conference on Reading at the beginning of my first trip to New Zealand in 1983. An earlier version had been published in the* Journal of Reading Behavior *the previous year. To enliven the research review for oral presentation, I added quotations from an intensely personal narrative of the experience of being changed by education:* Hunger of Memory *(1981), by a first-generation Mexican-American, Richard Rodriguez. Rodriguez summarizes his academic career in one sentence:*

> *The boy who first entered a classroom barely able to speak English, twenty years later concluded his studies in the stately quiet of the reading room in the British Museum. (p. 43)*

Chall (1982) first called attention to the significance of Rodriguez's memories of learning to read.

Hunger of Memory has received considerable publicity, perhaps less for the poignancy of his story than for the educational policy stands that Rodriguez takes: against affirmative action in selection for educational opportunities and against bilingual education in program planning. Quoting here from his literacy memories in no way implies my agreement with those recommendations.

Although Rodriguez writes of his life as a Mexican-American in California, his experiences seem to resonate with those in other cultures, even far away. After hearing these quotations, a Maori writer in New Zealand, Witi Ihimaera, spoke of the similarities with his own autobiographical story, "Catching Up" (1977).

In pedagogical disucssions, learning to read and write have traditionally been considered psychological processes—matters of the perception and interpretation of graphic symbols. Recently, two additional dimensions of literacy have received increasing attention: (1) literacy as a linguistic process, in which knowledge of the sequential probabilities of written text plays an important part—sequential probabilities not only of letters in words, but also of words in sentences and of sentences in paragraphs and larger units of particular genres of text, and (2) literacy as a social process that always takes place in social and culturally organized settings for social as well as personal ends. (Stubbs [1980] gives an excellent summary of these linguistic and social dimensions.)

Because aspects of the social dimensions of literacy are less discussed in education than are psychological and linguistic aspects, it would have been possible to focus this chapter entirely on recent research on the settings and activities in which children encounter written language in school. But to do so would perpetuate a separation of perspectives and might make it harder for teachers and those who work with them to integrate psychological, linguistic, and social perspectives on literacy in improving education. I have therefore defined "context" broadly enough to include both internal and external conditions that influence the nature of school literacy events and what children learn in them: "Context" is anything that affects the reader's or writer's response to the piece of written language that is the focus of immediate perceptual attention. Under this broad definition, I include the internal, mental context that the reader or writer brings—"contexts in the mind." And I also include the external social context that the reader or writer is in. I will talk about two aspects of contexts in the mind, then two aspects of contexts in the external social world of the classroom, then end with a few comments on one important intersection of internal and external contexts—the problem of motivation.

CONTEXTS IN THE MIND

Understanding The Structure of Larger Units of Text

Learning to read requires mastering a complex set of concepts and skills at many levels of a hierarchical system. According to one prominent theory of reading, reading is neither just a "bottom-up" process, driven by perceptions of letters and expectations of the words they may form, nor just a "top-down" process driven by hypotheses about what the text may be about. Rather, the processing of different levels of text structure proceeds in parallel and interactively—not sequentially and additively as we might suppose (Spiro, Bruce, & Brewer, 1981). The first meaning of context, then, is the internal psychological context provided by an understanding of larger units of text than the reader is perceptually focused on at any one moment. (See also Resnick [1987] on "reading as a higher-order skill").

Admittedly, descriptions of the mental operations of mature readers are not sufficient for planning how novices—child or adult—should be instructed: about the order in which their attention should be focused on different units in the hierarchical system and how an eventual integration can best be achieved. But I want to stress here the importance of supporting and strengthening the internal context of more holistic understanding even while the attention of the beginner is sometimes temporarily focused on letters and syllables in school instruction (Adams, Anderson, & Durkin, 1978).

Consider, as an analogy, learning to drive a car as it is described in terms of Soviet psychologist A. N. Leont'ev's (1981) theory of activity. In Leont'ev's theory, the structure of every human activity (which is energized by a motive) is composed of actions (which are directed by goals), and these actions in turn are composed of operations, selected and carried out automatically, depending on particular conditions. So, for example, shifting gears starts as a goal-directed action for a beginner; later, it recedes in status to an automatic operation done out-of-awareness under certain driving conditions (stopping at a light, changing speed and power on a steep hill, etc.). But even during the temporary learning period when the driver's focal attention is on the mechanics of shifting gears, the context in the mind of the learner of what the entire activity of driving a car is all about provides not only the motivation, but also the source of integration of all the separate operations and actions into a complex whole.

Imagine variation in the novice driver's previous experience with cars: has never seen a car, or seen one but never had a ride, or has ridden in a car but never up front to observe the driver, or has had much experience observing and talking about what driving is all about. With such variation in predriving experience, novice drivers will bring different internal contexts to the learning task. So with children learning to read and write: They will bring different experiences with texts, different internal contexts, from both the quality and quantity of the particular literacy events that they have participated in outside school.

The importance of this internal context, and variations in it, has several implications for school practice. First, teachers should know as much as possible about what children have learned from the literacy events they have participated in outside school—especially for those children whose experiences have not been primarily with books. There is growing interest in the United States in learning more about what preschool children learn from "environmental print" such as labels in the supermarket and on the kitchen shelves. There is no more important meaning to the pedagogical advice "to start where the child is." But second, while we build on such a base, we cannot rely on it to be a sufficient mental context for learning to read books. Evidence continues to accumulate that preschool experiences with books contribute significantly to school success. We must extend that context for all children by reading to them before and after they can read for themselves.

Reading to children can be an especially powerful way of increasing their understanding of written text structures, of increasing the top-down knowledge they bring to the reading task. At the level of sentence structure, consider a sentence one group of children had trouble with: "But Ricky', said his mother . . . " (McDermott, 1978). This is not a sentence structure one is apt to hear in ordinary conversation. Yet one can imagine encountering it often in books. If children have had many experiences of hearing such sentences, with the teacher's intonation supplying cues to the syntactic structure, then they should find them easier to comprehend alone. At the level of larger structures of different written genres—folk tales, for example, or newspaper accounts—the same benefits of oral experiences can be gained.

> It mattered that education was changing me. It never ceased to matter. My brother and sisters would giggle at our mother's mispronounced words. They'd correct her gently. My mother laughed girlishly one night, trying not to pronounce *sheep* as *ship*. From a distance I listened sullenly. From that distance, pretending not to notice on another occasion, I saw my father looking at the title pages of my library books. That was the scene on my mind when I walked home with a fourth-grade companion and heard him say that his parents read to him every night. (A strange-sounding book— *Winnie the Pooh*.) Immediately, I wanted to know, "what is it like?"

My companion, however, thought I wanted to know about the plot of the book. (Rodriguez, 1981, p. 52)

Fortunately, Rodriguez did hear books read in school, but in an unusual setting: in the remedial reading classes that were arranged for him with "a very old nun":

> At the end of each school day, for nearly six months, I would meet with her in a tiny room that served as the school's library but was actually only a storeroom for used textbooks and a vast collection of *National Geographics*. Everything about our sessions pleased me: the smallness of the room, the noise of the janitor's broom hitting the edge of the long hallway outside the door; the green of the sun, lighting the wall; and the old woman's face blurred white with a beard. Most of the time we took turns. I began with my elementary text. Sentences of astonishing simplicity seemed to me lifeless and drab: "The boys ran from the rain . . . She wanted to sing . . . The kite rose in the blue." Then the old nun would read from her favorite books, usually biographies of early American presidents. Playfully she ran through complex sentences, calling the words alive with her voice, making it seem that the author somehow was speaking directly to me. I smiled just to listen to her. I sat there and sensed for the first time some possibility of fellowship between a reader and a writer, a communication, never *intimate* like that I heard spoken words at home convey, but one nevertheless *personal* (Rodriguez, 1981, p. 60; emphasis in the original).

Third, we have to be sure that there's a balance of attention to all levels of text, for all children, in school instruction. Recent observational research in U.S. classrooms indicates that this is not always the case, and that the inner context of understanding larger meaningful units of text is apt to be neglected for those children who probably need it most.

In the United States, reading instruction in most classrooms of 30 children is conducted in three to five homogeneous reading groups of 6 to 10 children each. Allington (1980) audiotaped oral reading segments of reading lessons with the best and the poorest readers in 20 primary classrooms in three school districts in New York. He analyzed how the teachers responded to children's oral reading errors and found dramatic differences between the two reading groups in the 20 classrooms. There was a difference in the rate of teacher corrections of the errors: two-thirds of poor readers' errors were corrected, but only one-fourth of good readers' errors. There were differences in the timing of the correction: Teachers were more likely to interrupt poor readers immediately at the point of error rather than waiting for the next phrase or clause boundary. Finally, there were differences in the cues provided by the teachers to help the children read the right word: For the poor readers, the cues were more apt to be graphemic/phonemic, while the cues for good readers were more apt to be semantic/syntactic. At least in the United States, the top and bottom groups in ethnically and socioeconomically mixed classrooms will differ in ethnicity and social class. Thus there seems to be two theories in action of how to teach reading—one for the rich and one for the poor.

These observations do not suggest that the beginning reader's attention should never be focused on syllables and letters. Beginning drivers do have to focus temporarily on component skills, and so it seems do many beginning readers (Chall, 1979; Resnick, 1979). But the teacher, and thereby the children, must always have the larger internal context also in mind.

Knowledge of the World

As reading is an interactive set of parallel processes, attending simultaneously to different levels of text structure, it is also a constructive process. By this I mean that the reader's mind is not a blank slate on which the meanings of words and sentences are passively registered. Recent research on reading (Spiro et al., 1981) emphasizes the active work that readers do in constructing for themselves both the more literal meanings in the text and the inferences that go beyond the words themselves. A critical resource in constructing meaning is the knowledge of people and places, events and ideas, sometimes called scripts or schemata, that the reader brings to any reading task. Thus the second meaning of context is the internal psychological context of organized semantic networks of knowledge of the world that are in part reflected in the reader's vocabulary.

The importance of this knowledge even to adults is obvious to anyone who has tried to read an article on an unfamiliar topic. This knowledge base differs greatly among children who have had different life experiences and more or less contact with written language outside of school.

OPEN THE DOORS OF YOUR MIND WITH BOOKS, read the red and white poster over the nun's desk in early September. It soon was apparent to me that reading was the classroom's central activity. Each course had its own book. And the information gathered from a book was unquestioned. READ TO LEARN, the sign on the wall advised in December. I privately wondered: What was the connection between reading and learning? Did one learn something only by reading it? Was an idea only an idea if it could be written down? In June, CONSIDER BOOKS YOUR BEST FRIENDS. Friends? Reading was, at best, only a chore. I needed to look up whole paragraphs of words in a dictionary. Lines of type were dizzying, the eye having to move slowly across the page, then down, and across. . . . The sentences of the first books I read were cooly impersonal. Toned hard. (Rodriguez, 1981, p. 59)

The implications for reading instruction of the constructive conception of literacy are at least twofold: First, teachers must help children bring to mind whatever knowledge they have that is relevant to the text at hand; second, they need to find ways to help children acquire new knowledge and new vocabulary throughout their school career.

Most books on how to teach reading advise teachers to do some preparation for reading before actually assigning pages to be read. But in actual practice, this part of the reading lesson is often reduced to a few words written on the blackboard. One very successful and well-researched reading program has been developed in Hawaii in the Kamehameha Early Education Program (KEEP) for children of Polynesian descent in which phonics instruction is still included, but far more emphasis is put on prereading comprehension work.

Before any text is read, the KEEP teacher engages her small reading group in a preparatory discussion that is labeled "experience" (Au, 1979). The change in terminology from more general "preparation for reading" to "experience" signifies what is important in the content of the lesson. Discussion is focused directly on children's experiences relevant to what the teacher knows the content of the story to be. The teacher draws out the children's knowledge, clarifies misconceptions, and reinforces concepts she knows to be important in the text to come. For example, the preparation for a story called "Freddie Found a Frog" included discussion about what you would do with a frog, what frogs taste like, how frogs move, how it feels to touch a frog, where you can find frogs, and what kind of noises frogs make. Whereas many teachers include a brief presentation and discussion of new words, such extensive discussion of children's personal experiences related to the story topic is rare.

Alternative explanations for the success of the KEEP program are possible, and I will return to two other features below. But the "experience" discussion has two important consequences: For the children, it evokes and brings to the forefront of consciousness those concepts that will be most useful in comprehending the text to come; for the teacher, it displays the children's concepts so that misconceptions can be rediscussed and missing ideas introduced.

It is interesting to note fundamental similarities between the KEEP program for young children and Paolo Freire's method of teaching adults as adapted in the Nicaraguan campaign (Cardenal & Miller, 1981). In both, dialogue about ideas precedes phonemic analysis, and in both the dialogue draws heavily on readers' personal experiences.

Of course, more advanced stages of literacy require the ability to read material whose topics are increasingly remote from personal experience, so the second instructional problem is how to build children's knowledge base so that they can comprehend such texts more easily. In Chall's (1979) words, "The need to know some of the new, if more is to be learned from reading, becomes greater. Readers need to bring knowledge and experience to their reading if they are to learn from it" (p. 43). One kind of curriculum design that should be useful is the kind of unit organization centered around a social studies or science theme that makes it more likely for children to be reading texts that are about topics also encountered in nontext media.

Consider, as one example, a multiethnic classroom in Central Park East, a public school in New York City where the children have been studying ancient Egypt because the King Tut exhibit happened to be in town. Here reading and writing take place as children create a Monopoly-type board game called Loot-a-Tomb, write stories about a runaway slave that provoke a class discussion about similarities and differences between slaves in ancient Egypt and colonial America, write a cartoonlike series of picture stories about the pet classroom snake that died and was mummified and then buried with Egyptian funeral rites in nearby Central Park, and write diary entries that connect curriculum themes to personal experience:

Oni's story
We went to see the King Tut and his treasures. His treasures were beautiful. And when he was dead somebody—who?—I forgot his or her name, found Tut's body. My grandmother died because she had cancer and my grandfather died because he died in his sleep. And when I saw that I cried because I couldn't see him no more. And I always cry when I think of him and my grandmother too. I loved them so so so so much. And I wish he would come back but he is not dead as long as I love him. (from Holmes, 1980)

CONTEXTS IN THE CLASSROOM

Interactions with the Teacher

The obvious and most common social context for literacy in school (at least in the United States) is the reading lesson and the teacher–student interactions that take place in them. Detailed analyses of the language of lessons have been made by Sinclair and Coulthard (1975) in England, Mehan (1979) in the United States, and McHoul (1978) and Malcolm (1982) in Australia. And a historical survey indicates that, at least in the United States, the lesson—or recitation, as it is sometimes called—has persisted unchanged, pretty much in its present form (Hoetker & Ahlbrand, 1969).

We are all familiar with what lessons look and sound like—for example, the discussions before and after some text is read. The teacher controls talk on a particular topic with an entire class or some subgroup of it. She talks about two-thirds of the total time, primarily asking known-answer questions and evaluating children's answers. This means that only one-third of the time, or 10 minutes of a 30-minute lesson, is available to be shared among 30 or more pupils. In such conditions, talk is apt to get out of control, not only because children have a particularly hard time waiting their turn, but also because the lesson includes a demand for performance combined with limited possibilities for any one performer. And so an elaborate turn-taking apparatus is used (Mehan, 1979) to keep the talk under control.

In the last 10 years, there have been a series of studies in the United States documenting the problems that this typical lesson structure creates. If children try to participate too eagerly, more of everyone's time is spent in disciplinary talk, and less time is available for doing academic tasks. If children do not participate enough, teachers receive less information from which to diagnose their problems and children's opportunities to practice important skills are reduced.

These problems are exaggerated, of course, when children come to school not knowing the language of the school.

> Without question, it would have pleased me to hear my teachers address me in Spanish when I entered the classroom. I would have felt much less afraid. I would have trusted them and responded with ease. . . . [But] my teachers were unsentimental about their responsibility. What they understood was that I needed to speak a public language. So their voices would search me out, asking me questions.

Each time I'd hear them, I'd look up in surprise to see a nun's face frowning at me. I'd mumble, not really meaning to answer. The nun would persist, "Richard, stand up. Don't look at the floor. Speak up. Speak to the entire class, not just to me!" But I couldn't believe that the English language was mine to use. (In part I did not want to believe it.) I continued to mumble. I resisted the teacher's demands. (Did I somehow suspect that once I learned public language my pleasing family life would be changed?) Silent, waiting for the bell to sound, I remained dazed, diffident, afraid. (Rodriguez, 1981, pp. 19-20)

Then three nuns arrived at his home to talk to his parents and ask them to speak English, as best they could, even within the family.

Hunger of Memory is the autobiography of the exceptional immigrant working-class child who succeeds in a very traditional school, a school notable only—and this may have been the crucial feature—for the nuns' belief that he could learn:

With every award, each graduation from one level of education to the next, people I'd meet would congratulate me. Their refrain always the same: "your parents must be very proud." Sometimes they'd ask me how I managed it—my "success." (How?) After a while, I had several quick answers to give in reply. I'd admit, for one thing, that I went on to an excellent grammar school. (My earliest teachers, the nuns, made my success their ambition.) (Rodriguez, 1981, pp. 43-44)

Rodriguez believes that his public success was only possible at the private cost of alienation from home, that a high level of literacy inevitably distanced him from the intimate life he loved. But such a price need not be paid, and, if schools are changed, more than a few exceptional students can succeed.

In considering kinds of change, it is important to consider not only the language of instruction, but also the patterns of interaction. Fortunately, the KEEP program in Hawaii shows that change in the interactions between students and teachers in reading lessons can contribute to children's achievement. In the KEEP program, introduction of the "experience" discussions at the beginning of each reading lesson brought with it a simultaneous change in form. When comprehension was stressed in small-group discussions of the stories to be read, these discussions gradually took on an overlapping-turn structure similar to the overlapping speech that is common in ordinary Hawaiian Polynesian conversations, especially in the stylized speech event called "talk-story." In talk-story, a story is co-narrated by more than one person, and the speech of the narrators is also overlapped by audience responses. The KEEP children were familiar with this conversational structure in their lives outside school and gradually introduced it into the story discussions at school, when change in content of the lessons and a teacher who was willing to relax her control of turn-taking made it possible. Later, the new lesson form was analyzed by the KEEP research staff as a bicultural combination of indigenous conversational style and teacher-guided content, and it became an important feature of the KEEP reading program (Au, 1979).

In the KEEP program, the change in interactional patterns involved the relation of turn-taking rules to allow children to speak out without being called on—and to chime in even when another child was speaking, as long as the content was relevant to the teacher-chosen topic. These particular modifications were helpful to Polynesian children from one particular cultural background. Other modifications of traditional lesson structure may be needed for other groups of children.

Our general implication from ethnographic studies of classroom communication is that if children do not speak up in just the ways teachers expect, we should take as a first hypothesis not that the children are either stupid or rude, but that the ways of speaking children have learned at home have different rules. Beyond that generalization, teachers can learn by observing their children and by participating sensitively in the out-of-school life of the communities in which they teach.

Teacher–student interactions take a written form in what have come to be called "dialogue journals," which are written daily by the children and responded to at night by the teacher (Staton, Shuy, Peyton, & Reed, 1988). In contrast to most writing assigned in school, dialogue journals are interactive, self-generating as to topic, and functional in reliably eliciting a substantive (nonevaluative) response.

One particular language function found frequently in the journals, not surprisingly, is complaints. It is easy to consider children's complaints as trivial, but a second thought should remind us that complaints serve not only children but adults, to appeal for redress of grievances not only from family and friends, but from social institutions and governments as well. Shuy (in Staton et al., 1988) reports his analysis of all the complaints in one of the year-long dialogue journals in this classroom. He shows how these complaints develop in effectiveness, especially in providing supporting evidence of why the complaint is true. As the year went on, the proportion of effective complaints grew—first in October in interpersonal complaints about other students, and not until March about academic matters. For example, instead of just writing, "I thought what we did today was boring," the student writes:

> Everything has to be turned in on Wednesday. Our math our myth and our memorized poem. Now that is a lot of homework for just two evenings and that is not very much time to memorize anything especially since we have two extra things to do. (p. 159)

Shuy recommends journals as holistic writing that includes practice in narrative, descriptive, and expository components. He also values the interactive dialogic character of the journals, believing that the children's complaints become more effective over the year in response to the comments and questions in the teacher's daily response.

Interactions Among Peers

To adults, reading and writing are solitary and silent activities, moments of internal language processes that contrast with interpersonal talk. The contrast is not complete: In church, we read hymn books aloud and together; during lectures, we exchange notes, thus using reading as well as writing for immediate interactional ends; and we listen alone to talk on the radio or TV, thus making a solitary activity of the comprehension of speech. But usually we talk with others and read and write alone.

Not so with children, especially children just learning to read in the primary grades. Learning to read, like mature reading later on, is certainly an individual cognitive process; but it can be also a very social activity, and we should consider the value of allowing, even encouraging, collaborative work among students over reading and writing tasks. Traditionally, at least in the United States, despite the fact that school classrooms are unusually crowded social environments, such collaboration is rarely encouraged, perhaps in part because there has been no clear rationale for its value. My last meaning of context is thus the external social context of the peer group.

Recent observational research shows that children naturally want to work and talk with one another, and so there can be powerful motivational value in encouraging it in carefully planned literacy activities. Rodriguez implies that such collaboration may be especially important for children in communities where solitary book-reading is not a common part of out-of-school life.

In an elementary school in inner-city Philadelphia, Fiering (1981) wanted to understand the meanings of literacy for the children themselves, 90% poor and black. So she looked for all instances of what she called "unofficial" literacy, in which children read and wrote for their own purposes and in their own preferred interactional style. Because writing activities leave concrete products as reading does not, Fiering found it easier to study "unofficial" writing than "unofficial" reading.

Overall, Fiering (1981) found a tremendous amount and variety of unofficial writing; children were deeply involved in writing that their teachers paid little or no attention to. From her observations across the elementary school grades, Fiering drew several conclusions. First, while there was more unofficial writing in the higher-ability "tracks" in this homogeneously grouped school than in the lower-ability tracks (in the ratio of 2:1), the types of writing were the same. Second, the children spontaneously exploited, and played with, stylistic features intrinsic to the graphic medium—spacing and layout on the page, letter shapes and handwriting styles—that the teachers either didn't value or censored out of conventional norms of neatness. In other words, even after children learn the conventions of written language form, they enjoy violating them (as advertisements and TV do) in playful ways.

Third, the variety of kinds of writing was impressive. Of 184 pieces of unofficial spontaneous and unassigned writing, there were 45 labels and captions for objects or pictures; 23 imitations of "official" documents such as tickets; 15 notes and letters; 12 songs and poems; 13 lists; 8 word games; uncounted instances of copying from books, which Fiering sensitively and poignantly describes as a "phantom performance" of writing, a way to participate in literacy (p. 124) even without the actual skills; and more. In Fiering's words, "I am not arguing that this kind of writing should be considered equal to official literacy—stories, poems, compositions, etc., but only that it was a very real demonstration of the power of writing in the lives of children, some of whom were basically illiterate, at least in the official sense" (1981, p. 126).

Finally, she notes how often the children "turn literacy events into collaborative, oral and highly social-interactive phenomena. . . . Whereas the text-book (and adult) view of writing seems to emphasize the more personal, isolating functions of writing, treating audience as separate in time and space, these children seized opportunies to make writing one more tool for the kind of interactional work that is part of their daily lives." (1981, pp. 13, 51–52)

As part of her research, Fiering talked with the teachers about her observations of unofficial literacy and about ways to take advantage of the children's spontaneously expressed energy for literacy. To make the unofficial kinds of writing more official didn't seem to be the answer. To the extent that children's spontaneous writings were co-opted by official recognition, they would lose some if not all of their special meaning to the children. Moreover, teachers have legitimate agendas of official kinds of writing they want to support. But it did seem worthwhile to Fiering and some teachers to find ways to carry out the teacher's agenda but still permit more of the collaborative style of interaction that many of the children seemed to prefer. (Cazden [1988a] gives further discussion and examples of peer collaboration in reading and writing activities.)

That suggestion applies to all children. But it may have special importance for children like Rodriguez. Some of his most poignant passages are about the isolation he felt in learning to read and write in a nonbook home culture. About his home literacy environment, he writes:

> From an early age I knew that my mother and father could read and write both Spanish and English. I had observed my father making his way through what, I now suppose, must have been income tax forms. On other occasions I waited apprehensively while my mother read onion-paper letters airmailed from Mexico with news of a relative's illness or death. For both my parents, however, reading was something done out of necessity and as quickly as possible. Never did I see either of them read an entire book. Nor did I see them read for pleasure. Their reading consisted of work manuals, prayer books, newspapers, recipes. (Rodriguez, 1981, pp. 58-59)

Learning to read at school, Rodriguez felt the isolation of encountering written words alone:

> What bothered me most . . . was the isolation reading required. To console myself for the loneliness I'd feel when I read, I tried reading in a very soft voice. Until: "Who is doing all that talking to his neighbor?" . . . One day [at the end of a remedial reading class] the nun concluded a session by asking me why I was so reluctant to read by myself. I tried to explain; said something about the way written words made me feel all alone—almost, I wanted to add but didn't, as when I spoke to myself in a room just emptied of furniture. (Rodriguez, 1981, pp. 59-60)

Later, when reading had become easier and more familiar, there was the isolation and loneliness felt at home. Speaking in the third person, Rodriguez writes about the academically successful working-class student.

> Here is a child who cannot forget that his academic success distances him from a life he loved, even from his memory of himself.
>   Initially, he wavers, balances allegiance. . . . Gradually, necessarily, the balance is lost. The boy needs to spend more and more time studying each night enclosing himself in the silence permitted and required by intense concentration. He takes his first step toward academic success, away from his family. (Rodriguez, 1981, p. 48)

There are no easy answers for how to lessen the psychological and social distance between the love of books we hope to inculcate in school and nonbook (even nonliterate) home communities. But at least we can arrange learning environments so that reading and writing can more often be social and interactive, not isolating and silent, in school.

The Schoolboys of Barbiana (Italy) (1970) did just that. In a book called *Letter to a Teacher* (still very popular with young readers in Italy), a group of working-class students wrote about the importance of education and what they thought they should learn. They also described how they worked together, creatively and critically, in writing the book:

> This is the way we do it:
>   To start with, each of us keeps a notebook in his pocket. Every time an idea comes up, we make a note of it. Each idea on a separate sheet, on one side of the page.
>   Then one day we gather together all the sheets of paper and spread them on a big table. We look through them, one by one, to get rid of duplicates. Next, we make separate piles of the sheets that are related, and these will make up the chapters. Every chapter is subdivided into little piles, and they will become paragraphs.
>   At this point we try to give a name to each paragraph. If we can't it means either that the paragraph has no content or that too many things are squeezed into it. Some paragraphs disappear. Some are broken up.
>   While we name the paragraphs we discuss the logical order for them until an outline is born. With the outline set, we reorganize all the piles to follow its pattern.

We take the first pile, spread the sheets on the table, and we find the sequence for them. And so we begin to put down a first draft of the text.

We mimeograph that part so we each have a copy in front of us. Then, scissors, paste, and colored pencils. We throw everything back up into the air. Next sheets are added. We mimeograph again.

A race begins now for all of us to find any word that can be crossed out, any excess adjectives, repetitions, lines, difficult words, overly long sentences, and any two concepts that are forced into one sentence.

We call in one outsider after another. We prefer that they have not had too much school. We ask them to read aloud. And we watch to see if they have understood what we meant to say.

We accept their suggestions if they clarify the text. We reject any suggestions made in the name of caution.

Having done all this hard work and having followed these rules that anyone could use, we often come across an intellectual idiot who announces, "This letter has a remarkable personal style." (pp. 120–122)

INTERNAL AND EXTERNAL CONTEXTS:
THE ISSUE OF MOTIVATION

It is tempting for educators to consider motivation for literacy as something children either come to school with or do not—that is, as a characteristic of children determined by their out-of-school life. Without denying out-of-school influences, we should adopt the view of the Reading and Language Studies Division of the National Institute of Education, the former name of the research division of the U.S. Department of Education:

> *We view motivation as an attribute of situations and not as a character trait of individuals.* No one is "motivated" all of the time, for all kinds of learning. If we improve the content of instruction and the human interaction in classrooms, we will have made substantial progress toward improving motivation for learning to read. (Penny et al., 1980)

In discussing internal and external contexts for literacy, we have been considering specific aspects of "the content of instruction and the human interaction in classrooms." Changes in how the school affects the children's internal mental contexts of text and world knowledge, plus changes in the external social contexts of interactions with teacher and peers, should make "substantial progress toward improving motivation for learning to read" and to write as well.

Afterword. *Research on children's participation in one classroom literacy event suggests how subtly aspects of the classroom situation can affect motivation. In the early 1970s, the television show called "The Electric Company," designed to help children who were having trouble learning to read, went on the air. The producers (Children's Television Workshop, best known for "Sesame Street") wanted to know what environmental variables affected the viewing behavior of children watching in their elementary school classrooms (as we did in San Diego). A small research group at Harvard tried to find out (Cazden, 1973b).*

We defined viewing behavior as both visual attention and verbalizations in response to the screen. We observed 10 primary grade classrooms, five or six times each, while they watched the 30-minute show. Two independent and very reliable measures of attention were used: a scan of the entire class at 30-second intervals to count those visually oriented toward the TV screen, and continuous monitoring and recording of the visual attention of individual students with an instrument called an "event recorder." Verbalizations, often silent, were more difficult to record, but we did our best.

Because "The Electric Company" was designed especially for children reading below the norm for their grade, we were interested in the relationship between viewing behavior and reading level. Children's reading ability can be defined in two ways: ranked according to their relative standing in their class (high, middle, or low reading group) or more absolutely according to scores on a reading test. Because the range of reading levels varies from classroom to classroom, the best readers in one room may be only as able as the median reader in another room.

Without exception we found that children of any tested reading level showed more attention to the show when they were in a relatively higher reading group in their classroom than did children of a similar absolute tested ability who were in a realtively lower group in another classroom. In other words, lower relative standing in class (in terms of reading-group placement) adversely affected children's attention to televised reading material.

Seen in this way, a variable such as level of reading ability, which is usually considered a child variable in its absolute sense, becomes an environmental variable as well, affecting motivation through the child's relative standing in the classroom group. This may seem a surprising finding, but we are not alone in documenting this influence. Webb and Kenderski (1984) found a similar effect of relative, rather than absolute, ability on the frequency with which junior high school mathematics students gave explanations to their peers in cooperative learning groups.

Fiering's description of the urge to write shown by all children in one ordinary inner-city school argues strongly that the problem in greater literacy achievement is not so much in children's initial motivation, but in our efforts to direct their energy without killing it and to build their confidence in their own ability to learn.

5

◆ ◆ ◆

Play with Language and Metalinguistic Awareness
One Dimension of
Language Experience

Foreword. *This chapter is taken from a paper presented at a conference at the Bank Street College of Education in 1973 honoring the memory of one of its founders, Lucy Sprague Mitchell, and then published in* The Urban Review.

Bank Street is where I received my initial teacher training in 1946–47. Mitchell had just retired, but her influence was still powerful, especially through her ideas about children's language and children's literature. In the introduction to her Here and Now Story Book *(1948), in the section on form, Mitchell wrote:*

> There is no better play material in the world than words. They surround us, go with us through our work-a-day tasks, their sound is always in our ears, their rhythms on our tongue. Why do we leave it to special occasions and to special people to use these common things as precious play material? Because we are grown-ups and have closed our ears and eyes that we may not be distracted from our plodding ways. But when we turn to the children, to hearing and seeing children, to whom all the world is as play material, who think and feel through play, can we not then drop our adult utilitarian speech and listen and watch for the patterns of words and ideas? Can we not care for the way we say things to them and not merely what we say? (p. 50)

And so it seemed appropriate to honor her with further discussion of play with language—by her Bank Street colleagues (developmental psychologist) Barbara Biber and (nursery school teacher) Harriet Johnson, and others.

Most of the examples relate to young children's development of what we now call "emergent literacy."

Although the title of this chapter speaks of play and then metalinguistic awareness, I am going to discuss them in the reverse order—first, explain what I mean by "metalinguistic awareness" as a special dimension of language experience and its seeming importance in education; then describe one, and only one, conception of the function of "play" in general and play with language in particular; and finally ask how educators might encourage play with language in school.

METALINGUISTIC AWARENESS

It is intuitively obvious to us as language users that when either speaking or listening, our focal attention is not on speech sounds, nor even on larger units such as words and syntactic patterns. Our focal attention is on the meaning, or the intention, of what we or someone else is trying to say. The language forms are themselves transparent; we hear through them to the meaning intended. As the Duchess rightly says in *Alice in Wonderland*: "and the moral of *that* is—take care of the sense and the sounds will take care of themselves." In both speaking and hearing, complicated coordinations of phonetic, semantic, and syntactic processing are run off smoothly, resulting in the articulation of an idea into a sequential stream of sounds by the speaker, and the perceptual processing of such a temporal stream of sounds into an interpretation of an idea by the hearer. While we do not understand how human beings do this remarkable task, it is an indisputable fact that the processes usually do function successfully, and out-of-awareness, for adult and child alike.

In this way, speaking is like any other kind of skilled behavior, such as hammering a nail or playing the piano. In every case, we are aware of the parts of our body instrumental to the act only in a subsidiary fashion. Focally, we attend to the desired outcome of the act—the position of the nail or the music our fingers will produce (Cazden, 1972; Polanyi, 1964).

Occasionally in the course of communication, some aspect of language itself does come to our focal attention. As long as communication is working smoothly, this is not apt to happen. But when something interferes with the normally smooth process, our attention shifts, and the language itself loses its transparency and becomes for some moments opaque; we attend directly to it, more conscious of ourselves or others. As speakers, this often happens when we pause to search for a word (Goldman-Eisler, 1964).

Robert Coles (1973) gives a poignant description of the visible as well as audible evidence of one elderly Chicana woman's search. The woman lives in a small and isolated mountain community north of Santa Fe, has had virtually no schooling, and speaks "a mixture of Spanish and terse but forceful English." In Coles's words:

> She struggles not only with her mind but with her body—her whole being—to express herself. . . . When she searches for a word, be it in Spanish or English, she drops her needle and thread, drops her fork and spoon, drops anything she may have in her hand. She needs those old arthritic fingers. They flex and unflex. It is as if before her is a sandpile of words, and she must push and probe her way through it until she has found what she is looking for. Then the fingers can stop, the hands can relax and go back to other business or simply be allowed to rest in her lap. (p. 11)

Outside of normal communicative contexts, focusing attention on aspects of language forms themselves is also possible for adults, and gradually for children as their development proceeds. It is an important aspect of our unique capacities as human beings that we can not only act, but reflect back on our own actions; not only learn and use language, but treat it as an object of analysis and evaluation in its own right. Moreover, as David McNeill (1974) has pointed out, the shift between transparency (out-of-awareness) and opaqueness (in-awareness) is possible not only at the single contrast between meaning and form:

> The processing of language can be stopped anywhere. . . . Hence rather than a dichotomy between opaque meaning and transparent syntax or phonology, there is a series of opaque-transparent oppositions, depending on how far linguistic processing had advanced before it is stopped. (p. 224)

Metalinguistic awareness, the ability to make language forms opaque and attend to them in and for themselves, is a special kind of language performance, one which makes special cognitive demands and seems to be less easily and less universally acquired than the language performances of speaking and listening. Our concern as educators with this particular kind of language performance comes from increasing arguments that it is at least very helpful—and may be critically important—not so much in the primary processes of speaking and hearing as in what may be considered the derived or secondary processes of reading and writing. (Note that the human capacity for what I term linguistic awareness is here considered one kind of language performance, and not a means for ascertaining, in its more pure form, a person's language knowledge, or "competence.")

The idea that such awareness is related to literacy is not new. For more than 10 years, we have been reading in Vygotsky that literacy depends on, and in turn contributes to, making previously nonconscious or tacit knowledge more conscious. In Vygotsky's (1962) words:

> The child does have a command of grammar of his native tongue long before he enters school, but it is unconscious, acquired in a purely structural way, like the phonetic composition of words. If you ask a young child to produce a combination of sounds, for example, *sk*, you will find that its deliberate articulation is too hard for him; yet within a structure, as in the word *Moscow*, he pronounces the same sound with ease. The same is true for grammar. The child will use the correct case or tense within a sentence but cannot decline or conjugate a word on request. He may not acquire new grammatical or syntactic forms in school but, thanks to instruction in grammar and writing, he does become aware of what he is doing and learns to use his skills consciously. Just as the child realizes for the first time in learning to write that the word *Moscow* consists of the sounds m-o-s-c-o-w and learns to pronounce each one separately, he also learns to construct sentences, to do consciously what he has been doing unconsciously in speaking. (p. 100-101)

More recently, a conference resulting in the book *Language by Ear and by Eye* (Kavanaugh & Mattingly, 1972) focused directly on the differences that must exist between learning to speak and learning to read. Everyone learns to speak, but not all languages have written forms; even when they do, not all speakers become literate; when they do become literate, deliberate instruction is much more apt to be required. Why?

In his final "Reflections on the Conference," George Miller said,

"In my opinion, the most important issue we raised, chewed on, and returned to repeatedly was the issue Mattingly referred to as 'linguistic awareness' and Klima called 'accessibility'" (Kavanaugh & Mattingly, 1972, p. 376). Mattingly, in his chapter on "Reading, the Linguistic Process and Linguistic Awareness," says:

> Speaking and listening are primary linguistic activities; reading is a secondary and rather special sort of activity that relies critically upon the reader's awareness of those primary activities. . . . Linguistic awareness is very far from evenly distributed over all phases of linguistic activity. (p. 139) [E.g., awareness is greater for words than syllables; for syllables than sounds; and in general for units than for rules that govern their structural arrangements.] (Kavanaugh & Mattingly, 1972, pp. 133, 139)

Mattingly then suggests the relationship that is the focus of this chapter—the relationship to verbal play:

> There appears to be considerable individual variation in linguistic awareness. Some speaker-hearers are not only very conscious of linguistic patterns, but exploit their consciousness with obvious pleasure in verbal play, e.g., punning [and versifying, solving crossword puzzles, and talking Pig Latin] or verbal work (e.g., linguistic analysis). Others never seem to be aware of more than words . . . this variation contrasts markedly with the relative consistency from person to person with which primary linguistic activity is performed. . . . Our view is that reading is a language-based activity like a Pig Latin or versification and not a form of primary linguistic activity analogous to listening. (Kavanaugh & Mattingly, 1972, pp. 140-151)

Supporting evidence for this statement comes from Read's (1971) research on preschool children's invented spelling. His children, precocious only in their attempts to write, seemed distinguished more by their metalinguistic awareness than by their primary language ability per se.

If linguistic awareness is so important, what do we know about its development? Presumably, as a child's language develops, so does his or her conscious awareness of that language. Think of each addition to the child's linguistic knowledge as written in his or her mind in magic ink, or recorded there in magic sound. As these additions are growing in number and complexity of relationships, so they are also becoming gradually more visible, or audible, to the child himself or herself.

In looking for evidence of this gradual process, we should keep in mind Miller's distinction between two levels of awareness, called by Mattingly "awareness" and by Klima "accessibility." Miller suggests:

> I can conceive of some level of linguistic processing being accessible in the sense that some special transformations, like spelling or versification, could take advantage of it, and yet it might not be describable at the level of conscious awareness. (Kavanaugh & Mattingly, 1972, p. 378)

Whatever labels one thinks most appropriate, there clearly is a difference between having elements of language available for attention and playful manipulation outside of communicative contexts, and being able to evaluate and analyze those elements in other terms.

As an example of how difficult it is for even the eight-year-old daughter of a linguist to achieve this second level of verbal discussion of language forms, consider the answers given when Lila Gleitman asked eight-year-old Claire (Gleitman, Gleitman, & Shipley, 1972) if certain sentences sounded OK and, if not, why:

a. LG: *I saw the queen and you saw one.*
   C: No, because you're saying that one person saw a queen and one person saw a one—ha ha—what's a one? . . .

b. LG: How about this one: *I am knowing your sister.*
   C: No: *I know your sister.*
   LG: Why not *I am knowing your sister*? You can say *I am eating your dinner.*
   C: It's different! (shouting) You say different sentences in different ways! Otherwise it wouldn't make sense . . .

c. LG: How about: *George frightens the color green.*
   C: Sounds okay, but it's stupid, it's stupid!
   LG: What's wrong with it?
   C: The color green isn't even alive, so how can it be afraid of George? (pp. 149–151)

Even these three examples exemplify a general development trend: Claire could explain very well the anomalous meaning in the third example, while she could only recognize, but not yet adequately explain, the more grammatical deviation of the first two sentences. de Villiers and de Villiers (1972) found the same earlier importance of sematic, as opposed to syntactic, factors in judgments of the acceptability of sentences by 2- and 3-year-old children.

I assume that the simpler level of awareness, accessability, is all that is involved in learning to read. Here, too, there is evidence of a gradual developmental process. Specifically, for example, there is evidence that children of kindergarten age are not aware of the segmentation of their own speech into all the word units they are actually using. Marjorie Holden and Walter MacGinitie have been studying "Children's Conceptions of Word Boundaries in Speech and Print" (n.d.). In one task, they asked kindergarten children to repeat a sentence and then repeat it again, tapping one in a line of poker chips for each word. What they found, consistent with other research, is that young children are more aware of content words, especially nouns and verbs, than of function words—articles, prepositions, auxiliaries, and so forth. On the tapping task, the children tended to attach a function word to the content word before or after it. So, for example, out of 24 responses to the test sentence *You have to go home*, 12 children segmented it: You/haveto/go/home, and 5 children segmented it: You/have/togo/home.

It is striking that this sequence of content words followed by functors, which occurs at the level of awareness at around age 5 or 6, is also the sequence with which those words originally appear in children's "telegraphic" speech three or four years earlier. More specifically, Holden and MacGinitie found greater awareness of *is* as a copula (23 out of 27 tappings for *Snow is cold*) than as an auxiliary (only 11 out of 27 correct for *Bill is drinking soda*). In the emergence of these same forms in the speech of younger children, the copula also appears before the auxiliary (Brown, 1973, p. 274). One is tempted to hypothesize some kind of recapitulation, or vertical decalage in Piaget's terms, between the two stages of development.

Holden and MacGinitie then made the task more difficult by asking each child, after each item, to count the chips he had tapped and find the written sentence, one out of a set of four, that had the right number of visually separated units. Of 24 children, none was correct four out of five times in both segmenting the sentence conventionally and identifying the written version which was congruent with that segmentation. Nine of the children, however, could identify four out of five written sentences which were congruent with their own unconventional forms of segmentation—for example,

Redandgreen/balloons/popped.

It is true that Holden and MacGinitie's second task requires that the children know how to count. But at an even grosser level, where no counting is required, Lila Gleitman reports (personal communication) that more than half the children in one kindergarten could not choose correctly which word written on the blackboard might be *cat* and which word might be *hippopotamus* from the differences in temporal duration and visual length alone.

Clearly, as Holden and MacGinitie stress in their discussion, children beginning school are still developing an awareness of aspects of their own speech which many teachers probably assume they have, and which they probably do in fact need in order to make sense of instructions in phonics. An important question, therefore, is to discover contexts in which such awareness does or could develop.

The Soviet psychologist Elkonin (1971) argues against two notions which he feels have interfered with our understanding of the processes of language acquisition. One is the assumption of "special linguistic sensitivity, linguist instinct, and special linguistic giftedness, as non-analyzable internal forces" (p. 141), and the second is the so-called "glass theory." By glass theory, Elkonin refers exactly to what I have been calling the transparency of language. He argues with the following version of that theory written by his own Soviet colleague, Luria, in 1946:

> While actively utilizing grammatical language and while defining with words the corresponding objects and actions, the child still *cannot make a word and verbal relationships the object of his awareness.* During this period, the word may be used but not noticed by the child, and *frequently it presents things seemingly like a glass,* through which the child looks at the surrounding world, not making the word itself the object of awareness, and not suspecting that it has its own existence, its own aspects of construction. (italics by Elkonin, 1971, p. 141)

Elkonin agrees that "the development of awareness of the language's phonological aspect . . . represents one of the most essential preconditions for . . . learning literacy" (1971, pp. 168–169). But he asserts that children's playful manipulation of the sounds of words, apart from their meanings, is a natural, normal part of language development itself:

> Just as the mastery of objective reality is not possible without formation of activity with objects, exactly in the same manner is language mastery not possible without formation of activity with language as the material object with its concrete form. (1971, p. 141)

In other words, according to Elkonin, children, as part of their species-specific ability to learn language, will use elements of that language as the objects of one aspect of development not specific to humans—namely, play. Children may shift more easily than adults between using language forms transparently in interpersonal communication and treating them as opaque objects in play. Presumably, our overly instrumental attitude toward language for communication has dulled our ability and interest in attending to noninstrumental language elements for the joy of it (outside of the few poets and creative punsters, and the many more who enjoy crossword puzzles or games like Scrabble). When the child's intention is to communicate, he—like the adult—can "hear through" his language to that end; but, it is hypothesized, the child—more easily than most adults—can also intend to play with the elements of language for the very delight of self-expression and mastery. This brings us to consider more generally one function of play in development.

PLAY

In a paper on "Play and Human Evolution," Peter Reynolds (1972) categorizes all behavior into "affective-behavioral systems." Play is one such system, an inevitable part of the development process, with very special characteristics. In Reynolds's words:

1. "The playfulness of an act does not pertain to what is done but to the way it is done (p. 405). . . . Play possesses no instrumental activity of its own." (p. 12)
2. "In play, behavior, while functioning normally, is uncoupled [and buffered] from its normal consequences. . . . Therein lies both the flexibility of play and its frivolity." (p. 7) [Clearly, in the sense of playfulness, not frivolousness. CBC]
3. "Behavior patterns are elaborated and integrated in play but are returned to non-play affective behavior system control for utilitarian execution." (p. 12)
4. "In man, play is accompanied subjectively by a unique affect, as valid existentially as fear and anger, which is best characterized by joy." (p. 4)

In summary, play, according to Reynolds, is the performance of segments of behavior separated from their usual instrumental context, with the functional effect of elaborating and integrating that behavior, and the affective effect of joy.

This description seems related to familiar descriptions of the functions of play by Piaget and Erickson. Piaget and Inhelder (1969) speak of "exercise play":

> *Exercise play*, a primitive form of play, and the only kind that occurs at the sensorimotor level and is retained in part. It . . . consists in repeating, for the pleasure of it, activities acquired elsewhere in the course of adaptation. For example, the child, having discovered by chance the possibility of swinging a suspended object, at first repeats the action in order to adapt to it and understand it, which is not play. Then, having done this, he uses this behavior pattern for simple *"functional pleasure"* (*K. Bühler*) *or for the pleasure of causing an effect and of confirming his newly acquired skill.* (p. 59)

In *Childhood and Society* (1963) Erickson says, "the playing child advances forward to new stages of mastery. . . . The child's play is the infantile form of the human ability to deal with experience by creating model situations and to master reality by experiment and planning" (p. 222).

If children construct their reality by playful manipulation of objects in their world, why should not their construction of their language involve playful manipulation of verbal forms outside of use in meaningful communicative contexts? And if play is an essential part of the developmental process, then its presence or absence should make a difference. Reynolds suggests that "what is required is an assessment of the relative survival of rehearsed versus unrehearsed performances measured in terms of the particular selective system to which the action is coupled" (1972, p. 10). In our terms, the hypothesis to be tested is that a child's play with language makes one human adaptation, literacy, easier to achieve because the child's attention has been focused on the means, the forms of language, whereas in normal communicative contexts, attention is focused only on the end.

This hypothesis remains to be tested. Some suggestive evidence exists. Negatively, Ilse Mattick (1967), in her description of the language and cognitive development of "children of disorganized lower-class families," specifically mentions that "there was a lack of exploration of language and an absence of the usual play with words which facilitates increasing communicative skills and serves to extend knowledge" (p. 73).

More positively, we know that many young children do play with language and that many parents and teachers value that play. Consider just three examples: from a linguist-mother, Ruth Weir; a teacher-observer of preschool children, Harriet Johnson; and a Russian listener-writer of children's stories, Kornei Chukovsky.

Ruth Weir (1962) taped the presleep monologues of her 2-year-old son Anthony and found many examples of sequences of utterances where play with language sounds—of individual letters, of sequences, of syllables, and of stress—seems primary. For example:

1. Look at those pineapple	2. Blanket	3. Babette
In a pretty box	Like a	Back here
And cakes	Lipstick	Wet
What a sticks for cakes		
For the click	(pp. 103–105; numbers added)	

Second to sound play, Weir found examples of play with grammatical patterns. "The child finds great joy in practising his discovery that linguistic units can be combined freely up to a point but subject to rules which he is exploring" (p. 109). Examples of substitution games are frequent.

4. What color	5. There is the light	6. Listen to micro-
What color blanket	Where is the light	phone
What color mop	Here is the light	Go to micro-
What color glass		phone
	(pp. 109–112; numbers added)	

In her analysis, Weir separates a "poetic" function of language, in which "play with sounds" is primary [as in the first three examples], from a "metalanguage" function in which "speaking about language" is primary [under which she includes the last three examples of play with grammatical patterns]. In this chapter, I am including both as simply "play with language."

In her introduction to the reissue of Harriet Johnson's book *Children in "The Nursery School"* (1972), Barbara Biber emphasizes that Miss Johnson thought that "learning was soundest when the environment encouraged the child in his impulse to 'experiment' with the exercise of his growing powers in the widening world of experience" (p. xi), and she specifically included words as important objects for that experimentation. For example, Geordie, who at 24 months had a fair vocabulary, accompanied motoric activities with varied syllabication:

As he ran: Bee, bee, bee; Lee, lee, lee; Dub, dub, dub
At top of slide: Ma-wee, ma-wee, ma-wee, ma-wee, A-a. (p. 254)

Or Mathew, as he was being undressed:

Nolly lolly, nolly lolly, nilly lolly, sillie Billie,
nolly lolly. (p. 255)

And Donald as he ran around the roof:

Up a lup a dup, Up a dup I go. (p. 256)

Because Miss Johnson's children had companions in their play, as Anthony Weir did not, two children sometimes created joint changes. Note for example, 3-year-olds Philip and Caroline in the sandbox, where meaningful communication sometimes is inserted into nonsense chant play. (It is interesting, as Harriet Johnson points out [p. 260], that "Caroline does not echo Philip's pronunciation except in nonsense syllables," which suggests that Caroline separates sounds for play from sounds for communication and has the articulation ability to carry out that distinction.)

Philip: "Ees not."
Caroline: "Ees not."
Philip: "Eh."
Caroline: "Eh."
Philip: "Go 'way."
Caroline: "Go 'way."
Philip: "Go 'way ko."
Caroline: "Go 'way ko."
Philip: "Go 'way ki."
Caroline: "Go 'way ki."
Philip: "Aw dee, de wa, di geh."
Caroline: "Aw dee, de wa, di geh."
Philip: "My o ketty."
Caroline: "My o ketty."
Philip: "Ga de."
Caroline: "Ga de."
Philip: "Oh, see wain go in!"
Caroline: "Oh, see wain go in!"
Philip: "Eese no more holes."
Caroline: "Ees no more holes." (p. 260).

Finally, there is Chukovsky (1963), who speaks of children's delight with sounds and also their delight with "topsy-turvy" meanings. Play with sounds starts very early, and later "making up verses begins when the aimless pronouncing of rhymed and other sounds stops and meaning is introduced" (p. 64). For example, Chukovsky's 4-year-old son, running around the garden on a broomstick, shouted:

I'm a big, big rider
You're smaller than a spider. (p. 64)

Soon after, at dinner, he declaimed:

Give me, give me, before I die,
Lots and lots of potato pie. (pp. 64–65)

While these rhymes could communicate, that is not their primary purpose; often rhymes accompanying play do not. For example, 4-year-old Mura was pretending to be a Mommy hare with many babies and soon began to rhyme:

The little rabbit was fast and lean
He was chased by a Magazine. (p. 66)

While these rhymed chants are usually accompaniment to other play, topsy-turvies constitute verbal play in themselves, play not with sounds or grammatical patterns but with meanings. Examples of topsy-turvies include the simplest reversal of an animal and its sound enjoyed by a 2-year-old: "Daddy, doggy—meow!", and 4-year-old Mura's song:

I'll give you a piece of milk
And a jug full of silk. (p. 99)

Chukovsky explains the purpose of such play for the child:

His main purpose, as in all play, is to exercise his newly acquired skill of verifying his knowledge of things. We know that the child—and this is the main point—is amused by the reverse juxtaposition of things only when the real juxtaposition has become completely obvious to him. . . .
    When we notice that a child has started to play with some newly acquired component of understanding, we may definitely conclude that he has become full master of this item of understanding; only

those ideas can become toys for him whose proper relation to reality is firmly known. (pp. 101, 103)

Later—beyond the years described by Weir, Johnson, and Chukovsky, (and MacLean, Bryant, & Bradley [1987], and Garvey [1990]) —comes children's delight in puns and riddles; not just turning word meanings upside down, but playing with the effects of two meanings considered simultaneously, or the transformations of parts of words for new effects. A young friend of mine, John Rosenthal of Washington, D.C., knowing of my interest in word games, has been sending me examples of the current 7-year-old folk culture:

Q: What word has more letters than any other in the world?
A: Mailman.

Police: You can't park here.
Driver: Why not?
Police: Read that sign.
Driver: I did. It says, "Fine for parking."

Q: What did Tenne-see?
A: The same thing Arkan-saw.

Q: What time did the man go to the dentist?
A: Too-th irty.

Older children's playful use of language can be separated into verbal art, such as jump-rope rhymes, which are learned as finished products, and verbal games, such as Pig Latin, where the rules are learned and individual performances then creatively constructed in conformity with those rules. Probably because folklore collectors have concentrated on the collection of oral texts, collections of children's verbal art are more available than collections of verbal games.

Here is one example of each that I collected some years ago. The first, a jump-rope rhyme, has additional interest for the attitudes expressed toward race and sex roles. Yolanda Wilson, then 10 years old, learned it from a friend and taught it to me when we both happened to be visiting a daycare center for younger children in Boston:

Mý mother, yoúr mother
Líve across the wáy.
Év́ery night they havé a fight
Thiś is what they sáy:
Aćkle-backle sóda cracker,

Aćkle-backle boó;
Aćkle-backle sóda cracker
Í love yoú.
I wiŝh I had a niĉkle;
I wiŝh I had a dińe;
I wiŝh I had a cólored boy
Who loved me all the tíme.
I'll máke him do the diŝhes;
I'll máke him do the floór;
And íf he doesn't dó it,
I'll kiĉk him out the doór.
Hów many kiŝses dó you wiŝh?
Ońe, tẃo, thrée, foúr, fíve, siX́, seven, eiǵht, nińe, tén.

The second is the verbal game of "Categories," which some 7- and
8-year-old boys and girls on North Haven Island off the coast of Maine
had learned from the TV program "ZOOM" (a modern medium for oral
transmission) and taught me during recess when I was visiting their
school. Sitting in a circle on the floor, to a beat of four, each partici-
pant claps knees, claps hands, clicks right fingers and then left fingers,
while chanting on the first two beats examples of the category named
by the starter. Anyone who misses a word or a beat is out:

		(clap) (clap)	(click) (click)
			″ ″
Starter:	Cate-gories	″	″
	Such as	″	″
	Ca - ars	″	″
	Pon - tiac	″	″
Next:	Je - ep	″	″
Next:	Fo - rd	″	″
	etc.		

The social benefits of both kinds of verbal play are obvious: They
support and organize informal peer relationships. Cognitive benefits
are more controversial, especially for the verbal art. In a review of Opie
and Opie's collection of children's folklore in Great Britain, Bernstein
(1960) stressed the cognitive limitations of such well-rehearsed material. But Gilmore (1983) argues that "Mississippi," a black girls' street
rhyme in Philadelphia, is a spelling exercise recontextualized by the
performers, "declaring in dramatic expressive form their excellence as
literate spellers, as dancers, and as kids" (1983, p. 253).

The potential learning involved in the Category games was obvious when the children attempted "states" and then interrupted the game to argue whether Maine towns like Millinocket, or countries like Korea, were states. Even "cars" elicited some argument: "I know a jeep is a jeep, but a jeep's a car too."

IMPLICATIONS FOR EDUCATION

And so what can be suggested for education? I started out with the importance which the authors in *Language by Ear and by Eye* credited to awareness of language as critical for achieving literacy, and their hope that teachers could learn how to cultivate it. Elkonin suggested that language was in fact more opaque to children than to adults. Elkonin also urged that this opaqueness be kept alive at all ages by valuing and encouraging verbal play at home and school. Finally, Reynolds gave evolutionary support to the value of play and, by implication, of play with language for human children.

We can encourage verbal play and I think we should—not at the expense of stimulation of language for communication, but in addition to it. The danger is that when adults intervene in play, it may lose its critical characteristics and therefore its special value. In an article on "Nature and Uses of Immaturity," Bruner (1972) suggests that many special skills are first developed and practiced in play. He then quotes one study by Dolhinow and Bishop (1970) on play in chimpanzees that "occurs only in an atmosphere of familiarity, emotional reassurance, and lack of tension and danger" (quoted on p. 693) and refers to another study by Schiller (1952) of primate play which found that "attempting to direct play by reinforcing chimpanzees for play behavior had the effect of inhibiting play" (quoted on p. 693). Similar conditions should be important for human children's play as well.

Afterword. *With the increase in ethnographic studies of children's life in and out of school have come new glimpses of children's appropriation of written language forms for their own playful purposes. In addition to Gilmore's (1983) study of the street rhyme "Mississippi," Shuman (1987) found girls using "writing as play" in a Philadelphia inner-city junior high school, and McLane and McNamee (1990) describe "playful uses of writing" in a Chicago*

after-school program for elementary school children. Griffin and Cole (1987) analyze the eruption of a "written rap"—a genre outlawed in the local school—in the electronic communication between a group of working-class elementary school children in an after-school program and researchers at the university who mask their adult personas in the interests of more symmetrical, and therefore more liberating, language play.

For rich suggestions for more deliberate uses of language games in school, see two books by Margie Golick, for many years the chief psychologist at the Children's Hospital Learning Clinic in Montreal: Reading, Writing and Rummy *(1986) and* Playing with Words *(1987). And, as an example of language play for all ages in a computer program, there is* m__ss__ng l__nks *(Chomsky & Schwartz, 1983).*

6

◆◆◆

"The Electric Company" Turns On to Reading

Foreword. *Taking advantage of children's delight in language play for literacy education has an old and honorable history. Roskies (1975) describes the alphabet instruction in the* heder, *the primary schools of Eastern European Jews prior to World War I. And even earlier, she reports, were the spelling dramas in ancient Greece: "Actors were costumed, appearing as different letters. They danced in pairs, forming nonsense syllables which the student audience had to identify and chant according to a set meter" (p. 42).*

Television offers a new medium for these ancient strategies. Caleb Gattegno, best known for his Cuisenaire rods in mathematics and Words in Color *in reading, designed all his materials to build on children's strengths, what he calls "the functionings of children"—such as the power of "extraction," the power to make "transformations," and the power to handle "abstractions" (1985).*

In the early 1970s, Gattegno worked with a Canadian film producer, Joeseph Koenig, to create one-minute "pop-up" television films in which animation techniques are used to present raw data on how the English written language system works: its spatial ordering left-to-right, and the effects of transformations: insertion (mat/mast), reversal (nap/pan), substitution (map/mop), and addition (mop/mops).

The 8-millimeter "Sound Out" films that were part of Houghton Mifflin's Interaction *program developed by James Moffett were influenced by Gattegno's work. As I mentioned in Chapter 3, they were very popular with my children in San Diego for their zany sentences as well as the jazzy musical accompaniment.*

In general, animation techniques provide a powerful new way to make the abstract concrete and to portray the underlying structure of our written language in visual form. In the words of one television producer, "Fundamentally, the live-action camera represents the physical eye, and the animation camera represents the mind's eye" (Palmer, 1947, p. 26). Abstract form is made understandable through carefully designed concrete visualizations.

When Children's Television Workshop designed "Sesame Street" (which went on the air in 1969) and then "The Electric Company" (two years later), both live-action camera and animation were used to stimulate interest in, and knowledge about, reading. This chapter explains very briefly some of the thinking that went into planning "The Electric Company." It was published in the Harvard Graduate School of Education Alumni Bulletin *in 1972.*

When the Children's Television Workshop (CTW) decided to produce a half-hour reading show for children 7 to 10 years old who had not yet learned to read, it had to decide how to teach reading on television. In a field still full of controversy over teaching methods, CTW had to take a stand.

In characteristic CTW style, Harvard professor Gerald Lesser, chairman of the board of advisers, assembled a mixed group of people (October 1970) one year before the show was to go on the air to advise the staff on what the goals should be. Experts in the field of reading were there, but people in other fields participated freely. For example, my subgroup, one of four, consisted of Fred Calvert, a TV film writer; David Connell, a vice-president and executive producer for CTW; Lauren Resnick, a psychologist from the Research and Development Center at the University of Pittsburgh; Maurice Sendak, author and illustrator of children's books; Hercelia Tuscano, a staff development specialist at the Southwest Educational Laboratory; and Walt Wolfram, a research associate at the Center for Applied Linguistics in Washington, D.C. Two-day deliberations of four subgroups, all with an exciting mix of expertise, were developed by the CTW staff into a final set of goals that would guide the TV writers in producing the show and the Educational Testing Service (ETS) in evaluating it.

In order for the TV writers to do their job independently and creatively, we had to describe the reading process to them in a form they could use in writing the show. We hit on a threefold categorization that seemed to help. The three processes were termed *blending*, *chunking*, and *scanning for structure*. They operate both at the level of word recognition and at the level of deriving meaning from larger units such as sentences, or even paragraphs.

Blending means processing linear combinations in left-to-right sequence—letters in a word or words in a sentence. TV can show a slower focus on individual units, r-u-n, and then a faster blending into a larger whole as the letters visually come together.

Chunking means recognizing some combinations as indivisible wholes. At the level of combinations of sounds, this applies to diagraphs such as *sh*; at the level of meaningful units, it applies to verb endings such as *-ing*; and it also applies to a small sight-word vocabulary that the show would try to teach. These sight-words are selected according to two criteria: words important in the child's environment, such as *walk* on traffic signs, and words hard to learn but important in reading, such as *the*, *what*, and *if*.

On a recent program, the consonant diagraph *sh* was chiseled out of a stone slab and later appeared in the following laconic conversation in a basketball sequence: Shoot? Shy. Shoot! Shucks. Shoot! Shot. Show-off! On the same show a girl held *if* in her hand as she sang "*If*'s a word that makes you dream," and the dreams came to life in thought clouds over her head.

Scanning for structure means looking ahead to find helpful clues. Within words, the most common example is the silent *e*, which changes the sound of a preceding vowel. In phrases or sentences, there are punctuation marks and context clues in the language itself.

These were the reading strategies "The Electric Company" would try to teach, with all the means at its command. We hoped that the intellectual abilities that all children apply so successfully in learning the rules of their native oral language could be more effectively activated in learning to read.

Activation of these abilities of course depends on whether the children are excited about learning and feels they can succeed. Throughout the shows, "The Electric Company" tries to instill a belief that learning to read is a solvable problem with rewards of useful information and joyful delight for the successful "decoder." Fargo North, Decoder, helps people get needed information; Easy Reader reads just because he loves to. (Chapter 4 Afterword reports observations of children watching the show in school.)

CTW made one other decision that deserves thoughtful attention by educators and the public. Which variety of English should be used? Should nonstandard English ever be heard or appear in writing? If so, how should it be spelled? No issue aroused more debate in CTW planning meetings, and no aspect of the show has stimulated more mail since "The Electric Company" went on the air. Samuel Gibbon, producer of the show, explains (Children's Television Workshop, 1971):

> When we speak of dialect, it's important to distinguish between accented speech and real dialectal differences in syntax. As far as accents are concerned, we want children who speak with various regional or ethnic accents to understand that the correspondence of printed symbol to speech sound holds true equally well for their pronunciation as for so-called "standard network English" pronunciation. We will, therefore, include in the program segments in which a single word is pronounced with a variety of accents.
>
> The more difficult question is how to deal with the syntactic differences between standard English and the nonstandard dialect variants, such as what some linguists have come to call Black English. "The Electric Company" curriculum is based on the premise that printed language is simply an encoding into a graphic form of the spoken language system the child has already mastered. . . . Our advisors have recommended that it would be useful to the nonstandard-English-speaking child to reinforce his confidence in the printed code by occasionally showing him that his own speech patterns can be encoded in print.
>
> In showing nonstandard-English in print on the program, we will observe several guidelines. First, we will never misspell words in English in order to reflect accent. Only correctly spelled English words will appear. Second, presentation of dialect speech in print will be limited to dramatic situations in which that speech is appropriate and to speakers for whom the particular speech pattern is appropriate.

On "The Electric Company," written language has been matched to a wide range of accents, and colloquial (or "hip") vocabulary is often seen in print, for instance "Dig my sharp, shiny shoes" in a segment of *sh*. Nonstandard syntax has been heard but not seen, for instance the spoken punch line to one segment on silent *e* was "I have known me a lot of dudes who was duds."

Such a position has implications for the way ETS evaluates "The Electric Company." For instance, because some varieties of English speech simplify the pronunciation of constant clusters at the ends of words, testing children's comprehension of morphemes such as the past tense *-ed* must be separated from their pronunciation of them. A test for mastery of this morpheme might be constructed as follows (derived from W. Labov, 1969):

> "When John passed the corner, he read this sign." Children's pronunciation of *read* indicates whether they have processed the *-ed* on *passed*.

The goal of the show is to help children read standard English. The position on varieties of speech patterns was taken in order to make the show as relevant as possible to the children we hope to help. It was also taken to avoid penalizing children, as many tests now do, for nonstandard pronunciation in oral reading, which teachers often misinterpret as lack of comprehension. But beyond the children and the classrooms, the policy may also help the public to accept nonstandard varieties of English as normal language variation in a society as complex as ours, and to see they are of no importance in judging possible employees or friends.

Afterword.   *As I write this Afterword at the end of 1991, Children's Television Workshop is again designing a television show on literacy for children older than "Sesame Street" age. Called "Ghostwriter," it will be a dramatic series in which a group of children solve problems with the aid of reading and writing. In contrast to "The Electric Company," it will emphasize the forms of literacy less, and the functions of literacy more.*

Any one TV program can do only so much and do it well, and we can only hope that CTW will succeed in portraying reading and writing to its young viewers as powerful means to peer-group goals. For schools, however, the continuing challenge can be described as combining the best of "Ghostwriter" and "The Electric Company": wholistic activities for functional use plus periodic, and just as carefully planned, attention to formal parts.

7

◆ ◆ ◆

Spontaneous and Scientific Concepts
Learning Punctuation in the First Grade

Patricia Cordeiro, Mary Ellen Giacobbe,
and Courtney Cazden

Foreword.   *Like spelling, punctuation is part of our conventions for*
transcribing oral language into print. And, also like spelling, it
appears early in the timetable of most language arts programs. In
this research, we followed the progress of one group of first-graders
in a whole language classroom.

   Mary Ellen Giacobbe was one of the classroom teachers in
Donald Graves's (1983) research on children learning to write (and
is pictured on the cover of that book). The writings analyzed here
come from the year after the Graves research team had left. When
Giacobbe enrolled at the Harvard Graduate School of Education,
she brought—with her children's permission—a complete set of all
their writings from the previous school year. In my course on Child
Language she met Patricia Cordeiro, then a classroom teacher
from Cape Cod; as a collaborative term project, they started this
analysis.

   We reported this research in two versions, one for Language
Arts *in 1983, and the second for* Language and Learning: An Inter-

national Perspective, *edited by Gordon Wells and John Nichols (1985). This chapter is a composite of the two.*

More than ten years ago, one of us wrote that, "One reason why language is such a difficult subject for curriculum planners is that we do not understand the relationship between what is in some way *learned* and what can be *taught*" (Cazden, 1973a, pp. 135–136). Emig (1981), quoting that statement in a recent article, goes on to caution against what she calls (after Piaget) "magical thinking"—the belief that we have, by our actions, caused something that in fact has an independent source. In the case of writing, she cautions against the tempting belief that children learn only because, and only what, we as teachers explicitly teach. Our intent here is not to argue about the relative importance of learning versus teaching, or—to use Vygotsky's terms—spontaneous versus scientific concepts, but to ask again about the relationship between the two.

In *Thought and Language* (1962b), Vygotsky defined spontaneous concepts as those—like *brother*—that are learned directly from experience, unmediated by definitions or explanation: scientific concepts, by contrast, are those—like *exploitation*—that begin in the verbal definitions and explanations of a more knowledgeable other. What we call "teaching" is necessary for the latter, but they cannot be absorbed ready-made in parrotlike repetition. Vygotsky (1962b) reminds us that both spontaneous and scientific concepts evolve with the aid of strenuous mental activity on the part of the child:

> In working its slow way upward, an everyday [or spontaneous] concept clears a path for the scientific concept and its downward development. It creates a series of structures necessary for the evolution of a concept's more primitive, elementary aspects, which give it body and vitality. Scientific concepts in turn supply structures for the upward development of the child's spontaneous concepts toward consciousness and deliberate use. Scientific concepts grow down through spontaneous concepts; spontaneous concepts grow upward through scientific concepts. (p. 109)

For concrete material with which to consider this relationship, we will describe a longitudinal study of 22 first-grade (6-year-old) children's progress in coping with one set of written language conventions—three punctuation marks: possessive apostrophe *s*, quotation marks, and periods. We focus on punctuation not at all because we think it should become more important to young writers or their teachers. Punctuation, like spelling and handwriting (or typing), is an aspect of the transcription—not the composition—process. (See Bartlett [1981] and F. Smith [1982] for excellent discussions.) It is the composition of ideas, not their transcriptions on paper, that is the first focus of writers' attention. Nonetheless, a longitudinal analysis of children's learning of punctuation, especially of periods, illuminates some details of the relationship between spontaneous and scientific concepts, even here where one might assume that explicit adult instruction in the conventions of written English could be the only source of growth.

We will first describe the classroom in which this learning took place, and then report children's learning by means of both summary statistics and examples of texts. When children's actual spelling is irrelevant to the discussion, our standardized translation is presented in lowercase letters. Later, in examples 5–12, we preserve children's spelling in SMALL CAPS. We will then refer briefly to related research on children's early learning of both spelling and punctuation, and end with suggested implications for teaching.

THE CLASSROOM AS A WRITING ENVIRONMENT

Giacobbe's was an activity-centered classroom where children viewed themselves and their classmates as individuals who had thoughts and ideas worth communicating to others, and who knew writing was a powerful aid in this communication. From the first day of school, these children were writing; not dictating to the teacher but writing themselves (Giacobbe, 1982).

Given a 9-by-12-inch blank journal to draw and write in, they all drew pictures and wrote about them. When the children finished their initial journals (in four to six weeks), they shifted to picture story paper, booklets, and so forth. There was a writing center with an assortment of writing materials for rehearsing, drafting, revising, and editing. With this encouragement, these children wrote far more than first-grade workbooks are likely to require: 5,997 sentences, or 272 per child, or 1½ per child per school day.

Giacobbe's role as teacher was to conference with the children about their writing. She held four types of conferences, with content always the first focus and skills the last. About the skills or editing conference, she says:

When the content is as the writer intends it to be, the child is taught one skill in the context of his writing. For instance, if there is a lot of dialogue in a particular story, I might teach the child how to use quotation marks. If the child uses that skill in the next piece of writing, I ask about the usage, and the child decides if it should be added to the list of skills s/he is responsible for during the editing stage of future writing.

Located in the writing center were two writing folders for each child. The first folder, for work in progress, served as a record-keeping device for both the writer and the teacher. All the titles of books written are listed on the cover. Inside the cover on the left is a list of possible topics to write about (compiled by each child). On the right is the list of skills the writer is responsible for during the editing stage of any piece of writing. On the back of the folder is space for the teacher to keep a record of skills known and skills taught. The other folder was for accumulated work.

As the children read their work aloud to the teacher, she retranscribed the text in conventional spelling and punctuation in small print at the bottom of each page. So, even at some distance, we can be sure of each child's intended message.

CHILDREN'S LEARNING

The material for our study of the learning of punctuation comes from these two sets of folders. We had the complete folders of all 22 children for the entire first-grade year, and we had information on just when (from September to May) each child was taught (and sometimes retaught) a particular skill. We realize that, especially in a classroom like this, children have many sources of information in addition to the teacher—notably, other children and a wide variety of written texts—and we have no way retrospectively to track children's use of these sources for information about punctuation. But we can locate the time when an individual child received explicit individual instruction from the teacher.

From the list in each child's folder, we can tell that the three punctuation marks taught to most children were periods (13 of the 22 children), possessive apostrophes, and quotation marks (six children each). The only skill taught to as many children was the spelling of the verb ending *-ing*, and it is worth stopping to look at the pattern of learning here for later contrast with the more difficult punctuation tasks.

Between September and May, 13 of the 22 children were taught how to spell -*ing*. Typically, Giacobbe would say: "We really write the sound at the end of words like *coming* and *going* as *i-n-g*" (writing as she speaks). The first section of Table 7.1 presents the children's learning over the entire year: the number of times the children used a present progressive verb and the number of times the ending was correctly spelled. Describing children's progress as a percentage of the total number of opportunities that are correct is adapted from research on the development of noun and verb inflections in oral language (Brown, 1973; Cazden, 1968). To put the first section of Table 7.1 into words: for the 13 children who were taught, their texts included 238 verbs requiring -*ing*. Forty-nine of these were spelled correctly, or 21 percent. There were 42 verbs in the 13 stories about which the teaching took place. Then from the time of teaching until the end of the year, these same 13 children's texts included 706 -*ing* verb forms, of which 655 were correctly spelled, or 93 percent. For the nine children not taught, their spelling of -*ing* is summarized once for the entire year: 358 instances, of which 293 were correct, or 82 percent.

Table 7.1   Learning to spell the verb ending -*ing* and use punctuation marks

Learning to:	No. of children	% correct before teaching	% correct throughout year	opportunities at time of teaching	% correct after teaching
Spell the verb ending -*ing*					
Taught	13	21(49/238)[a]		42	93(655/706)[a]
Not taught	9		82(293/358)[a]		
Use possessive apostrophes					
Taught	6	16(3/19)[a]		10	56(31/55)[a]
Not taught	16		12(29/243)[a]		
Use quotation marks					
Taught	6	0(0/28)[a]		12	53(73/138)[a]
Not taught	16		17(14/81)[a]		
Use periods					
Taught	13	25(267/1056)[a]		154	57(1692/2966)[a]
Not taught	9		49(817/1821)[a]		

[a]The numbers in parentheses are the ratios of correct answers to the number of opportunities.

The data for punctuation are presented in this same form. Note that Table 7.1 shows only opportunities and the number of them filled correctly; that is, it shows only errors of omission. For the punctuation marks, errors of commission, placing the marks where they do not belong, will be discussed separately.

It is clear from Table 7.1 that -*ing* gave these children little trouble. The 13 children who were taught it obtained virtual mastery usually in the next story. And the nine children who were not taught, presumably because the teacher felt they didn't need it, achieved nearly the same mastery from other sources of help.

The three punctuation marks Giacobbe decided from their texts that the children most needed were periods, possessive apostrophes, and quotation marks. Concidentally, these exemplify the two major purposes of punctuation in English: *segmentation* of words into units by periods, commas, and so forth, and *identification* of units such as a possessive ending (and not a plural) by an apostrophe. Quotation marks share both functions—both separating and identifying direct speech (Quirk & Greenbaum, 1973). While the need for these (and other) punctuation marks seems so natural to us, it is important to realize that our English system is only 400 years old. In earlier writing, letters ran on continuously, as children today may do when they begin to write. Because periods pose problems that are especially difficult for the children and especially interesting to us, we leave them until last.

Possessive Apostrophe

Six children were taught to use an apostrophe to mark possession. Typically, Giacobbe would say, "When something *belongs* to someone else, we put one of these little marks [showing as she speaks]. We call that an 'apostrophe' and we add the *s*. That lets the reader know that *my friend's house* [pointing to the child's text] means the house belongs to your friend; it doesn't mean 'lots of friends.'"

We counted as correct any mark floating above the line followed by an *s*. The summary story presented in Table 7.1 shows slower learning and a more significant role for instruction for the use of possessive apostrophes than for the -*ing* ending.

Quotation Marks

Six children were taught to use quotation marks. Typically, Giacobbe would say, "Someone is talking on this page. If we could hear her talking, what would she say? [Child reads] Well, we have some marks that we put around the words people say, before the first word and after the last."

We counted as correct any floating marks of any shape. Table 7.1 presents the summary story. In quantitative terms, the children's progress in learning to use quotation marks is similar to their progress in learning to use possessive apostrophes: Teaching makes a big difference, but the children are correct after teaching only about half the time.

Periods

Periods were taught to 13 children, and they were retaught more often than the other three conventions combined: once to five children, and twice to one child. Typically, in the editing conference, Giacobbe read aloud a child's story without pauses; when the author objected, she said, "You read it the way you want it to sound. When you come to a stop, that's probably where we need to put a period."

We counted as a period any dot between words, grounded or floating. To divide the children's text into sentences for analysis, we were guided by Giacobbe's transcriptions made during her conferences, and she in turn was guided by the child's oral rendition of the text. So, for example:

(1) My Dad docked the boat and me and my friends on the boat.

was punctuated as one sentence in Giacobbe's transcription and accepted as correct in our analysis. On the other hand,

(2) We went downtown. and to the store.

was counted as one opportunity for a period (after *store*) and one correct (and one incorrect) use. (The number of opportunities for correct use of periods is thus also the number of sentences in the total set of compositions according to Giacobbe's judgment.) Children were given credit for deviations from a strict criterion of sentencehood when their use would be considered a legitimate stylistic decision in adult writing. For example, one child wrote a 200-word sentence about his family's "Cousin convention" in which it was clear that he hated sausage. When he then wrote:

(3) We are having pancakes for breakfast. Without sausage.

both periods were both considered correct, even felicitous, use. The many instances of incorrect placement of periods, as after *downtown* in (2), are not counted in the summary figures and will be discussed separately.

Table 7.1 presents the summary picture for periods. Overall, required periods were not supplied more than half the time. In this respect, children's progress is not very different from their progress with apostrophes and quotation marks, except that the untaught children do relatively better from other knowledge sources, whether published texts or their own intuition about structural units. We return to the latter possibility below.

Now to the errors of commission—punctuation marks that were supplied, but in the wrong place. First, a one-chart summary of errors of comission for all three punctuation marks (Table 7.2), and then we look at some actual texts to see what the numbers represent.

With quotation marks, there is little confusion: There were only four instances, such as the following, where the writer mistakes where the quoted speech ends.

(4) We are at
my Aunt Susie's
house. I said

"Hello to Danny
Stephen Mickey and
Tommy."

With possessive apostrophes, the number of errors is much greater, both absolutely and proportionally. These errors are largely what we call overgeneralizations toward formal similarities of sounds that have different meanings: to plurals like *parade's* and *thing's* and

Table 7.2 Misplaced punctuation marks

Punctuation	Number	% of total (correct and mistaken)
quotation marks	4	4 (4/87 + 4)
possessive apostrophes	38	38 (38/63 + 38)
periods	475	17 (475/2776 + 475)

to verbs like *like's* and *live's*. Any system of transcribing speech into writing is necessarily based on a mixture of sound and meaning principles (Stubbs, 1980). The teacher taught the possessive apostrophe on the strong meaning basis of "belonging." But the children—with their attention focused on sounds in their invented spelling—sometimes acted on the basis of sounds here too.

With periods, possibilities for error are more complex. Consider possible answers to the question the children face: When should words be separated not just by a space but also by a period? Five patterns appeared frequently in these first-graders' texts:

(5) I.AM.WOKEING.MY.BAEK.AP.THE.HEL.   interword
I am walking my bike up the hill.

(6) WE PRT ON THE.   endline
FORTH FOR.
We parked on the fourth floor.

(7) WAN THE BOWNE WOBPAK IS GON THE   endpage
CHKDE. (end of page)
When the downy woodpecker is
gone, the chickadee comes and
takes his hole. He is too lazy to
make his own hole.

(8) ON THE WA HOME. MI CAR IT SPLODID   phrase structure
On the way home my car it ex-
ploded.

(9) WON DAY WAN I WAS OWT SID PLAING.   1 end line
KERRY CAM OVR. TO PLAY WATHE ME.   1 phrase structure
                                                     (after OVR)
                                                     1 correct

(10) WE ARE PACING. TO.   1 phrase structure
GO TO LON MOWTIN.   (after PACING).
We are packing to go to Loon   1 endline, 1 correct
Mountain.

(11) WE ARE SILE (still) DRIVING TO NEW YOK.   1 phrase structure
WE TOK MY GRAMS CAR. MY DAD MY MOM   (after list of names)
AND MY BROTHR MY GRAMY AND MY   3 correct
GRAPY. WAT TO NOW YOK WATH ME.

(12) PETER PAN LIFFS WITH THE LIST BOS. AND   1 phrase structure,
WENDY.   1 correct

All the children tried out more than one of these hypotheses, often more than one in a single story. Fewer children included the syllabic possibility: DN.USOS (dinosaurs), RAS.ING (racing), and BL.DID (builded.)

Cognitively, the most interesting alternative, even though no more correct by our conventional standards than the others, occurred between groups of words we call phrases or clauses, structural units intermediate between words on the one hand and full sentences on the other. We refer to this intermediate constituent level as "phrase structure" placement. We have given several examples of this placement (8–12 above) because of its importance as evidence of children's implicit awareness of constituent structures above the level of the word. By "awareness" we mean more than is evidenced simply by spontaneous speech production; by "implicit" we mean that it has not been taught and could not be verbalized with labels for adult categories.

Here are two more examples, showing longer texts. Example (13) is from a long, multipage story about fishing. In this case the phrase structure placement of a period occurs at the end of a complete sentence but before the *because* clause:

(13) if you are fish
      ing under a bridge
      all you are going to
      catch is a sun
      fish. because
      you are in shallow
      water.

Example (14) includes several pages from a multipage story about space shuttle problems, written over several days as the action unfolded on television. Here the phrase structure placement occurs after the pilots' names and after "on Tuesday."

(14) I hope they fix the computer.
      The shuttle took of Sunday
      morning John Young and
      Bob Crippin. They were the
      pilots.
      It went around the earth.
      We saw the shuttle land
      on Tuesday. On TV in
      Mrs. Claveon's room
      It was a good landing
      It landed in Houston, California.

Third, there was evidence of phrase structure awareness in some children's division of a text into lines—with or without periods. Here is a particularly clear example from another child, in which each line—without exception—ends at the end of a phrase or clause. Figure 7.1 gives both the original and a more readable translation:

The important point is that not all groups of words dismissable as "sentence fragments" have the same structural status, and evidently

Figure 7.1

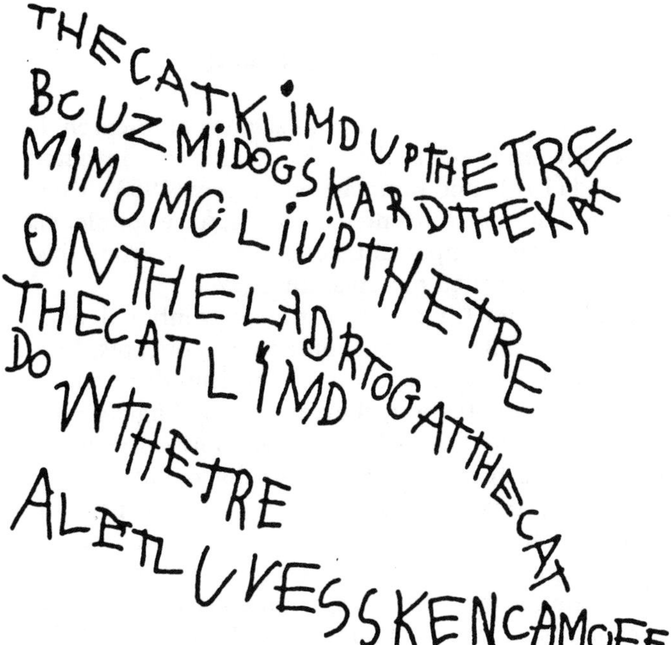

The cat climbed up the tree
because my dog scared the cat
My mom climbed up the tree
on the ladder to get the cat
The cat climbed
down the tree
A little of its skin came off.

children intuitively know some important distinctions. They have somehow learned more than we might have thought possible about what Frank Smith (1982) calls "the structure of meaning" that punctuation indexes, and more than we could have explained even if we had tried. We suggest that the groupings of words we call phrases or clauses are somehow represented in children's internal language structure as spontaneous concepts in Vygotsky's sense, but that externalized evidence of that structural knowledge is apt to get overlooked in our attention to "shaping" children's behavior to our own conventional standards.

RELATED RESEARCH

Our work builds on three previous strands of research. First, there is the extensive and well-replicated research on invented spelling begun by Read (1971) and summarized by Clay (1983). Examples (5)-(12) above contain many invented spellings, for example, BLDID, BAEK, CHKDE, WA, MI. Some important generalizations from this research seem to apply to invented punctuation as well.

Children's errors (in terms of the conventional adult system) provide vivid externalizations of spontaneous concepts. In the case of invented spelling, the concepts are about English phonology; in the case of invented punctuation, they are about English syntax. These errors do not become "bad habits" as behaviorist psychologists would have us believe. Instead, they are gradually replaced by closer and closer approximations to the adult system. At what point in this progression the children can benefit most from explicit teaching of the adult system is an important instructional question. (We do not suggest that the relationship between spontaneous and scientific concepts is the same across domains of knowledge. Hawkins [1978], for example, finds more discontinuity, and even interference, in the transition from everyday concepts to scientific concepts within science itself.)

Second, imaginative experiments on oral language also find evidence of children's phrase structure knowledge. Read and Schreiber (1982) show that 7- and 8-year-old children can easily learn to repeat only the subject noun phrase of a sentence—"*My best friend and I* are selling lemonade."—but could not learn to repeat a nonconstitutive sequence of the same length. From this evidence, Read and Schreiber argue that "major surface constituents are, in various senses, psychologically real and accessible" (1982, p. 84).

Third, there is a small set of studies on punctuation itself. Bissex (1980) mentions her son's early use of periods between syllables and between words. Edelsky (1983) provides many examples of phrase structure segmentation and punctuation in her rare study of the writing—in Spanish and English—of Hispanic farm worker children in first-, second-, and third-grade bilingual classroom environments that were similar in some ways to Giacobbe's. It was her work that first alerted us to the presence of phrase structure usage. Weaver's (1982) analysis of compositions from grades 1 to 6 gives further evidence that punctuation errors are neither random nor mindless. She found that "sentence fragments" that are punctuated erroneously by our conventional standards change qualitatively with age. Merely counting errors thus masks significant growth. Furthermore, if anyone thinks that children wouldn't make these errors if teachers just gave more drill and practice on proper use, Calkins (1980, as part of the Graves project) compared the knowledge of punctuation in classrooms like Giacobbe's and those where more traditional instruction was given. She found that third-graders who were only taught punctuation during conferences about their own compositions:

> could define/explain an average of 8.66 kinds of punctuation. [But] the children who had studied punctuation through classwork, drills and tests, but had rarely written, were only able to define/explain 3.85 kinds of punctuation. (p. 569)

Cronnell (1980) includes a review of other research on punctuation instruction.

IMLICATIONS FOR TEACHING

In her skills conferences, Giacobbe gave her children explanations of punctuation marks that were based on *meaning* and *function*: the meaning of belonging and of what someone says, and the function of where you want your reader to stop. Such explanations make excellent sense from everything we know about child language acquisition.

Slobin (1985), generalizing from research on the acquisition of some 40 different languages, concludes that rules based on consistent meaning—like the regular past tense in English, or the Turkish direct object inflection—are more easily acquired than rules which do not exhibit a one-to-one mapping of meaning onto surface form. A criterion of consistent meaning fits -ing and quotation marks and possessive apostrophes too (if we forget for the moment their use to identify contractions). But unfortunately, it won't work for periods, which may seem to be the most important punctuation of all.

For periods, no criterion of meaning or function intelligible to a first-grade writer is a valid guide to the adult system. A "sentence" is in the end a formal syntactic category, and explanations that rely on nonsyntactic criteria inevitably produce errors. The semantic criterion of a "complete thought" is meaningless. The speech production criterion of "where you stop" or "where your voice falls"—which this teacher used—may well be the most useful approximation for young writers. But one's voice stops, or drops, at the end of many groups of words that are significant phrasal or clausal constituents but are not sentences. And particular rules (not taught in this classroom but often invoked) like "You can't start a sentence with *because*" are just plain wrong. In speaking we start *utterances* with "because" all the time (in answer to *why* questions), and even in the most formal writing, sentences can start with "because" if the "because" clause is followed by an independent clause (for example, if the first two lines of the text in Fig. 7.1 had been reversed).

The formal difficulties inherent in the correct scientific concept of a sentence should certainly make us reconsider why we usually try to teach periods so early. (See Kress [1982] for an important discussion of the development of the concept of "sentence" in children's writing.) And whenever we do try to teach them, one new teaching possibility is suggested by the evidence of intuitive knowledge of constituent structure in the children's phrase structure errors, and in some of the children's division of text into pages (in the journals) and lines later. Where such evidence exists, maybe it would be helpful to go back to it with the child and explain where to put periods ostensively, by pointing: "Here [lines 2, 4 and 7] but not here [lines 1, 3, 5 and 6]" (Figure 7.1).

It is possible that until children are old enough to understand terms like "phrase" and "clause," both "independent" and "dependent," appeal to intuitive structural knowledge provides a firmer basis for growth in understanding than externally imposed definitions that do not take this knowledge into account. As F. Smith (1982) says:

> How then does a child ever learn to recognize a question, a clause, a sentence . . . ? The answer is in the same way that children come to recognize dogs, cats, chairs, tables, and just about everything else in the world. Adults do not often try to define for children what

constitutes a cat, dog, chair, or table. They do not attempt to teach rules of catness, dogness or whatever. They simply point our instances of each category and leave the children to work out the rules themselves, implicitly. (p. 190)

As regards children's learning of punctuation, teachers should realize that progress—while real—is not steady. Especially with periods, alternative hypotheses coexist, and seemingly correct usage in one composition is followed by errors of both omission and commission in the next. The important message is not to despair, and not to blame either oneself or the child. We must remember that writing is truly a complex activity and that attention at one level can divert attention from another level, and make previously demonstrated knowledge temporarily disappear from performance (Scardamalia, Bereiter, & Goelman, 1982). Moreover, while errors have been our focus in this analysis, the most compelling observation is of how much in these compositions was right. Often, in the face of seemingly monumental concerns, even these beginning writers remembered not only the big ideas but the little details.

Afterword. *This report about how one group of young writers began to use punctuation illustrates important issues in the relationship between development and instruction.*

In planning any instruction, we need to know as much as we can about learners' conceptions and how they are changing over time. As Judith Langer points out in one of her editorial columns, "Musings," in Research in the Teaching of English, *comparisons of experts and novices are sometimes converted into instructional programs that focus only "on 'adding' the missing skills to the novice's repertoire" (1984, p. 341), ignoring existing conceptions that may make excellent sense from the learner's point of view. The children's invented punctuation in Giacobbe's classroom, like their invented spellings and like all children's earlier oral language forms like mines and goed, are child (not childish) forms that represent significant cognitive work and that may seem temporarily impervious to even the best instruction.*

The difference between developmental and (at least some) instructional sequences is vividly shown in a student paper from Donald Graves (personal communication, October 1982). To inves-

tigate "the psychological validity of the conventional sequence of teaching punctuation," the author (whose name was unfortunately missing from the paper) compared the punctuation "mastery" (that is, consistently correct use) of her son, Shane, in a learning environment much like Giacobbe's, with the grade norms assumed in two professional textbooks (P. S. Anderson, 1964; Otto & McMenemy, 1966). Both sequences are given in terms of chronological age in Tables 7.3 and 7.4. Because the period is the last of these 10 marks that Shane mastered, the author asks why it should be the first that teachers expect.

Cordeiro (1988) also found late learning of periods when she returned to her Provincetown, Massachusetts, classroom and compared Giacobbe's first-graders with her own third-graders in a similar language arts program. In third grade, she found only a slight increase in the overall percentage of sentences with periods placed correctly at the end. But she also found a large increase in the percentage of misplaced periods that children had used to separate what we had called phrase structures: 54 phrase structure placements out of 965 total misplacements in the first-graders' writings, but 161 out of 174 in the third-graders' writings. Just as interesting was her qualitative finding that by far the most frequent kind of phrase so punctuated by both groups of children was adverbial. Here are two third grade examples:

I went downtown. with my mother.
We might have a Christmas play. if we be good.

Table 7.3 Shale's mastery of punctuation

Punctuation mark	Chronological age, in years				
	6	7	8	9	10
period (terminal)		X	X	X	X
question mark			X	X	X
comma (limited use)			X	X	X
capital letters			X	X	X
period (abbreviations)		X	X	X	X
comma (listing)			X	X	X
apostrophe (contraction)		X	X	X	X
apostrophe (possession)			X	X	X
exclamation point			X	X	X
hyphen			X	X	X

Table 7.4 Age of instruction in two language arts textbooks

Punctuation mark	Chronological age, in years				
	6	7	8	9	10
period (terminal)		X	X	X	X
question mark			X	X	X
comma (limited use)			X	X	X
capital letters			X	X	X
period (abbreviations)				X	X
comma (listing)				X	X
apostrophe (contraction)				X	X
apostrophe (possession)				X	X
exclamation point					X

As it happens, professional writers do sometimes punctuate in exactly that way, usually at the end of a paragraph or a whole piece, for special emphasis. For example, at the end of the first paragraph of the chapter on "The Ending" in On Writing Well, Zinsser (1985) writes, "In fact, you should give as much thought to choosing your last sentence as you did your first. Well, almost as much" (p. 77). And, as I write this Afterword the day after the ground war started in the Gulf, Anna Quindlen ends her Op-Ed column in the Sunday New York Times (2/24/91): "(F)or some time the war in the Persian Gulf has made the world a simpler place. . . . But not for long." Such professional usage is why we gave full "credit" to the first-grader who hated sausage: "We are having pancakes for breakfast. With out sausage."

Such nuanced use is admittedly not for most beginners, and even professionals leave such "fragments" standing alone only sparingly. But the overall picture of mature usage is not the rigid rule-governed system that is sometimes taught in schools. So we have to face again the difficult instructional question of how to teach periods, and later all the other segmentation marks—commas, colons, semicolons, dashes, parentheses—that cue readers to relationships among units of meaning, some of whose rules are even fuzzier.

Just because of this complexity, Frank Smith (1983) says it is impossible for any teacher to be explicit about rules, and the only way to learn is to "read like a writer." But there is, it seems to me, a middle way. Although I think I do read that way, noticing how authors whose texts are a pleasure to read go about their craft, I did not figure out just when fragments stand alone in professional writing until an adult class and I set out to collect examples and analyze them inductively. Only then did we discover patterns of form (most frequently a phrase that could be attached to the preceding sentence but wasn't, like the examples given above); function (emphasis); and placement (almost always at the end of a paragraph or larger unit).

The field of second-language acquisition makes a useful distinction between "input" and "intake": Input is what is available in the language environment; intake is what learners in fact attend to and incorporate into their action systems. Learners need different amounts of help in focusing their attention on what is available to be learned and in learning the general strategy of such attending. That's what I mean by "whole language plus": minilessons that avoid both the oversimplification of textbooks' rigid rules and overreliance on students' tacit learning.

8

◆ ◆ ◆

Adult Assistance to
Language Development
Scaffolds, Models, and
Direct Instruction

Foreword. *The metaphorical term* scaffold *has now become iden-*
tified with Vygotsky's ideas, although he never used the term. The
word was first applied to forms of instruction by Wood, Bruner, and
Ross (1976). But surprisingly, that article does not cite Vygotsky at
all, though Bruner had been familiar with his work at least since
writing the introduction to Thought and Language *(as recounted in*
Bruner, 1985).

In Metaphors We Live By, *Lakoff and Johnson (1980) discuss*
how "we tend to structure the less concrete and inherently vaguer
concepts (like those for our emotions) in terms of more concrete
concepts, which are more clearly delineated in our experience"
(p. 112). In keeping with that direction of transfer, Bruner appro-
priated the concept of scaffold, and also ratchet, from the more
concrete domain of material construction in order to conceptualize
the vaguer domain of verbal interaction.

The ideas in this chapter were first put together as a plenary
talk at the 1979 Stanford Child Language Research Forum, with
the more vivid title of "Peekaboo as an Instructional Model: Dis-
course Development at Home and at School," and printed in the
annual proceedings of that conference, Papers and Reports on
Child Language Development.

This version was given during 1980 to groups of early child-
hood educators in several states, and then published in Developing

Literacy: Young Children's Use of Language, *edited by Robert Parker and Frances Davis (1983). It gives evidence for the active role of parents, thereby supporting arguments for a similarly active role for teachers.*

In her beautiful book on the problems of inexperienced adult writers, Mina Shaughnessy (1977) writes of their difficulty in composing passages "beyond the sentence":

> "There is not a sentence," writes Whitehead, "which adequately states its own meaning." The statement suggests that the quality of an idea is not to be found in a nucleus or thesis statement but in the sentences that follow or lead up to that statement. An idea, in this sense, is not a "point" so much as a branching tree of elaboration and demonstration.
>
> This distinction is useful in approaching the difficulties BW [Basic Writer] students have beyond the sentence, for it is not accurate to say, although many teachers say it, that BW students have no ideas, if by "idea" they mean what is conventionally meant by an "idea"—that is, a "point" or general statement. Not only do BW students produce essays that are full of points but the points they make are often the same ones that more advanced writers make when writing on the same subject. The differences lie in the style and extent of elaboration. (p. 226)

Shaughnessy is talking about the particular forms of elaboration expected in academic discourse: the convention of ranging widely but predictably between cases and generalizations, and the conventions of marking the rhetorical relationships between larger units of composition. But these problems must have their antecedents in earlier school years, and be open to help then too.

Consider two sharing-time narratives from a California first grade observed by Michaels (1981). She identified two styles by which sentences are combined into a larger oral text: topic-centered and topic-chaining. (St. T is the student teacher.)

Topic-centered	Topic-chaining
Jenny: Yesterday	Deena: I went to the beach Sun-
my mom	day

and my whole family
went with me to a party
and it was a Thanks-
giving party
where and we

St. T: mm

Jenny: my mom
we had to get dress up
as Pilgrims
and my mom made me
this hat for a Pilgrim

St. T.: Oh great.

and to McDonald's
and to the park
and I got this for my
birthday
My mother bought it for
me
and I had two dollars for
my birthday
and I put it in here
and I went to where my
friend named Gigi
I went over to my grand-
mother's house with
her
and she was on my back
and I and we was walking
around
by my house
and she was heavy
She was in the sixth or
seventh grade

St. T: OK I'm going to stop you.
I want you to talk about
things that are really,
really very important

(from unpublished transcripts by Michaels, 1981)

Whereas Jenny's topic-centered narrative receives a confirming "Oh great," Deena's topic-chain is cut off with criticism for what the teacher refers to as her "filibuster." Even though she is one of the best readers in the class, her oral discourse style may, in time, interfere with her ability to produce literate-sounding prose.

As with many language abilities, the ability to construct such prose develops very early in supportive environments. As one example of what is possible, here is the Scollons' account of their daughter Rachel's ability to tell the kind of narratives they, like Michaels, believe to be related to later acquisition of literacy in school. A few days before her third birthday, Rachel silently "wrote" a story in circular scribbles and then "read" it to her parents. Here's the story, with division into lines to indicate pauses, dots (.) to indicate breaths, and double slashes (//) to indicate an intonation contour of high rise and then fall, which serves to close an information unit and yet communicate an intention to continue reading.

There was a b-
girl
she
went out to get snow//

.

she
she made a hole//

.

she

.

she went back
she cried//
she went back in tell m-

.

her
her mom to get
tel—old her Mom, to
give her apple//
so she gived her apple//

.

she got

.

she went out again
got sn-
some more snow//

(Scollon & Scollon, 1979, pp. 12–13)

Rachel's ability to tell a third person narrative about an incident in her own life a few days before is impressive. Note her self-corrections from "M-" to "her Mom" and from "tell" to "told." Understandably, problems remain: the referents for the same-sex pronouns in "she gived her apple" are ambiguous, but that specific problem in anaphora persists well into the elementary years (Bartlett, 1981).

While most discussions of oral preparations for what the Scollons call "essayist" literacy focus on what children learn from being read to and being around adults and older children who read and write frequently and happily, they acknowledge such influences and go beyond to suggest what additional assistance Rachel received through adult–child interaction. I will report their observations and then generalize to three broad kinds of adult assistance: scaffolds, models, and direct instruction—first with examples from young children's language development at home, and then at school.

SCAFFOLDS

A scaffold is a temporary framework for construction in progress. One kind of scaffold is what the Scollons call "vertical constructions," in which the adult asks the child for additional new information in each utterance. The result has what Bruner calls a ratchetlike quality (personal communication, 1980) with the adult helping to "hold" each previous utterance in focal attention while asking the child to say more. In the Scollons' words:

> The child says something. The mother asks about it and the child says something further. The first can be seen as a topic statement, the mother's question as a request for a comment, and the child's answer as giving that comment.
>
> As the child develops she begins to take over both roles. That is, Brenda [the subject of R. Scollon's previous study, 1976] soon began to say both the topic and the comment. As soon as these became prosodically linked as a single utterance the whole process shifted up a level. The whole topic-comment pair was taken as a given and the interlocutor sought another comment. An example of one of these more elaborate pairs follows:
>
> Brenda: Tape recorder
>   Use it
>   Use it
> Int.:   Use it for what?
> Brenda: Talk
>   corder talk
>   Brenda talk
>
> Two things are important for this discussion. One is that this development is based on interaction with other speakers. The other is that it involves the progressive incorporation within a single tone group of greater amounts of new information. (Scollon & Scollon, 1979, pp. 43–44)

R. Scollon (1976) first described "vertical constructions" in his study of Brenda. At that time he believed them to provide assistance to the child's development of syntax. Because of intervening evidence from other researchers that children develop syntax in the absence of this particular form of interaction, the Scollons (1979) now believe that "the vertical construction is a discourse process as is the information structuring of essayist literacy. We now see the former as an important means of teaching the latter" (p. 45).

The interaction with Brenda is about the tape recorder, present at the moment of speaking. New problems confront the child who, like Rachel, is struggling to encode a narrative of a past event. Stoel-Gammon and Cabral (1977) describe the development of the "reportative function" in Brazilian children 20–24 months old. Attempts to construct narratives of past experiences usually occur first in a dialogue in which the adult asked questions that acted as prompts. For example, when a 20-month-old child reported "fell ground," the adult prompted more information by asking how and where it happened and "who pushed you down?" These early reports were most successful when the adult had been with the child at the event and later asked the child to relate what had happened to a third person. The companion's questions not only elicit progressively more information from the child, they also indicate to the child what aspects of the past event are significant and notable, focusing the child's mental image on those aspects that should be replayed in the present account.

Another kind of interactional scaffold appears in adult–child conversations in these early years, in proto-conversations with infants and in the language games such as peekaboo and picture-book reading, where the adult creates a sequential structure with slots of certain shapes in which the child comes to speak. In a different domain, that of learning to play a musical instrument, comparable assistance is supplied by special chamber music records, called "add-a-part" or "music minus one," each with a missing part to be played by the novice, in a graduated series of difficulty. Neither scaffolds nor add-a-part records are as dynamic and interactional as these language games; moreover, the games are very special scaffolds in self-destructing gradually as the need lessens, to be replaced by a new support for a more elaborate construction. But if these limitations are kept in mind, both metaphors may be helpful.

In proto-conversations with infants, mothers work hard to maintain a conversation with their 3- to 18-month-old babies, despite the inadequacies of their conversational partners (Snow, 1977). At first they accept burps, yawns, and coughs as well as laughs and coos—but not arm-waving or head movements—as the baby's turn. They fill in for the babies by asking and answering their own questions, and by phrasing questions so that a minimal response can be treated as a reply. By 7 months, when the babies become more active, the mothers no longer accept all the baby's vocalizations, only vocalic or consonantal babbles. As the mother raises the ante, the child's development proceeds.

In peekaboo and picture-book reading, as in the proto-conversations, the adult first produces the entire script, then gradually relinquishes parts as the child develops the ability to speak them. In peeka-boo, the mother starts by doing the hiding (usually herself) as well as the talking—answering as well as asking questions about who and where. The child gradually takes over the actions and then the speech, reverses roles and asks, "Where's Mommy?" Finally, there is a solo performance with objects the child has made to disappear (Ratner & Bruner, 1978).

As peekaboo is a routinized speech situation, structured around the physical activities of hiding and finding, so picture-book is a ritual-ized speech event, where talk is the primary purpose—not just phatic communication and greetings as in peekaboo, but labeling for which the book provides clear and present referents. In one common form, book reading in the children's second year has a four-part structure:

An attentive vocative, such as *Look.*
A query, such as *What's that?*
A label, such as *It's an X.*
A feedback utterance, such as *Yes, that's an X* (if the child has provided the label). [paraphrased from Ninio & Bruner, 1978, p. 6]

As the child's development proceeds, the adult encourages the child to speak more of the script.

A larger set of early language games played by nine English and 16 Dutch families has been analyzed by Snow, Dubber, and de Blauw (1982), and their analysis confirms and extends that of Bruner and his colleagues. Their conclusions speak to the benefits of the scaffolds provided in all these routinized situations.

Several years ago, in a study of social class differences in mothers' speech (Snow, Arlmann-Rupp, Hassing, Jobse, Joosten, & Vorster, 1976), we found that mothers' speech was more complex in book-reading than in a free-play situation. At that time, we suggested that this resulted from the greater contextual support for speech avail-able during book reading; the presence of the book served to focus attention and determine topics, so these tasks need not be fulfilled by maternal utterances. The automatic establishment of joint atten-tion to an agreed-upon topic freed the mother to make more sophis-ticated, and thus linguistically more complex, comments than would be possible during free play.

While this explanation cannot be ruled out, I now feel that a much more potent reason for the greater complexity of "book talk" can be found in the accompanying routinization. Routines enable participants to deal with complexity. We think of routines as simple and unsophisticated—the produce of memory, not of rule use. But their simplicity allows for the introduction, into the slots created by the routine, of fillers considerably more complex in structure and-or content than could possibly be dealt with elsewhere. The slot, by its predictability, provides the opportunity for novel, complex, and creative fillers to be inserted. (pp. 68–69)

Thus the two kinds of scaffolds—vertical constructions and gamelike routines—provide different kinds of support for the child's growing ability in both language and social interactions.

Before turning to the second kind of assistance, the provision of models, it is important to think about the similarities and differences between these scaffolds at home and at school.

In formal terms, similarities between the basic book-reading structure and classroom lessons (Mehan, 1979) are striking. With the mother's attentional vocative replacing the teacher's turn-allocation procedures, the remaining parts of the book-reading event fit exactly the initiation–reply–evaluation sequence of the lessons. Moreover, the initiations in both events are questions to which the adult asker knows the answer. In studies of antecedents of school success, many people have found a high correlation between being read to and succeeding in school and have remarked on the special linguistic features of written text (Chomsky, 1972) or of the conversation interpolated into the text-reading scene (Snow et al., 1982). The structural similarities suggest that picture-book reading may, in addition to its substantive contribution, be the basis for transfer to participation in the discourse structure of classroom lessons several years later.

But there are differences too: Classroom lessons are notably less responsive to the child's growing competence. Instead of self-destructing, the structure remains much the same across grades, and only the content of the slots—the teacher's questions and students' answers—increases in complexity. Furthermore, students do not get a chance to take over the adult role. For such opportunities, peer dialogues are essential.

There can be an analogue to "interference," or negative transfer, between earlier and later discourse patterns in this early learning. As Ninio and Bruner (1978) point out, picture-book reading has a different structure if the mother reads a nursery rhyme and leaves a slot for the child to fill in at the end of each line. A graduate student at Harvard, Sharon Haselkorn, reported interference between the patterns of mother and researcher that she encountered over book reading at this early age. Sharon is used to playing the What's That? game, but one of her young subjects had learned the Fill-in-the-Blank game, and they had a very hard time getting their speech event together (personal communication, 1978). Even very young children are acculturated beings, and these cultural differences increase in importance by school age. Part of the reason that Deena's teacher evaluates her narrative ability so negatively, and does not help Deena with interpolated questions as she does Jenny, may be because of such a mismatch in expectations (Michaels, 1981).

MODELS

As we talk to children, how we speak indicates how texts are constructed for particular purposes and in particular situations. In adopting the term *model* for this form of assistance, we must remember that the child's task is to acquire an underlying structure; imitation of the model itself does not suffice. The texts we supply are examples to learn from, not samples to copy.

Caretakers who are literate themselves not only supply models through reading to children, but also coach young children in such narrative accounting by speaking for them before they can speak for themselves—by giving a running account of an activity as it is taking place: "See, look, we throw it up and we catch it . . ."; or by telling the child a story about herself after an event has taken place, "Once upon a time there was a little girl named Rachel . . ." (Scollon & Scollon, 1979).

Such narratives, the Scollons believe, help the child develop what they call "fictionalization of the self": the ability to distance oneself from participation in an event and as an observer describe it to someone else. By extension, the provision of such models—jokes and arguments as well as narratives—should aid the acquisition of the structure of different genres of oral and written texts. Knowledge of such structures is not only necessary for composition, but can make that composition an easier task by providing some decisions ready-made (Bartlett, 1981).

Of course, models and scaffolds are much less separate in conversation than they are in this analysis; and in classroom practice they should be deliberately combined to help children learn the particular discourse forms valued in school. One excellent example of such a combination comes from Heath's work (1982) with teachers in a southeastern U.S. black community she calls Trackton. When the teachers complained that the Trackton children did not participate in lessons,

Heath helped them understand what she had learned from five years of ethnographic fieldwork in the Trackton community. For example, the children were not used to known-answer questions about the labels and attributes of objects and events. As one third-grade boy complained, "Ain't nobody can talk about things being about theirselves." Heath then worked with the teachers to try out changes in their classrooms, in the following sequence:

- Start with familiar content and with familiar kinds of talk about that content.
- Go on to new kinds of talk, still about the familiar content, and provide peer models, available for rehearing on audiocassettes.
- Provide opportunities for the Trackton children to practice the new kinds of talk, first out of the public arena and also on tape, and then in actual lessons.
- Finally, talk with the children about talk itself.

Ideally, we should provide opportunities for children to practice a growing range of discourse functions (explaining, narrating, instructing)—first in situations where models and supports are available, then gradually with less help. Imagine the kind of help Heath's teachers gave children for answering questions being available for the children telling narratives in the classroom observed by Michaels. One might start with narratives about content known to the teacher—as in retelling stories or reporting on a classroom trip—and then go to narratives of children's personal experiences, where the teacher's guiding questions necessarily must be more general. For such assistance, the show-and-tell or sharing time is probably not the most helpful event. For children like Jenny, who don't need help, it is fine. But for children like Deena, the teacher needs more private time to give sustained help without worrying about losing the attention of the rest of the class; and Deena, like the Trackton children, needs a more private time in which to try.

DIRECT INSTRUCTION

The third kind of adult assistance is direct instruction, in which the adult not only models a particular utterance but directs the child to *say* or *tell* or *ask*. In spontaneous adult–child conversations, direct instruction seems to focus on two aspects of language development: appropriate social language use and correct vocabulary.

As peekaboo is the prototypical scaffold, so "say bye-bye" is the prototype of direct instruction. As described by Gleason and Weintraub (1976), "Even when the child is only expected to open and close its fist, the adult, who may shake the baby's arm, is liable to say, 'Say "Bye-bye"'" (p. 130). Other routines considered important for polite social life and taught in this way are greetings, thanks, and other farewells, as well as routines for special occasions such as trick-or-treat on Halloween (Greif & Gleason, 1980).

But direct instruction is not limited to teaching children to be polite; it seems to be used to teach whatever interpersonal uses of language are considered essential for young children in a particular community. In some families, the focus will be on learning to be polite; in others, the focus may be on learning to speak in self-defense.

For example, P. J. Miller (1982) heard poignant examples of how three young white working-class mothers in south Baltimore taught their young children appropriate compliance and assertiveness in what they know to be a harsh world. One form of this instruction is giving the children lines to say to a third person, sometimes in play situations with dolls. For example, when 5-year-old Kris took a doll from Amy, Marlene (the mother) helped Amy to reassert her claim by giving her the appropriate lines to say:

Amy	*Marlene*
	Oh, what did she [Kris] do?
my baby	
	Tell her [Kris], say "Keep off."
keep off	
keep off	
	Say "You hurt it."
you hurt it	
	(Miller, 1982, p. 115).

Preschool teachers often consider it part of their role to teach appropriate interpersonal language, such as how to substitute speech (assertive, but politely so) for physical action or cries. In a toddler class in one daycare center, Isler (1981) observed that if a child begins to cry when another child attempts to pull a toy away, the teacher might intervene, "Can you use words and tell him/her 'I'm using this'?" In three observations in this class in November, December, and March, Isler followed the teachers' instructions and their results. In general, the children's cries and one-word holophrases decreased and phrases increased. More interesting were the qualitative differences between November and the two later observations:

> The phrases recorded in November tended to be those which were frequently modeled in the class, such as "I using that," "Don't do it," and "Is mine" (or variations of those forms). Although the children certainly used all of these forms in December and March their repertoire seemed to have expanded considerably. Phrases recorded in December included "I sitting right here," "Too heavy people" (child was telling another child not to sit in a wagon she was pulling), "No banging floor," and "I eating that cracker." Phrases recorded in March included, "Becca's sleeping on me," "I wanna go there now," and "Dat not for you, dat is for Jonathan." It appears as if the children may not only learn the phrases modeled by the teachers but may also learn to recognize the situations in which it is appropriate to use verbal assertions. This understanding of the situational characteristics of language might then allow the child to expand his communicative skills as his vocabulary grows. (Isler, 1981)

As with all models, children must generalize beyond the particular utterances and the particular situations in which the instruction is provided; and in these reports of direct instruction in real-life situations there is clear evidence that such generalizations take place.

The second focus of direct instruction in spontaneous adult–child conversations is vocabulary. In conversations about first-hand experience and in book reading, adults often say, "That's an X. Can you say X?" This is undoubtedly useful assistance, as long as we remember that direct instruction can give only the word itself, a seed from which rich conceptual meanings must grow more slowly. In Brown's (1958) felicitous phrase, the word is "an invitation to a concept," inviting attention to itself and to the related verbal and nonverbal context when it is heard again; but it must be heard again and again, and in varying contexts as well.

IN CONCLUSION

While most of my examples of adult assistance are from middle-class families in the United States, I want to suggest that the kinds of assistance I have called scaffolds, models, and direct instruction are universally provided, with the particulars of each varying from culture to culture. For whatever behavior is considered important, adults will provide scaffoldlike frameworks within which children at an early age can participate in weaving or fishing or speaking. Either as part of these scaffolds or separately, models of more mature behavior are always available as long as children have the opportunity to be around more competent members of the community, even if only as onlookers and eavesdroppers. Where direct instruction to "do" or "say" is given, that is probably an especially significant indicator of valued learning.

Afterword. Of these three labels for kinds of adult assistance— scaffolds, models, and direct instruction—the last is the most controversial. "Direct instruction" has unfortunately become identified with one particular instructional program called DISTAR; *and teachers who don't like that program may avoid considering how some kinds of direct instruction can be very helpful.*

The critical meaning is explicitness: Direct instruction means being explicit about what needs to be done, or said, or written— rather than leaving it to learners to make inferences from experience that are unmediated by such help. In addition to the parental examples given in this chapter, we saw classroom examples of direct instruction in Giacobbe's teaching of possessive apostrophes and quotation marks in Chapter 7:

> *When something belongs to someone else, we put one of these little marks [showing as she speaks]. We call that an "apostrophe" and we add the s. . . . We have some marks that we put around the words people say, before the first word and after the last.*

The problem with direct teaching of periods is not with the idea of direct teaching itself, but with the concept of sentencehood, which is so complex.

In Australia, a controversy analogous to that between whole language versus phonics in the United States centers on the teaching of writing. In opposition to proponents of "natural language teaching" (e.g., Cambourne & Turbill, 1987) are the "genre" educators (e.g., Derewianka, 1991). One member of the genre group, Joan Rothery (1989), has extended the application of all three terms— scaffolds, models, and direct instruction—to the help that needs to be given in the teaching of writing.

Another Australian educator in the genre group, Brian Gray, has developed another metaphor, "concentrated encounters." Its history has no Soviet ancestry, but it illustrates how ideas about education cross national boundaries. Cazden and Bartlett (1973) first used the term in a review of an oral language program based on Basil Bernstein's theory of language use (Gahagan & Gahagan, 1970). By concentrated encounter, we referred to the Gahagans activities, like games and role playing, in which opportunities for practice in a wide range of language functions can be created in school.

Then, in 1974, for a conference on language and learning in early childhood at the University of Leeds (England), I adopted "concentrated encounters" as a label for assessment situations, such as two-person communication games, which are concentrated forms of familiar interactional experiences and which contrast with the "contrived encounters"of more typical tests (Cazden, 1975b).

Finally, Brian Gray, working in an Aboriginal school in central Australia, imaginatively reappropriated the term for curriculum development (1985). Here is an extended example from his program to develop Aboriginal children's knowledge of English language and culture:

> *When a class of children were working on a cattle station theme in preparation for a visit to a local station, one of the situations we explored was "saddling a horse." In order to develop this as a series of concentrated encounter sessions, we brought horses into the school over several days and listened as their owner explained and demonstrated how to saddle them. Then teachers and children practised doing it and talked through the process together. Photographs were taken of the sequences of steps involved. Each day, in addition to working with the horses when they were available, the teachers and children discussed the picture sequences, practised putting them in order, and mimed the steps involved in the process.*
>
> *The concentrated encounter sessions on "saddling a horse" created a specific context in which the meaning requirements for communication were shared by all parties involved. The sequence was complex, but it was worth learning and the children were happy to work on it until they had mastered it, and once they had mastered it they were happy to explain it to others and in fact were willing to create an expository text which displayed their knowledge. This series of concentrated encounters was one of a number—for example, riding, mustering, branding, butcher-*

ing cattle, putting bridles on, and leatherwork—all of which served as a focus for the classroom cattle station theme. (Gray, 1985, p. 92)

More schematically, the curriculum sequence in this and other examples of Gray's concentrated encounters (from toast making to hospital clinics) seems to be roughly as follows:

- Children have extensive first-hand experience with real objects and events, in situ and in the classroom, and with related books and other written documents.
- Teacher and children together role play, sometimes many times, the significant role relationships involved in that experience and their appropriate language use.
- After both first-hand and role-playing activities, children engage in discussions, with and without photographs.
- Teacher helps children construct a group report (or experience chart).
- (Eventually) the children do independent writing on the topic.

There are important structural similarities here to Heath's (1982) descriptions of curriculum in which black and white children in Appalachia learned to answer particular kinds of teacher questions.

As in parent–child interactions, scaffolds, models, and direct instruction are all integrated in these complex classroom group activities.

9

♦♦♦

A Vygotskian
Interpretation
of Reading Recovery

Marie M. Clay and Courtney B. Cazden

Foreword. In Chapter 2 I referred to Reading Recovery as one clear example of instruction that calls the learner's attention to parts (features of how our system of written language works) in the context of whole language (reading good children's literature and writing down the learner's ideas). It is one way to teach children who need, in the words of one teacher, "more than an implicit approach to reading" (Amanda Branscombe, personal communication, February 1990). And it has become for me the prototypical example of "whole language plus," although that phrase does not appear in this chapter.

The chapter was coauthored with the originator of Reading Recovery, Marie Clay, now professor emeritus at the University of Auckland (New Zealand) and 1991–92 president-elect of the International Reading Association. It was written in response to an invitation to contribute to a volume on Vygotsky and Education, edited by Luis Moll (1990).

This is an analysis of one tutorial program, Reading Recovery (RR), for children who have been in school for one year and have not yet "caught on" to reading and writing. RR was designed and evaluated by Clay in New Zealand (1985a, 1991) and is becoming available to children who need it throughout that country. Because of its success there, it is being tried out in the United States, notably through Ohio State University (DeFord, Lyons, & Pinnell, 1991; C. A. Lyons, 1987; Pinnell, 1985). Cazden learned about RR while on extended stays in New Zealand during 1983 and 1987 and became interested in features of its instructional design after viewing videotapes of New Zealand RR lessons.

Reading Recovery was designed from Clay's theory of the nature of reading, observations of children's behavior in learning to read, and collaboration with experienced New Zealand infant school teachers. Although no thought was given to Vygotsky's theories during this program development, it is possible to interpret features of RR in Vygotskian terms. At first it seemed to Cazden that RR was simply an elegant example of scaffolded instruction. As we worked together on this article, more relationships to Vygotsky's ideas appeared.

After a brief introduction to the theory of reading that guides literacy instruction in both regular New Zealand and RR classrooms, we analyze features of RR that require teacher and child to collaborate in shared tasks—reading a new book and writing the child's story; we present evidence in both cases of a shift from teacher/child interindividual functioning to increasingly complex intraindividual functioning by the child. We then suggest Vygotskian interpretations of RR as a system of social interaction organized around the comprehension and production of texts that demonstrably creates new forms of cognitive activity in the child.

A THEORY OF READING

According to Clay's theory of reading and writing instruction (1991), all readers, from 5-year-old children attempting their first book to the efficient adult reader, have to monitor and integrate information from multiple sources. Readers need to use, and check against each other, four types of cues: semantic (text meaning), syntactic (sentence structure), visual (graphemes, orthography, format, and layout), and phonological (the sounds of oral language) (see Figure 9.1).

The endpoint of early instruction has been reached when children have a *self-improving system*: They learn more about reading every time they read, independent of instruction. (Stanovich [1986] calls

Figure 9.1   Relationships among multiple sources of information during reading

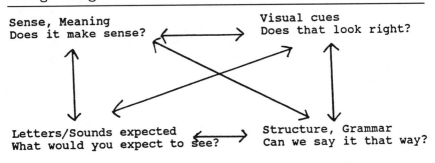

this "boot-strapping.") When they read texts of appropriate difficulty for their present skills, they use a set of mental operations, strategies in their heads, that are just adequate for more difficult bits of the text. In the process, they engage in "reading work," deliberate efforts to solve new problems with familiar information and procedures. They are working with theories of the world and theories about written language, testing them and changing them as they engage in reading and writing activities.

By the age of 6, after one year of instruction, high-progress readers in New Zealand classrooms operate on print in this way. As cue users, not just oral language guessers, they read with attention focused on meaning, checking several sources of cues, one against the other, almost simultaneously. When such higher-level strategies fail, they can engage a lower-processing gear and shift focus to one or another cue source in isolation—such as letter clusters or letter–sound associations—while maintaining a directing attention on the text message at all times.

Low-progress readers, on the other hand, operate with a more limited range of strategies—some relying too much on what they can invent from memory without paying attention to visual details, others looking so hard for words they know or guessing words from first letters that they forget what the message as a whole is about.

For all children, the larger the chunks of printed language they can work with, the richer the network of information they can use and the quicker they learn. Teaching should only dwell on detail long enough for the child to discover its existence and then encourage the use of it in isolation only when absolutely necessary.

OVERVIEW OF READING RECOVERY

RR addresses a problem of concern to most Western educational systems. It selects young children who have the poorest performance in reading and writing and, in daily individual teaching sessions over 12-15 weeks, brings most of them to average levels of performance and teaches them how to improve their own reading and writing skills when they are no longer in the program.

Children are selected for the RR program by a diagnostic survey (Clay, 1985) administered by RR teachers and by consultation among the school staff. No child in ordinary classrooms is excluded for any reason—intelligence, limited English proficiency, possible learning disability, and so forth.

Children's rate and amount of progress in the program in New Zealand (where three-year follow-up research yielded evidence of continued average achievement) is similar to that achieved in Bloom's one-to-one tutoring programs (B. Bloom, 1971, p. 60). With the exception of 1 to 2 percent of the entire age-class cohort who need more help than RR provides, pupils from the low end of the achievement distribution are moved into the average band of performance. In other words, a significantly different population becomes not statistically different from the average group.

In order to achieve such accelerated learning, attention of teacher and child must be on strategies or operations—mental activities initiated by the child to get messages from a text. If the teacher becomes involved in teaching items rather than strategies—particular letter-sound correspondences or sight vocabulary words, for example, rather than the strategy of checking a word that would make sense in the context against information in the print—the prospect of accelerated learning is seriously threatened. Letter-sound correspondences and spelling patterns are learned, but in the course of reading and writing meaningful text, especially writing. RR teachers praise children for generative strategies, not for items learned.

The following activities, usually in this order, constitute the daily RR lesson:

1. Rereading of two or more familiar books
2. Independent reading of yesterday's new book while the teacher takes a running record
3. Letter identification (plastic letters on a magnetic board)
4. Writing a story the child has composed (including hearing sounds in words)

5. Reassembling cut-up story
6. Introducing a new book
7. Reading the new book

When a child no longer needs to work on letter identification, the third slot is deleted or used for other word-breaking or word-building work.

We will present a detailed analysis of reading activities 6 and 7 and writing activities 4 and 5. All examples are from videotapes of RR lessons in New Zealand and Ohio. The teachers, like all RR teachers (infant teachers in New Zealand, primary teachers in the United States) have received a year of training and practicum. Because of this training and subsequent monthly meetings while RR teachers are on the job, there is much less variation across teachers than in most program implementations. The children—Melanie, Larry, and Premala—are all from the lowest 10 percent in their school cohort.

READING A NEW BOOK

During the first two weeks of a Reading Recovery program, the teacher does not try to teach the child anything new, but rather initiates activities that allow the child to use and explore further the repertoire of behaviors that he already controls. Teacher and child discover many things about each other during these two weeks. The teacher discovers what the child already knows; and the child learns how book-sharing will occur in the lessons to come. A format for book-sharing interaction between this child and this teacher is created.

Excerpts from Melanie's book introduction illustrate this (see Figure 9.2). Because the teacher takes the initiative in these early lessons, her moves are given on the left, categorized by kinds of help, with the child's responses on the right. Oral reading is transcribed in small capital letters.

The Teacher's Introduction of a New Text

In RR, the child is not usually expected to sight-read novel text without preparation; that is more appropriate after children have learned how to read. A new book is both carefully selected and carefully introduced. What may seem like casual conversational exchanges between teacher and pupil are based on the teacher's deliberate teaching decisions for a particular child. These are based on her records, obtained from the daily individual teaching sessions, of each child's

Figure 9.2   Melanie: Book introduction during the first week

TEACHER	CHILD

Setting the topic
THE CHOCOLATE CAKE.
(*T reads the title for M*)

Maintaining interaction
Let's read this together.

Increasing accessibility
(*She provides a model*).
'MM' and GRANDMA.

Supporting performance
    (*T and M complete the page together.*)
       'MM, MM' SAID GRANDMA.
Prompting constructive activity
(*T pauses . . .*)

                                        (*and M continues reading the
                                        next two pages.*)
                                        'MM, MM' SAID GRANDPA. 'MM,'
                                        SAID MA AND 'MM,' SAID BABY.

Working with necessary knowledge
and what did they do?

                                        Eat it.

That's right. They all ate it.
(*T confirms M's response, while
changing the verb tense to match
the text.*)
Providing a model and prompting
completion
And so they said, 'IT'S ALL . . .'

                                        (*M anticipates and generates*)
                                        . . . GONE.
                                        (*Then she goes quickly to the
                                        next page and anticipates and
                                        generates a relevant oral text.*)
                                        We want more.

Accepting the partially correct
response
(*T accepts this, but revised it in
her reply to match the sentence in
the text.*)

                                        (continued)

Figure 9.2 (*continued*)

TEACHER	CHILD

'MORE, MORE, MORE,' THEY SAID.
Maintaining shared interaction
   (*Pointing to the page, T invites M.*)
Calling for reflection or judgement
about the story

> (*T and M discuss what will happen—will another cake be baked? This focuses M's attention on comprehension of the story as a whole.*)

---

response repertoires—what Wood, Bruner, and Ross (1976) refer to as "performance characteristics" (p. 97), the observable aspects of the child's reading and writing action system.

Setting the topic. The teacher has selected the new book to challenge the pupil in specific ways. She has previewed the story and its challenges. She sets the topic, title, and characters with minimal interaction; too much talk confuses. Titles are treated as labels; they often have tricks in them and tend to use language from which redundancy has been stripped. Discussion may relate to the conceptual context of the new story or to a related book the child has read.

Increasing accessibility. The teacher may sketch the plot, or the sequences in the text, up to any climax or surprise. Using new or unusual words in context, she introduces things which the child might not understand or language the child might not be able to anticipate. She may carefully enunciate unusual syntax (for example, when the text uses a full form, *cannot*, where the child might expect *can't*). Or she may use a sentence pattern two or three times to help the child hold it in his mind. If the child generates a relevant phrase, the teacher confirms it and alters it where necessary to match the text (as one teacher does when Melanie says "Eat it" in Figure 9.2 and another teacher does when Larry makes the same error in Figure 9.3 below).

In these ways, teacher and child rehearse what is novel in the story without the child actually hearing the text read. It is typical of all RR instruction that features of texts receive attention not in isolation but within the complexity of that text for this particular individual child.

Maintaining interactive ease.   To repeat and amplify what the child says maintains interactive ease, but it also models for the child that discussion of the story is expected. It may create more conceptual context, add new information, or remove ambiguity and possible confusion.

Prompting the child to constructive activity.   In general, the teacher urges the child to actively search for links: links within the story (by pausing for the child to generate the ending: "It's all_____" [*gone*] or guess *grandpa* and *baby* by analogy with *grandma*); links within the print (asking, "How did you know . . . ?"); and links beyond the book into the child's experience ("Have you ever done that?" "How do you think X felt?").

Teachers may think that such questions are intended to arouse the child's interest and motivation, but they play a more instrumental role in beginning reading. Such questions both provide signals to the child that reading requires active interaction with texts and bring relevant experiences and knowledge to the child's "context in the mind."

Working with new knowledge.   The teacher checks to see whether the child has relevant knowledge and ensures that it has been "brought to mind" and is accessible for use in reading the book. When the teacher suspects that the child does not have the ideas or word needed for a particular text, she may explain some part of the story, or contrast a feature of the story with something she knows the child knows in another book. For example, she may help the child discriminate between two things like a school desk and an adult-type writing desk. Such help may be either anticipatory or responsive to signals from the child. When teachers expect a word to be unfamiliar to a child, they first talk toward the meaning, describe some relevant object, setting, or use, and only last label or name the word; cognitive context is necessary in order for the child to "receive" the new word with understanding.

Because constructive activity is so important, the teacher gently pushes the child toward actively working with the new knowledge in some way—for example, by checking the new information with the pictures in the book.

Accepting partially correct responses.   The teacher promotes emerging skill by accepting and reinforcing responses that are only partially correct. Rarely does the child's response come out of thin air; it is a response to some part of the text and/or some part of his understanding. If a response is correct in some respect, it is in the interests of both the child's economy in learning and his increasing self-confidence as a reader for the teacher to recognize this, and then help the child change where necessary. If the teacher cannot tell what strategy the child has used, her response will be deliberately general: "I liked the way you did that but did you notice . . ." At other times, she praises the use of a particular feature or type of information (such as attention to the first letter).

In this way the teacher creates a lesson format, a scaffold, within which she promotes emerging skill, allows for the child to work with the familiar, introduces the unfamiliar in a measured way, and deals constructively with slips and error. The teacher calls for the comprehension of texts and for the detection and repair of mismatches when they occur. She passes more and more control to the child and pushes the child, gently but consistently, into independent, constructive activity.

In Figure 9.3, Larry is introduced to a new book, *The Great Big Enormous Turnip*, in the ninth week of his daily lessons. Following this introduction shown in Figure 9.3, the teacher expects Larry to read the book for the first time by problem solving as independently as possible.

Figure 9.3   Larry: Introduction of a new book in the ninth grade

TEACHER	CHILD
Setting the topic, theme, and characters Let's look at our new book. This story was about a big turnip, wasn't it (T knew L had heard the story somewhere but had not read it.) THE GREAT BIG ENORMOUS TURNIP. Let's see what happened. Here's a little old man and he's . . . Prompting constructive activity What's he doing?	
	He's telling it to grow.
Accepting the child's involvement That's right! He's telling it to grow. Good! Prompting constructive activity and then what's he trying to do?	

Figure 9.3   (*continued*)

TEACHER	CHILD
	Pull it out.
Pull it out. Can he pull it out?	
	(Shakes his head).
No. Who does he ask to help him?	
	The little old woman.
And what do they do?	
	Pull it?
Did they do it?	
	(Shakes his head.)
No. Who do they ask next?	
	(no reply)
Working with new knowledge They're asking the granddaughter, aren't they? Prompting constructivce activity And do they all pull? Does it come up?	
	No.
Who do they ask next?	
	The dog.
Accepting partially correct responses The black dog, that's right. And still it doesn't come up. Prompting constructive activity Who do they ask next?	
	The cat.
Playing with the climax effect And does it come up? Does it? I think it might, and they all . . . (turns the page) . . . Oh, no! Not yet. Prompting constructive activity Who do they have to ask?	
	The mouse.
The mouse, that's right. And they're all pulling, aren't they And then what happened?	
	It came out.
It came out, and what did they all do? Accepting partially correct responses	
	Eat it.
That's right. they all ate it. You read it to me.	

Teacher–Child Interaction During the First Reading

Over the course of each child's RR program, there are shifts in how much control of the task he is able to take as a result of such introductions, and how independent his first reading of a text can be. In the early weeks, the child will generate an oral utterance, inventing and reconstructing a text from the introduction or memory of past readings, the pictures, and what little he knows about print. He will spend the next 12 to 15 weeks mapping oral language onto printed text. Through the child's constructive cognitive activity, visual perception of print, oral language, and world knowledge work together, with meaning as the goal and the teacher as monitor and guide.

Larry's first reading of *The Great Big Enormous Turnip*, immediately after the teacher's introduction, is shown in Figure 9.4. On two occasions, the teacher directs his attention to the subword level of analysis—"sw-" [eet] and "str-" [ong], without losing the textual emphasis of the interchange. (Sometimes a first reading will contain more new teaching than this one does.) The teacher attends only to what she believes is critical for a correct reading of the text the next day; she decides not to work on some errors. Because the child now has the initiative, his reading is placed on the left in Figure 9.4, with the teacher's responses on the right.

A running record would be taken when the child reads the book independently the next day, and this teacher could be reasonably confident that the child will read it at or above 90 percent accuracy. When this does not happen, then the teacher's choice of book, or the way she introduced it, or her teaching around the first reading has not been appropriate.

After this first reading, each book is reread several times during the first activity in subsequent lessons. During these rereadings, there will be opportunities for the child to return to, and discover, more aspects of the text than he understood the first day.

WRITING A STORY

During each RR lesson, the child composes a "story" (usually just one sentence) and writes it, with help from the teacher, in an unlined notebook. Then a sentence-strip version of the same story, copied and cut up by the teacher, is given to the child to reassemble immediately and then take home to reassemble again "for Mum." Much of the

Figure 9.4   Larry's first reading of the new book

CHILD	TEACHER

THE GREAT BIG ENORMOUS TURNIP
ONCE AN OLD MAN PLANTED A TURNIP.

> Good.
> (*T ignores the omission of "Once upon a time."*)

HE SAID, GROW, GROW LITTLE TURNIP,
GROW . . . (*pauses at the next word*)

> How does that word start?
> Can I help you start it
> off? How does it start?
> s . . . He tells it to grow
> sw . . . sweet. (*T could
> have anticipated this word
> in her introduction.*)

(The child does not re-read the
prompted text but moves on.)
GROW LITTLE TURNIP, GROW S . . .
(pauses at another word.)

> How else does he want it
> to grow? He wants it to
> grow sweet and he wants
> it to grow str . . .

(*Child is now working at both the
word and story level*) . . . STRONG

> Good boy, that's lovely.
> Grow strong.

AND THE TURNIP GREW UP SWEET AND
STRONG AND . . .

> (*No attention to the
> omission of "big."*)
> What's the other word
> that begins with "e"?
> Enor . . .

ENORMOUS

> Good.

AND THEN . . . (*self corrects*) THEN ONE
DAY THE OLD MAN WENT TO PULL IT UP.
HE . . .

> (*No attention to the
> self-correction, so as*

(continued)

Figure 9.4   (*continued*)

CHILD	TEACHER
	not to detract from meaning.) What's he doing?
PULL . . .	
	That's right.
AND PULLED AGAIN BUT HE CAN'T	
	(*Teacher ignores the uncorrected "pulled," and attending to the present problem-solving, accepts the partially correct response.*) Nearly right. It starts like *can't* but he c . . .
COULDN'T	
	(*Models*) could
COULD NOT PULL IT UP.	
	That's right. He could not pull it up.
I can't	
	(prompts story structure) What did he do?
HE . . .	
	Look! What is he doing, do you think? He . . .
HE CALLED THE OLD WOMAN	
	Right, he called the old woman.
THE OLD WOMAN PULLED . . .	
THE OLD WOMAN PULLED THE OLD MAN	
	Good, I like the way you went back and did that again (*confirming check*).
THE OLD MAN PULLED THE TURNIP	
AND THEY PULLED AND PULLED AGAIN	
BUT THEY COULD NOT PULL IT UP.	
	Well done. We got that word (*they*). Jolly good.
SO THE OLD WOMAN CALLED HER	
GRANDDAUGHTER.	
	Good boy!
	(continued)

Figure 9.4 *(continued)*

CHILD	TEACHER
THE GRANDDAUGHTER PULLED THE OLD WOMAN. THE OLD WOMAN PULLED THE OLD MAN. THE OLD MAN PULLED THE TURNIP AND THEY PULLED AND PULLED AGAIN BUT THEY COULD NOT PULL IT UP.	
	(The teacher skips to the end. This is a timed session being recorded.) Right! Let's find where they pulled it up. . . . and it came out.
THEN THEY . . .	
	(Steadying) That's right.
. . . THEY PULLED AND PULLED AGAIN AND UP CAME THE TURNIP AT LAST.	
	That's very good. Do you like that book? What would you like to do to finish off?

child's learning of sound-letter relationships and spelling patterns is prompted and practiced in these activities.

For one child, Premala, we have three videotapes taken near the beginning, middle, and end of her 15-week RR program (Premala I, II, and III). Here are the stories she composes:

    I. *A little girl is cuddling a cat.* (about a book)
   II. *The little red hen made a cake.* (about a book)
  III. *I am going swimming at school now.* (about a personal experience; New Zealand children do swim at school!)

Figure 9.5 shows how these three sentences got written down. What the child (C) wrote is on the top line; what the teacher (T) wrote is underneath. If the child wrote the letter, but only after some kind of help from the teacher, the letter appears on the child's line with a circle around it. The "boxes" around letters in *hen* and *made* are explained below. Premala's progress in transcribing her stories can be summarized in the increasing number of letters written correctly by the child,

Figure 9.5 How Premala's sentence got written down

I	(C)	A ①	g		k		a	c t.
	(T)	ittle	irl	is	cuddling		a	

II	(C)	The	little	red	h e n	m a d e	c	
	(T)						some cakes.	

III (C) I am going swimming at school now.

alone or with help, and the decreasing number written by the teacher
(T), as shown in Table 9.1.

To achieve this progress, the teacher gives various kinds of writing
help that are analogous in function to her help in reading:

- Calling attention to the sounds of words and spelling patterns in
  writing
    I. "Do you know how to start writing *little*?"
    III. [After Premala has written *s* for *swim*] "Let's listen to it. What
    can you hear?"
- Prompting visual memory of previous experience with written words.
    II. "Something needs to go on the end [of *little*], doesn't it."
- Drawing boxes (Clay, 1985; adapted from Elkonin, 1973) to correspond to the sounds (phonemes, not letters) in the word, and showing the child how to push counters into the boxes, left to right, while
  saying the word slowly: h-e-n, m-a-d-e. When these boxes are first
  introduced, the teacher accepts letters in any order, as long as they
  are in the correct place. The numbers under the boxes show that
  Premala placed the letter for the final sounds in both words first.
  Later the teacher will encourage the child to fill in the letters in left-

Table 9.1 Premala's progress in writing, in numbers of letters

	C alone	C with help	T	(total)
I	5	1	19	(25)
II	9	10	9	(28)
III	19	8	0	(27)

to-right order and will draw the boxes to correspond to letters rather than sounds.
- Asking the child to develop and use her visual memory.

In II, the teacher asked Premala to write *red* several times, first with a model available to copy, then with the model covered, then to walk over and write it on the blackboard from memory, and finally to finish it after the teacher had erased the last two letters.

In III, there was similar practice for a harder word, *school.*
- Praising strategies, even if the result is only partially correct.
  I. "That's a good guess, because *cuddling* sometimes sounds like that" [when Premala has written a *k*].
  II. "Good thinking. You remembered that" [*e* on *little*].
  II. "I liked the way you checked it all through" [referring to the child's reassembly of her cut-up sentence].
  III. "You don't need to look because you've got it inside your head, haven't you?" [referring to writing *school* from memory].
- Introducing new information
  I. "Let's have a look and I'll show you what else *cuddling* can sound like."
- Increasing the difficulty of the task

Because the child composes the sentence that is written during each RR lesson, the teacher cannot increase the challenge of the overall writing task as she does in selecting a new book. But she does increase the challenge of the reassembly of the child's sentence from sentence-strip pieces. Slash lines show her segmentation of the sentences for II and III. (There was no sentence strip in I):
  II. The / little / r/ed / hen / made / some / cakes. (Note the relationship between the segmentation of *red* and the writing Premala did from memory at the blackboard.)
  III. I / a/m / go/ing / swi/mm/ing / a/t/school / now.

Although both sentences have seven words, the teacher increases the number of segments for Premala to reassemble from 8 to 12. In both lessons, Premala succeeds, rereading and checking as she goes.

GENERAL FEATURES OF READING RECOVERY

Generalizing from these examples of RR activities, we suggest features that distinguish RR from other reading programs and features that may apply to other curriculum areas.

For teachers in the United States, this program should be differentiated from both "whole language" and "phonics." It differs from most whole language programs in recognizing the need for temporary instructional detours in which the child's attention is called to particular cues available in speech or print. It differs from phonics in conceptualizing phonological awareness as an outcome of reading and writing rather than as their prerequisite, and in developing children's awareness of sounds in oral language rather than teaching letter–sound relationships. It differs from both in the frequent observation and recording of the reading and writing repertoire of the individual child as the basis for teacher initiative (as in choosing the next book) and response (in moment-to-moment decisions about when, and how, to help).

There are three reasons for these features. First, especially when children have limited strengths relevant to the task at hand, it is important to use those strengths. Five-year-old children have oral language resources; RR draws on those resources in developing the child's sound awareness that can then be used to check against visual cues in print. Second, at-risk children who are taught letter–sound relationships often cannot use that information, because they cannot hear the sounds in words they say or read. So the harder skill must be taught, and the easier one seems to follow. The most pragmatic place to teach sound awareness is in writing, where segmentation is an essential part of the task.

Finally, in the case of vowels, teaching any one-to-one relationship between letters and sounds in English words must eventually be confusing to the child. Reading requires flexibility in handling such relationships, and writing provides rich practice. For example, children who learn to write five high- and medium-frequency words containing the vowel a—a, at, play, father, said—have implicitly learned a one-to-many letter–sound relationship (Clay & Watson, 1982, p. 24). The teacher helps the child use this knowledge, first learned in writing, during reading.

RR was designed specifically to teach reading and writing to children who are still low achievers after one year of school. In developing programs of problem solving with adult guidance for other low-achieving learners in other curriculum areas, six pedagogical premises may have wider significance:

1. The teacher works with what she knows the children can do alone, or with assistance, and brings them by different paths to patterns of normal progress, with which she had extensive experience.
2. The interactions occur daily for a substantial block of time, and daily records ensure that at any one time the teacher knows exactly what the child can now do independently, and what he is currently learning to do with support.

3. The lessons address a wide range of subroutines and types of learning, all of which have been shown in research on normal children to play a role in the desired outcome behaviors, even though they may not be highly interdependent at this particular stage of learning. Most obvious is the example of reading and writing: Both occur in the daily lessons from the beginning, although their reciprocal value may not be utilized by teacher or child until later in the program.

4. At all times, the achievement of a task requires that the child see it as meaningful, because only then can the child control the task and detect errors when the message doesn't make sense.

5. The child is encouraged to work independently in some way from the first week of the program.

6. Because task difficulty is constantly being increased, the types of interactions between the child and teacher do not change greatly throughout the program, even though the child assumes more control. What does change is the problem solving done by the child and the strategies that the child is called upon to use.

VYGOTSKIAN INTERPRETATIONS

The Teacher's Role as Scaffold

The metaphorical term "scaffold," though never used by Vygotsky, has come to be used for interactional support, often in the form of adult–child dialogue, that is structured by the adult to maximize the growth of the child's intrapsychological functioning. In their shared activity, the teacher is interacting with unseen processes—the in-the-head strategies used by the child to produce the overt responses of writing and oral reading. For any one child, the RR program as a whole is such a scaffold. On a more micro level, we have seen many examples of the child functioning independently, both in reading and writing, where earlier collaboration between teacher and child was necessary.

But it would be a mistake to think of the scaffold as simply being removed as the child's competence grows. Considering RR as a whole, that does happen, and the child becomes able to continue learning to read and write as a "self-improving system" within the regular classroom, without the finely tuned support of the RR teacher. But within the program, because the teacher selects texts on an increasing gradient of difficulty, the scaffold of teacher support continues, always at the cutting edge of the child's competencies, in his continually shifting zone of proximal development.

Changes in the Forms of Mediation

According to Vygotsky, major turning points in development are connected with the appearance, or transformation, of new forms of mediation. Reading Recovery is designed to help the child accomplish just that: the integration of the semiotic codes of oral language and English orthography, plus world knowledge, into the complex operations of reading and writing. It includes the presence of stimuli created by the child (in the self-composed sentences) as well as those given to the child in teacher-selected texts. And it includes a shift from pointing as an external psychological tool (Wertsch, 1985) that the child is initially asked to use to focus his attention on each word in sequence, to later internalization when the teacher judges the child to be ready to "Try with just your eyes" (as she said in Premala III).

The Special Case of Conscious Realization

Wertsch (1985) discusses four criteria that Vygotsky used to distinguish higher mental functions: their social origins, the use of sign mediation, voluntary rather than environmental regulation, and the emergence of conscious realization of mental processes. The role of the last in learning to read (perhaps in learning any skill) is not a simple linear development toward increasing consciousness.

It is true that during RR, as the child becomes familiar with lesson procedures and text-solving processes, the teacher imposes demands for conscious realization by asking "How did you know . . . ?" She needs to understand what information the child is using. And the child, by being prompted to talk briefly about text processing, learns that we can know about how we know and thereby control our mental processes more effectively.

But there are two qualifications to the growth of conscious realization in the RR teaching procedures and their outcomes. First, while conscious manipulation of signs to mediate higher mental functions should be available when needed for problem solving, it should recede into automatic processing when the reader/writer is attending to text meaning, which is most of the time. (We do not drive in low gear when we do not need to.)

Second, certain behavior developed and checked initially at an explicit interpsychological level (such as directional behaviors and most visual perception learning of written language forms and formats) are properly run off as automatic subroutines without conscious attention. Most cognitive psychology models of reading capture the trend toward conscious manipulation in some form. What are often neglected are the perceptual, directional, sequential sign-processing operations that operate outside conscious awareness but must be learned, since they are specific to the script in use. Learning to read and write can be considered a prototypical example of what Rommetveit (1985) calls "the cultural development of attention" (p. 194).

Development, Instruction, and Diagnosis

Vygotsky applied the concept of a zone of proximal development to both instruction and diagnosis. In his well-known words, "the only good kind of instruction is that which marches ahead of development and leads it; it must be aimed not so much at the ripe as at the ripening function" (1962, p. 104).

Reading Recovery is designed for children younger than those in many "remedial" programs, and teachers may ask why children are placed in the program after only one year in school. Wouldn't some children "catch on" to reading and writing in the regular classroom in their own time? For a few, such development might happen. But for most children identified as low achievers after one year in school, time will bring an increasing gap between them and the rest of their age cohort, thus reinforcing their self-image as incompetent in important school skills. In short, many will learn—unnecessarily—to be "learning disabled" (Clay, 1987). With RR, instruction supports emergent development rather than waiting for it.

With respect to diagnosis, Vygotsky (and Soviet psychologists working with his ideas) used the concept of zone of proximal development to differentiate among a group of underachieving learners. While RR is most obviously and intentionally a program of instruction, it also can serve as a form of what Brown and Ferrara (1985) call "dynamic assessment."

According to the New Zealand experience, within the 10 percent of each 6-year-old cohorts who are assigned to RR, the effects of 15 weeks of instruction lead to the differentiation of two groups of children. One group, approximately 9 percent of the entire age group, benefits sufficiently from the program to progress as average learners in the regular classroom, at least for the three-year period for which follow-up research has been done. The other group, less than 1 percent of the entire cohort, needs further specialist help. Although the two groups of children have similar levels of independent performance at the time of the six-year diagnostic survey, their response to RR instruction is very different:

> Reading Recovery is a programme which should clear out of the remedial education system all the children who do not read for many event-produced reasons and all the children who have organically-based problems but who can be taught to achieve independent learning status in reading and writing despite this, leaving a small group of children requiring specialist attention. (Clay, 1987, p. 169)

In the United States, the percentage of children requiring specialist attention may be somewhat different than in New Zealand, but the benefits of making assessment decisions on the basis of each child's response to carefully designed instruction should be the same.

Afterword.   In a discussion of this interpretation of Reading Recovery with faculty and students at Ohio State University, where transplanting the program from New Zealand to the United States was initiated, I realized that the two segments described here—introducing a new book and writing down the child's sentence—call attention to two different phases of scaffolds, with different temporal relationships between the adult's actions and the learner's.

In the analysis of introducing a new book, the focus is on how the teacher constructs the scaffold ahead of time, like building a jungle gym and then helping a child climb it. She talks the child through the book, looking at pictures, using particular words that she thinks may be difficult for the child and particular phrases that she knows are going to appear in the text. In that way, she gets these words and phrases into the air and, she hopes, easily available in the child's mind as he or she tries to read the text for the first time. She may also ask about related experiences that the child has had (just as we saw the KEEP teacher do in Chapter 4). Through these means, the teacher-created scaffold is in place when the child starts reading.

A different temporal relationship is analyzed in the writing segment. Here, after the child has orally composed a sentence, the scaffold gets built word by word, even letter by letter, as teacher and child together get the sentence written down.

Considered in context, these two phases occur together, one after the other. Introducing the new book is followed by page-by-page support if needed. The Elkonin boxes are drawn for the entire word, and markers pushed into place for all the sounds, before the child is asked to supply individual letters.

Both kinds of scaffolds, separately or together, can help older students too. Wolf gives some secondary school examples of the first kind in Reading Reconsidered (1988). For example, a junior high school teacher draws her class into Lord of the Flies through a discussion of good and evil, British boarding schools, and being shipwrecked. That's like the semantic, comprehension part of the new book introduction in Reading Recovery: a scaffold built by the teacher (with student oral participation, to be sure) before reading begins.

As a contrast, imagine learning to use a computer program with the help of an on-screen tutorial. In its temporal relationship, the assistance given by the tutorial would be like the teacher's assistance during the writing segment of Reading Recovery (though not as individually tailored)—a scaffold available to the learner step by step (even though prepared by the program designer in advance) as he or she goes along.

I suspect that at all levels of education a good deal of effective instruction fits one or both of these partnerships. They differ in temporal relationship to the learner's actions; but they are alike in pointing the way to strategies that the learner gradually internalizes and comes to use independently with entirely new content.

Scaffolds are, after all, only a temporary aid. To be true to the meaning of their metaphorical label, the need for their support must diminish so that they can eventually disappear or be replaced by a new scaffold for a more complex construction.

Part III

◆ ◆ ◆

Texts in Contexts

10

◆◆◆

The Myth of
Autonomous Text

Foreword. *For a long time I have been bothered by the notion of "decontextualized language" as an educational goal for writing and thinking (Cazden, 1988a). So in preparing a paper for an international conference on thinking in 1987, and for publication in the conference volume* Thinking Across Cultures *(Topping, Crowell, & Kabayashi, 1989), I attempted a counterargument. Assuming David Olson's widely cited paper, "From Utterance to Text," (1977), would be familiar to many in that audience, I expressed the arguments in his term, "autonomous," which raises the same issues as "decontextualized."*

I invite you to step back and see ourselves as a moment in the unending conversations that constitute human history. In the words of literary critic Kenneth Burke (1941/1973):

> Imagine that you enter a parlor. You come late. When you arrive, others have long preceded you, and they are engaged in a heated discussion, a discussion too heated for them to pause and tell you exactly what it is about. In fact, the discussion had already begun long before any of them got there, so that no one present is qualified to retrace for you all the steps that had gone before. You listen for awhile, until you decide that you have caught the tenor of the argument; then you put in your oar. Someone answers; you answer

him; another comes to your defense; another aligns himself against
you. . . . The discussion is interminable. The hour grows late, you
must depart. And you do depart, with the discussion still vigorously
in progress. (pp. 110-111)

For centuries, conversations were all oral. And so most contributions to these conversations existed only in the context in which they
were spoken. Exceptions were utterances that reappeared as reported
speech or became texts that were memorized and repeated by others—
for example, as folk tales. But as soon as there were written texts, they
could reappear in many contexts, recontextualized in many subsequent conversations.

Some texts have a continuous life—religious scriptures, for example—although conversations about them, or their roles in the conversations, may change dramatically. Other texts die out, and some are later
reborn, sometimes after a long silence. Vygotsky's writings are one
example: *Thought and Language* (1962) was written in the 1930s;
then, for reasons of Soviet political history, died, and has now had a
remarkable new life in conversations around the world, including
resurrection within the Soviet Union.

The typical pattern of text life is different in different domains. In
natural science, texts are cumulative, and older ones are more quickly
replaced and less apt to have either a continuous life or a resurrection
(Kuhn, 1970), except in those conversations where the primary topic is
intellectual history. But in the social sciences, and even more in the
humanities where some texts become "classics," there are both continuous and resurrected lives.

Relationships between written texts and their contexts in these
conversations can be analyzed in many ways. The term *autonomous
text* in the title of this chapter is from an influential article by David
Olson. In "From Utterance to Text," Olson (1977) argued that there
has been a historical progression, and that there should be educational
progression, toward the construction of texts in which meaning is
explicitly and unambiguously expressed in words and syntactic patterns. He wrote:

I shall repeatedly contrast explicit, written prose statements, which I
shall call "texts," with more informal oral-language statements,
which I shall call "utterances." . . . My argument will be that there is
a transition from utterance to text both culturally and developmentally and that this transition can be described as one of increasing

explicitness, with language increasingly able to stand as an unambiguous or autonomous representation of meaning. (1977, p. 258)

Later in the same article, Olson describes the effect of this historical development on the writer: "[The writer's task] now was an adequate explicit representation of the meaning, relying on no implicit premises or personal interpretations" (p. 268).

As evidence for his argument, Olson drew on a moment in the history of written texts—seventeenth-century England—in the domain in which text explicitness should be the most complete: natural science. I will reexamine that history; look carefully at another moment from the same natural science domain (the first report, in 1953, by microbiologists James Watson and Francis Crick of their discovery of the structure of DNA); explore briefly the special problems faced by very distant readers; and then, on the basis of two meanings of *myth*, suggest implications for the teaching of writing.

SEVENTEENTH-CENTURY ENGLAND

In his 1977 article, Olson quoted a famous document from seventeenth-century England about the kind of discourse that the developing science of that time required: Thomas Sprat's *History of the Royal Society of London*, commissioned in 1663 and published in 1667, just a few years after the Society was founded in 1660. Here are the paragraphs quoted by Olson (and others) as a significant comment about language use:

> There is one thing more, about which the Society has been most solicitous; and that is the manner of their Discourse. . . . Eloquence ought to be banished out of all civil Societies, as a thing fatal to Peace and good Manners. . . . this vicious Abundance of Phrase, this Trick of Metaphor, this Volubility of Tongue, which makes so great a noise in the world. . . .
>
> They [members of the Society] have therefore been more rigorous in putting in execution the only remedy that can be found for this extravagance; and that has been a constant resolution to reject all the amplifications, digressions, and swellings of style; to return back to the primitive purity and shortness, when men delivered so many things, almost in an equal number of words. They have exacted from their members a close, naked, natural way of speaking, positive expressions, clear senses, a native easiness, bringing all

things as near the mathematical plainness as they can and preferring the language of artisans, countrymen, and merchants before that of wits or scholars. (1667/1966, pp. 111-113)

Here is a text that exemplifies these prescriptions: a report from one of the early *Philosophical Transactions* published by the Royal Society of an air pump experiment by Robert Boyle:

> But when after this, the feathers being placed as before, we repeated the experiment by carefully pumping out the air, neither I nor any of the bystanders could perceive anything of turning in the descent of the feathers; and yet for further security we let them fall twice more in the unexhausted receiver, and found them to turn in falling as before; whereas when we did a third time let them fall in the well exhausted receiver, they fell after the same manner as they had done formerly. (quoted in Dear, 1985, p. 152)

Note some of the features of Boyle's report: Details of the setting up of the experiment are described in the passive ("the feathers being placed" or, later, "this pipe, being hermetically sealed at one end was, at the other, filled . . . "). But the experimenter's or observer's role is always in first person active voice ("we repeated . . . , we perceived . . . , we let fall . . . "). The report's veracity depends on the actual experiences of specified persons on particular occasions.

The experiences that the Royal Society wanted to encourage were both experiments, like Boyle's, and the observations of seamen and other travelers. The first volume of *Philosophical Transactions* included a set of directions to seamen for keeping diaries on their voyages and a request that a copy be delivered to the Society on their return. Parenthetically, some recent readers of the *Transactions* have noted that if the reporter was of high social status—nobleman rather than seaman, for instance—the Royal Society seemed to expect fewer circumstantial details!

Reading about the book of nature and writing about it in these prescribed ways were part of the larger drama of seventeenth-century England, part of a new structure of authority in politics, religion, and science. Politically, there was a shift of authority from the feudal monarchy and church to Parliament. In religion, one of the radical sects that began in the seventeenth century and continues today, the Quakers, still maintains a discourse norm of knowing and speaking "experientially," out of personal, first-hand experience with the "inner light." Scientifically, the Fellows of the Royal Society were making a decisive break with the previous authority of ancient texts and scholastic arguments. In their place was put the authority of the individual report of first-hand experience; and the rhetorical form that the society requested in part served to establish that the reported experience did in fact take place.

The changing norms of scientific discourse during the seventeenth century are even more vividly exemplified in three revisions of a single piece—a philosophical text on the nature of knowledge by Joseph Glanvill. Within a 15-year period, he published *The Vanity of Dogmatizing* (1661), *Scepsis Scientifica* (1665), and *Several Important Subjects in Philosophy and Religion* (1676). Recently, the three versions have been brought together by Steven Medcalf (1970) of the University of Sussex with a lengthy introduction, and I draw on his analysis here.

At the time of the first version in 1661, Glanvill was not a member of the Royal Society, but he hoped to become one. In 1665, he dedicated the second version to the Society and, in its preface, writes that he "had grown discontented with his youthful taste for the musick and curiosity of fine Metaphors and preferred manly sense, flowing in a natural and unaffected Eloquence" (Medcalf, 1970, p. xxi). The Society responded by electing him to membership at the same meeting at which it established a "committee for improving the English language." But two years later, in 1667, the secretary of the Society still referred to him as "a florid writer" (Medcalf, 1970, p. xxii). A decade after that, Glanvill made his second and more drastic revision.

Here is one idea—the difficulty in thinking about the soul—as expressed in all three versions (Medcalf, 1970):

It's a great question with some what the soul is. And unlesse their phancies may have a sight and sensible palpation of that more clarified subsistence, they will prefer infidelity itself to an unimaginable Idea. (1661 version, p. 18)

. . . most have been deceived in this Speculation, by seeking to grasp the Soul in their Imaginations; to which gross faculty, that purer essence is unpalpable. (1665 version, p. 14)

Men would form some Image of the Soul in their Fancies, as they do in the contemplation of corporeal objects. (1676 version, p. 2)

Whether we agree with Glanvill that he has eliminated metaphor in the final version depends in part on the difficult decision about what counts as metaphorical as opposed to literal meaning. For example, if we accept the *Oxford English Dictionary* as authority, *grasp* was used only for action of the hand, not for mental activity, until 1680. So Glanvill's use in the second (1665) version should be metaphorical, and its absence in the third version a possible indication of Glanvill's attempt to conform to the Society's dictates. But the result is less an increase in Olson's ideal of explicitness and precision than a shift toward conformity with John Locke's conception of knowledge. In Medcalf's (1970) interpretation, the change (from the second version to the last) from *grasp* to *form some Image* "indicates a change from a notion of imagination as apprehensive, as directly grasping at its object, to a notion of imagination quite dissociated from its object and merely forming images of it" (p. xxxvi).

The first-hand accounts favored by the Royal Society were not the only seventeenth-century attempts at a precise denotative language. There were two others, neither of which seems to have had the Society's stamp of approval at that time. One is mathematics. Despite the notable absence of ambiguity that characterizes the language of mathematics and its favorable mention in the excerpt from Sprat's history, very few mathematical formulations were included in the early *Transactions*, presumably because they fit neither the norm of first-person accounts nor Locke's empiricism. There is even one report of Newton giving a lecture on optics at Cambridge in 1670 with his conclusion at the beginning as a postulate to be proved, and then inventing a discrete personal experience for a presentation to the Royal Society two years later (Dear, 1985).

The second alternative language had a much shorter life. It was a curious attempt to construct an artificial language of exact denotation that would provide the same kind of precision for qualitative phenomena, especially in botany and zoology, that mathematics was providing for quantifiable phenomena, notably in physics (Slaughter, 1982). It worked like zip codes today, with characters assigned to successive levels in a taxonomy. The characters were letters of the alphabet, rather than numbers as in zip codes, and the result was a set of nonsense strings, like ZAB, that denoted particular elements in a botanical or zoological hierarchy. But even though the foremost advocate of this artificial language was the Royal Society's first secretary, John Wilkins, it never became popular within the Society. Even John Locke, dissatisfied as he was with "the cheat of language," realized such an attempt was doomed:

> I am not so vain as to think that any one can pretend to attempt the perfect reforming the language of the world, no not so much as of his

own country, without rendering himself ridiculous. To require that men should see their words constantly in the same sense, and for none but determined and uniform ideas, would be to think that all men have the same notions and should talk of nothing but what they have clear and distinct ideas of; which is not to be expected by any one who hath not vanity enough to imagine he can prevail with men to be very knowing or very silent. (quoted by Slaughter, 1982, pp. 206-207)

I conclude from this brief historical exploration that just as speakers must observe appropriate ways of using language when entering any oral conversation at a particular time and place, the same is true for writers. Seventeenth-century England was a moment of conflict in ways of writing about the "book of nature." As Medcalf summarizes the importance of Glanvill's work:

Two epochs and two extremes of the human mind overlap in the three books: roughly, the end of the scholastic era with the beginning of the scientific, and a metaphorical and figurative with an abstract non-figurative way of describing the world. . . . The last version, still recognizably the same book in structure and matter, is rendered wholly different by its spare and abstract diction: one can see in it the beginning of a style of thought and language which lasts into our own time, the classic style of English rational empiricism. (1970, p. xiii)

The changing expectations about the proper forms for written texts do not progress toward explicitness and autonomy, as Olson suggested, but rather express and reinforce changing ideologies about both content and form.

WATSON AND CRICK ON DNA

It is of course possible that Olson is wrong with respect to seventeenth-century history but right with respect to his more general assertion about the norm of explicitness and autonomy in formal writing today. To examine this claim, skip three centuries to our own, to one of the most famous scientific texts of the mid-twentieth century: the first report by Watson and Crick of their discovery of the structure of DNA, work for which they later received the Nobel prize, published in the prestigious British journal, *Nature*, April 25, 1953.

The general format of *Nature* is similar to that of the U.S. journal *Science*. Although Watson and Crick's report appears in the section of

News and Views, not in the Letters to the Editor, it has both address and date at the end. The date is April 2, and so we know that there was a publication lag of only 23 days. Here are the first three paragraphs of Watson and Crick's (1953) report on "Molecular Structure for Nucleic Acids":

> We wish to suggest a structure for the salt of deoxyribose nucleic acid (D.N.A.). This structure has novel features which are of considerable biological interest.
>
> A structure for nucleic acid has already been proposed by Pauling and Corey. They kindly made their manuscript available to us in advance of publication. Their model consists of three intertwined chains, with the phosphates near the fibre axis, and the bases on the outside. In our opinion, this structure is unsatisfactory for two reasons: (1) We believe that the material which gives the x-ray diagrams is the salt, not the free acid. Without the acidic hydrogen atoms it is not clear what forces would hold the structure together, especially as the negatively charged phosphates near the axis will repel each other. (2) Some of the van der Waals distances appear to be too small.
>
> Another three-chain structure has also been proposed by Fraser (in the press). In his model the phosphates are on the outside and the bases on the inside, linked together by hydrogen bonds. This structure as described is rather ill-defined, and for this reason we shall not comment on it. (1953, p. 737)

These three paragraphs constitute about one-third of the whole report. The full text includes a diagram of what came to be called the double helix, seven footnotes that are mostly references to competing work, and a paragraph of acknowledgments. (Retrospectively, we know that those acknowledgments came to play an important part in another set of conversations—here about the role of women in science. One of the people thanked is "Dr. R. E. Franklin"—Rosalind Franklin, whom others have argued should have been a co-recipient with Watson and Crick of the Nobel prize.)

How autonomous is this text? Who is it addressed to and what does it assume on the part of its readers? My comments draw on an analysis by Bazerman (1981), who has compared this text with one from the social sciences by Robert Merton and one from the humanities about a Wordsworth poem.

Some features of Watson and Crick's report are matters of conventions about form:

- The use of first person—"We wish to suggest. . . . In our opinion. . . . We believe"—expressing their personal role in coming to know this object that exists out in the world; and also, in the case of "we wish to suggest," expressing an attitude of humility, whether or not sincere, toward nature and/or their colleagues.
- " . . . features which are of considerable biological interest." and, in the next to last paragraph, "It has not escaped our notice that what we are postulating suggests a pairing mechanism for genetic material." Together, these comments imply that their work is of great significance but express that implication in very understated form.
- The early acknowledgment of (Linus) Pauling and colleague, and their "kindly" act of making "their manuscript available to us in advance of publication." Though the two groups were intense competitors, the audience is assured that the game of science is being played according to the proper rules.
- Finally, just before the acknowledgments, they promise that "full details . . . will be published elsewhere." With these words, Watson and Crick acknowledge a debt to the scientific community for fuller disclosure. From Watson's later autobiography, *The Double Helix* (1968), we know more about the scientific race, and we understand the importance of the publication lag of only 23 days for the public certification of Watson and Crick's position in that race.

In pointing out these stylistic features, I am not suggesting that Watson and Crick's style is the norm for *Nature* in the 1950s. It is clear from a perusal of the one issue in which their report appeared that significant variation exists. In one Letter to the Editor, for example, avoidance of first person active verbs, which Watson and Crick use freely, is carried to the extreme of leaving a dangling participle: "Having found . . . , a theoretical value can be calculated." Figuring out the structure underlying this variation would require a more thorough analysis of many issues of *Nature*, plus knowledge of the status of the various authors and the views of the journal's editors and peer reviewers. Watson and Crick's more personal style may be idiosyncratic, or it may be related to their status in their field.

Other features of Watson and Crick's report are matters not of form but of presuppositions about the substantive knowledge of their audience. At an obvious level, one has to know the referents for the technical terms, and we who are not molecular biologists will lack some or all of that knowledge. But there is a deeper meaning to the presuppositions:

- " . . . the salt of deoxyribose nucleic acid (D.N.A.)" implies there is preexisting agreement that this object exists; and its very name incorporates an accepted theory of elements and their chemical combination.
- There is also an assumption throughout the report not just that the object of their investigation exists and is known to the audience, but also that there is, within the community they are addressing, a slot for knowledge as yet unknown, a slot that is already both well-defined and of agreed importance.

Overall, this is a very short report, and the amount of detail must be contingent on assumptions about audience. The elegance and economy—the seeming autonomy—of this text is possible precisely because of how much the authors can assume about the knowledge, the contexts in the minds, of their readers—the other participants in the race and, beyond them, widening circles within the scientific community. Because of the competition, the conversational drama is here intensified. But I am asserting that the essential feature is always present: What is said or written is only explicit with reference to, and in relationship to, what is unsaid and unwritten but presupposed about an audience, about a particular interpretive community.

The term 'intertextuality' refers to the important role of such presuppositions (Culler, 1976), not just to explicit allusions inserted within the text (to "Pauling and Corey" and "Fraser" in the Watson and Crick excerpt). The short form of my argument is that intertextuality inheres in all writing and that the notion of autonomous text is just plain wrong. No one is ever successfully writing a truly autonomous text, to a completely generalized other. Outside of school exercises, texts that matter—that are part of some living tradition, a contribution to some ongoing conversation—always assume both substantive knowledge on the part of the audience and shared assumptions about matters of both value and form.

Of course, oral utterances and written texts are contextualized in different ways. Spoken utterances are contextualized in part with respect to the physically present situation that both the speaker and hearer are in. Written texts are indeed decontextualized with respect to that physical situation; it is not available as a resource for understanding. But they are massively contextualized with respect to contexts in the mind—contextualized first in the mind of the writer and then recontextualized in the minds of readers.

Such contextualization is no less true of scientific reports and scholarly essays than of other kinds of writing. In Burke's (1941/1973) metaphor of human action as drama,

> An essayist treatise of scientific cast, for instance, would be viewed as a kind of Hamletic soliloquoy, its rhythm slowed down to a snail's pace, or perhaps to an irregular jog, and the dramatic situation of which it is a part usually being left unmentioned. (p. 103)

It can even be argued that expository prose is relatively more shaped—not less—by the writer's "sense of audience" (the term is from Britton, Burgess, Martin, McLeod, & Rosen [1975]), whereas fiction and poetry are more shaped by criteria internal to the piece.

WRITERS AND DISTANT READERS

If, as I'm arguing, writers always write with some audience in mind, then texts that have to be recontextualized by distant readers pose special problems. Two domains in which distant readers facing these problems have to find some interpretation on which to act, and where the grounds of their decisions are subject to public discussion, are theater and constitutional law.

In the theater, I was personally startled to realize how immediately Ibsen's *Ghosts*, written in 1881 about a young man dying of syphilis, is heard today as a play about AIDS. And evidently Arthur Miller's *The Crucible* can be reexperienced in the same way. Originally using material on the seventeenth-century Salem witch trials to make a statement about the McCarthy period of the early 1950s, it can now be heard as a play about the AIDS hysteria (*Washington Post*, June 12, 1987).

In a rich and fascinating book entitled *Subsequent Performances*, J. Miller (1986) discusses decisions about interpretation that a theater director has to make during what he calls the "afterlife" of a play. After explaining how copies of works of visual art—whether made for purposes legitimate or nefarious—"invariably betray the period in which they were painted" (p. 51), Miller comes back to the theater:

> If we agreed that the function of the director is to restore as much of the information of the original performance as he could, what he would infer as being important about the original production would not provide a faithful copy of its original but merely tell us what he

thought was important in it. He would automatically and unavoidably be introducing an interpretation, and even at his most obedient would introduce preconceptions. I believe that it is better to be conscious of your preconceptions rather than simply to be the victim of them. (p. 53)

In constitutional law, controversy over judicial interpretation became daily newspaper copy during the selection of a successor for Supreme Court Justice Powell in the summer of 1987. On July 1, Attorney General Meese was quoted as explaining the selection process to a meeting on the Constitution:

We [the Reagan administration] don't have any test. . . . We don't care about the political or ideological allegiance of a prospective judge. We are concerned with how they interpret the Constitution. (*New York Times*, p. A18)

The audience is reported to have laughed at Meese's denial of any ideological test. And the next day, Tom Wicker started his Op-Ed column with that laughter.

In a speech nearly two years earlier, at a "Text and Teaching Symposium" at Georgetown University, Justice Brennan (1985) explained why, for the Reagan administration, the single criterion of constitutional interpretation may be sufficient:

Because judicial power resides in the authority to give meaning to the Constitution, the debate is really a debate about how to read the text, about constraints on what is legitimate interpretation. There are those who find legitimacy in fidelity to what they call "the intentions of the Framers." . . . [But] while proponents of this facile historicism justify it as a depoliticization of the judiciary, the political underpinnings of such a choice should not escape notice. . . . Those who would restrict claims of right to the values of 1789 specifically articulated in the Constitution turn a blind eye to social progress and eschew adaptation of overarching principles to changes of social circumstance. (pp. 3–5)

I know nothing about Brennan's audience at Georgetown. But the larger public context for his talk was even then a matter of public record. Just a few weeks before the symposium, Meese had asserted that the Supreme Court was overstepping its proper role, and that the judges should just go back and figure out what the founding fathers meant. But Justice Brennan, like theater director Miller, shows us how arguments for such a return to the intent of the author(s) are in actuality arguments for an alternative, and no more ideologically neutral, interpretation.

TWO FEATURES OF MYTH

Myth is defined as: "belief or notion commonly held to be true but utterly without factual basis . . . belief given uncritical acceptance by the members of a group, especially in support of existing or traditional practices and institutions "(Webster's *Third International Dictionary*). In other words, although their truth value is dubious, myths have a significant social function, often in supporting and justifying the status quo. In Barthes's terse words, "Myth has the task of giving an historical intention a natural justification, and making contingency appear eternal" (quoted in Emerson, 1986, p. 27).

Brennan argues as much with respect to Meese's views on the Constitution. And at least one British historian, Christopher Hill (1972), has suggested that the same may have been true of Sprat's history of the Royal Society. The Society was founded in 1660, immediately after the restoration of the monarchy, ending the 20 years of the Commonwealth in which radical groups with marvelous names like Ranters and Levellers tried to establish wider democracy but ultimately failed "to turn the world upside down." The commissioning of a history of the Society only three years later, surprisingly soon for an institutional history, suggests that it might have been part of a public relations effort to gain social respectability and assure the Crown that the new science was uncontaminated by radical ideas.

By naming the notion of autonomous text a "myth," I intend to raise both features for discussion. I believe that the myth of autonomous text is worth arguing about not only because it is wrong, but also because it can have the effect of supporting another status quo: in this case, certain practices for the teaching of writing.

Tony Burgess, a colleague in Britton and colleagues' (1975) influential study of secondary school writing in England, describes the research teams findings:

> There is good sense to the requirement that students move on from conversational and imprecise uses of language and learn the conventions of more formal kinds of writing. Much school writing, however, does not remotely fit the optimistic picture implied by this. Often expectations are left implicit or unexplained; or the *critical*

and ultimately cultural awareness which should accompany young writers' choices are short-circuited. Instead, iron conventions are imposed without rationale or grounding in communicative intent. Much writing in school proved on investigation not to be real and continuous writing at all but routine, unreal and mystifying—a busywork succession of trivial exercises. Development at secondary level looked more like an apprenticeship to a narrowing range of requirements for presenting information than a spreading mastery over writing of different kinds. (1985, condensed from p. 54; emphasis added)

Teaching "the critical and ultimately cultural awarenesses that should accompany young writers' choices" (which Burgess and I both recommend) is not any easier than trying to teach something called "explicitness" (which notions of autonomous text entail). But it requires different learning environments and raises different questions for the classroom.

A full discussion of issues in the design of a writing curriculum is beyond the scope of this chapter. Briefly, whereas the myth of autonomous text justifies decontextualized exercises for the practice of generic skills of explicitness, an alternative program based on a more situationally specific "sense of audience" needs two ingredients: first, continuous opportunities for writers to participate in some bit of the unending conversation—for example, with their peers (Heath & Branscombe, 1985)—thereby becoming part of a vital community of talkers and writers in a particular domain; second, periodic, temporary focus on conventions of form, taught as cultural conventions expected in a particular community.

The latter in turn raises important questions not only about how best to teach the conventions, but what they realistically are. As I tried to suggest with respect to both seventeenth-century England and 1953 molecular biology, answering the "what" requires an ethnography of significant forms and a critical analysis of the ideological assumptions implicit in each one.

◆ ◆ ◆

Afterword. *David Olson and I have both continued to mull over these issues, and so have others (e.g., Halverson, 1991; Nystrand & Wiemelt, 1991). Olson has written one reply to his critics (1990) and is working on a book tentatively titled* The World on Paper. *In the former, he writes, "I had some difficulty, and certainly considerable counter argument as to the status of 'autonomous text,' most critics identifying it with the positivistic view of the objective 'givenness' of the world and of the objective givenness of meaning. . . . In fact, I never wanted to take sides on so fragile an issue" (1990, p. 56). And specifically to my criticism, he writes:*

> *I now notice, perhaps for the first time, that I meant something quite different by "autonomous" than you do. You quote Brennan approvingly for saying that meaning of a text cannot be determined by the authorial intention (of the writers of the Constitution). . . . That is precisely what I argued about "autonomy," namely that the putative authorial intention becomes detached from the text, which comes to take on a life and meaning of its own. For me, autonomy never meant a sort of Hirsch "correct interpretation"; it meant a detachment from authorial intention. (personal communication March, 1991, used with permission)*

Perhaps our main difference is that I am simply more concerned with the instructional connotations of terms and the implications of these issues for the teaching of writing. One trouble with characterizing writing as more "decontextualized" than speech in discussions about teaching is that the implied difference then becomes a matter of subtraction, of something having been taken away—namely, the particular speech event setting that both speaker and hearer are in. It seems to me that, in teaching writing, it is more important to emphasize what has to be added—namely, writers' mental sense of audience: the knowledge about content and expectations about form that will constitute the contexts in the minds of their readers.

The apt phrase "sense of audience" comes from James Britton. He and his colleagues include a quote from British linguist John Lyons (1963) about how "the idea of context . . . should be incorporated in any linguistic theory of meaning" (p. 83). Here is Lyons's discussion:

> *The situational context of utterance cannot simply be identified with the non-verbal matrix of the 'speech event,' as some authors [footnote to Bloomfield and Malinowski] have suggested. A much wider and more abstract notion of context must be adopted; one that brings the verbal and non-verbal 'components' together*

under one head. The context of the utterance must be held to include, not only the relevant external objects and the actions taking place at the time, but the knowledge shared by speaker and hearer of all that has gone before. More 'abstractly,' it must be held to comprehend all the conventions and presuppositions accepted in the society in which the participants live, insofar as these are relevant to the understanding of the utterance. In particular, the context of the sentence in a written work must be understood to include the conventions governing the literary genre of which the work in question is an example. . . . (telling a story, philosophizing, buying and selling, praying, writing a novel, etc.). (Lyons, 1963, pp. 82–83; quoted in Britton et al., 1975, pp. 75–76)

"Conventions governing the literary genre of which the work in question in an example" constitute an important aspect of written language that student writers need to learn (Bartlett [1981, ch. 2] is still an excellent discussion). Whether, or when, explicit teaching of genre forms is the best strategy is the subject of a major controversy over the teaching of writing in Australia. (See, for example, the arguments between Australian and British language educators in Reid [1986]).

The next chapter stresses the importance of a critical perspective in reading. In a British book, Knowledge About Language and the Curriculum, *Ron Ivanic (1990) suggests the importance of critical awareness for writing too:*

With a critical view of language, accuracy and appropriacy are not things to be learned, but things to be questioned and understood. Learners will want to know what the conventions are, but not be drilled into reproducing them. Instead, they want to be in a position to choose confidently when and if to conform to them. . . . This means that a good language user is not just an accurate reproducer of patterns, nor someone who conforms to conventions of appropriacy. Rather the good language user understands how language is shaped by social forces and in turn affects other people, and acts accordingly. . . . The aim is not accuracy or appropriacy but socially responsible language use. (pp. 127–128)

In other words, conventions once understood can then be violated, or at least adapted—as Watson and Crick seem to have done—for particular rhetorical effects.

11

Information and Education
The Need for Critical Understanding

*Foreword. This chapter was written for an interdisciplinary con-
ference on "Information and Its Functions" at the University of
Tokyo in 1986 and circulated only in unpublished conference
proceedings.*

*As I thought about my writer's task in the terms suggested in
the preceding chapter, I realized I had no "sense of audience." I
had never been to Japan before and, regarding the conference
topic, had only a general concern that "information" might be
treated as just a literal matter of (too many) "facts."*

*So I developed arguments for the importance of critical under-
standing, returning to "concepts in the mind" introduced in Chapter 4 and continuing the argument against "autonomous" texts.
Where the last chapter focused on implications for writing, here the
focus is on reading—of texts (especially textbooks) and computerized databases.*

◆ ◆ ◆

There have been many reports on the state of U.S. education in the last
few years: reports by researchers and reports by groups commissioned
by the federal government or private organizations. One of the most
recent, commissioned by the Carnegie Forum on Education and the
Economy (1986), is entitled *A Nation Prepared: Teachers for the 21st
Century*. The introduction to this report, entitled "A Time of Fer-

ment," expresses the theme of this conference, "Information and Its Functions," in terms that pose a great challenge to education:

> Much of our system of elementary and secondary education evolved in the context of an economy based on mass production. It emphasized development of the routinized skills necessary for routinized work. These are skills that are now called "basic," [such as] the fundamentals of computation and the reading of straightforward texts.
>
> The skills needed now are not routine. Our economy will be increasingly dependent on people who have a good intuitive grasp of the ways in which all kinds of physical and social systems work. They must possess a feeling for mathematical concepts and the ways in which they can be applied to difficult problems, an ability to see patterns of meaning where others see only confusions, a cultivated creativity that leads them to new problems and new services.
>
> Such people will have the need and the ability to learn all the time, as the knowledge required to do their work twists and turns with new challenges and the progress of science and technology. They will, of course, have to have a basic stock of facts and know how to carry out basic procedures, but it will be essential for them to understand how those facts were derived and why those procedures work. They will spend a lifetime deciding which facts are relevant and which procedures will work for a constantly changing array of problems.
>
> We are describing people who have the tools they need to think for themselves, people who can act independently and with others, who can render critical judgment and contribute constructively to many enterprises, whose knowledge is wide-ranging and whose understanding runs deep. (shortened from pp. 15, 20)

Let me repeat and emphasize: The problem that the information explosion poses for education is not simply teaching students how to "manage" that information by means of such procedures as computers can provide, but, as the Carnegie Forum urges, teaching them to

- Understand that information, including how it was derived
- Decide which new facts are relevant and how to get them
- Render critical judgment

I will explore this problem in three sections: the meaning of "understanding," the special case of understanding textbooks and computer programs, and the problem of transfer in teaching complex cognitive skills.

THE MEANING OF "UNDERSTANDING"

Consider first the cognitive process called "understanding." It is important to realize all that is involved. As one British linguist, Stephen Levinson, defines understanding language:

> Understanding an utterance involves a great deal more than knowing the meanings of the words uttered and the grammatical relations between them. Above all, understanding an utterance involves the making of inferences that will connect what is said to what is mutually assumed or what has been said before. (1983, p. 21)

It is obvious that understanding utterances spoken in face-to-face conversation requires inferences about mutual, but unspoken, assumptions. Sometimes this shared knowledge is about the visually present situation, as when one says,

Please leave it closed.

to someone who has just opened the door to come in. The proper referent for the pronoun *it* (the door) is mutually assumed. At other times, the referent has become mutual knowledge because of what has been said before. For example, the referent of *it* is clear if someone says,

I left my book in the kitchen. Could you get it for me, please.

At still other times, the mutually assumed knowledge is not available either from the physical context or the immediately preceding words. It exists only in what I call the "contexts in the mind" of speaker and addressee—contexts that have been constructed from previous verbal and nonverbal experience. The precise origins of these mental contexts is hard, often impossible, to specify; but they are extremely significant for human understanding.

For example, I saw a certain student on the streetcorner outside my office after 6:00 o'clock on a Thursday evening. I greeted him with a smile:

CBC: Why aren't you at dinner?
S: I'm not on the Board anymore.

To understand this short conversation, spoken in very simple English, decoding the sentences is not enough. Understanding depends on our mental contexts at the moment of meeting. I knew that he was a member of the student board of the *Harvard Educational Review* that meets for dinner on Thursdays; in fact, smells of cooking had reminded me of that weekly event as I left the building. Just as importantly, he knew that I knew he was on the Board, and also that I feel close to the *Review* (as a student editor myself 25 years ago), and so would be likely to refer to it. This was our shared world, our mutual assumptions, as we correctly not only decoded but understood each other's remarks. The physical place of our meeting, close to the site of the Board dinner, may have increased the probability and speed of the appropriate inferences, but the substantive knowledge was already there as contexts in our minds.

So much is obvious. It is perhaps less obvious that understanding written texts is just as context-dependent as understanding oral conversation. Because understanding texts does not depend on the immediate context of situation, they are sometimes considered decontextualized, or "autonomous." But this seriously underestimates the educational problem of teaching for such understanding. Texts are decontextualized only with respect to the physical situation in which we read them; they can never be independent of mental contexts essential for their understanding.

Again, an example may clarify. I am spending this fall in London and so have been reading London newspapers. The club where I am staying gets three papers each morning. My understanding of them is completely independent of my situation at the moment of reading; it does not matter whether I am in the reading room with other residents or alone in my room. But such independence from one kind of context does not mean that my understanding is the same as that of British readers, or that it depends only on our shared ability to decode the English language.

Think about what you would do in a comparable situation. A comparison of the three papers helps, particularly a comparison of their reports on material one knows best—in my case, news from the United States:

What is included in one paper but omitted in another?
If reported, on what page?
In what detail?
In what terms?

From the pattern of answers to such questions over several days, one constructs a mental picture of the reporter and editors, and the contexts in their minds as they select and organize and write. Without such inferences, understanding in Levinson's sense is impossible.

But, you may be thinking, of course inferences about point of view, and the assumptions that underlie it, are important in understanding daily newspapers. But, outside of politics, can't reports on other phenomena be understood as long as one knows the meanings of words and the grammatical relations? I suggest that the answer is no. Even when there is not the problem of biased interpretations, there is always the problem of partial pictures. When we deal with complex phenomena, we cannot avoid studying about, writing about, and therefore reading about, some partial picture. That is why "understanding" requires that we know as much as possible about the perspective and assumptions of the person who has done the selecting and organizing of information for us.

Sometimes this mental context of speaker or listener, writer or reader, is called a "frame of reference." That is a good label, because the referents of the words in the text, the definitions of the phenomena being discussed, depend on a selection, usually not made explicit, of one frame and not another. (Parenthetically, scholarly discussion across disciplines at conferences such as this one can be difficult for just this reason. As British sociologist Paul Atkinson [1985] puts it, "disciplines construct the objects of their own discourse" [p. 123]. Are we all referring to the same phenomena by the term *information?*)

In my own field of language development, the two terms *language* and *development* both exemplify this problem; in neither case is the referent obvious from the word alone. To some linguists, *language* refers narrowly only to knowledge of the grammatical system; to others, it refers more broadly to knowledge of how to speak appropriately as well as grammatically. To some psychologists, *development* is a synonym for *acquisition* and focuses on the child's mental activity in constructing the grammatical system; to others, *development* is a synonym for *learning* and focuses on the assistance provided to the child by the surrounding language environment. To still others (more influenced by anthropological perspectives), the referent of *development* includes simultaneous "socialization" into a culture as well as a language. One cannot fully understand texts about language development, no matter whether they are written for specialists or teachers or parents, unless one can somehow determine the perspective of the author and the "interpretive community" he or she is a part of, and read the text with that knowledge, that context, in mind.

Any act of referring requires a selection of what Wertsch (1985) calls a "referential perspective." Wertsch's examples come from observations of conversations between mothers and their young children as the mothers help the children complete a jigsaw puzzle. Pieces of the puzzle may be called by different names. A round piece may be a "circle" or a "wheel" of a truck; a rectangular piece may be a "rectangle" (or for an even younger child, a "square") or a "window" of a house. Labels like "circle" or "square" can be considered "common referring expressions": They apply across a wide range of situations but carry no information about any of them, would be considered "unmarked" by linguists, and may seem to express what the referent "really" is. By contrast, labels like "wheel" and "window" are what Wertsch calls "context-informative referring expressions": They provide more information about the perspective from which the referent is being described; they communicate effectively in a narrower range of contexts and are only understandable to those who see the situation in the same way; they thus require, and contribute to, a higher degree of intersubjectivity between speaker and listener, writer and reader.

A great deal of education is devoted to teaching students to see phenomena in a new way, to recontextualize circles as wheels, or wheels as circles. Once such recontextualizations, or alternative frames of reference, are learned, then the choice of labels can convey meaning, beyond the indicative pointing of reference, about the perspective that is being invoked. The ability to make such inferences is one test of the degree of understanding of the listener or reader.

In different fields, the shared mental context that I am calling simply "perspective" has different names: in the domain of scientific theories, Kuhn (1970) speaks of "paradigms"; in the domain of literary theories, Fish (1980) speaks of "interpretive communities." I am extending their ideas to the everyday theories underlying what everyone acts on and speaks from in everyday life.

Before leaving this issue of the nature of understanding, I want to be clear on two points. First, the problem here is not one of bias; it is rather a matter of the selectivity inherent in human perspection, human understanding, and human communication. Second, I am not arguing that knowledge is inherently subjective and relative to the viewer or researcher; I am rather asserting that the only sure basis of objectivity—crucial as it is—lies in the public, and publicly debatable, nature of the perspectives, assumptions, conventionalized procedures, and so forth, in whose terms all information exists and has its meaning. These are not problems to be cured by education, but phenomena to be understood. I believe that such understanding is what the Carnegie Forum calls for when they call for

- Understanding how facts are derived
- Deciding which new facts are relevant and how to get them
- Exercising critical judgment

I am calling this set of abilities "critical understanding."

THE SPECIAL CASE OF SCHOOL
TEXTBOOKS AND COMPUTER PROGRAMS

Before turning to the question of how to teach for critical understanding, I want to say a few words about the particular kinds of text students read in school, and then about computer programs.

In the United States, students read textbooks, packages of information about history, chemistry, and so forth that have been written for school use by a team of writers and subject-matter specialists. The names of the authors are always given, but those names will not be sufficient to provide cues to their referential perspective and point of view. The intent of the publishers, concerned as they are with obtaining as large a share as possible of a very diverse market, is to seem to have no perspective or, alternatively, to have an all-inclusive one. But, however honest the intent, the attempt will fail. Selectivity cannot be avoided; it can only be made harder to discover.

I am personally less familiar with computer programs and computerized databases, and so have to rely more on the views of others. (I am a devoted word processor, but not otherwise a computer user.) But I want to raise a question about what "understanding" entails in the computer world. In comparison with textbooks, is the perspective that controls the selection and organization of information in databases even more hidden? One computer scientist, Joseph Weizenbaum (1976) of the Massachusetts Institute of Technology, answers yes in his book *Computer Power and Human Reason*:

> Our society's growing reliance on computer systems that were initially intended to "help" people make analyses and decisions, but which have long since both surpassed the understanding of their users and become indispensable to them, is a very serious development. It has two important consequences. First, decisions are made

with the aid of, and sometimes entirely by, computers whose programs no one any longer knows explicitly or understands. Hence no
one can know the criteria or the rules on which such decisions are
based. Second, the systems of rules and criteria that are embodied
in such computer systems become immune to change, because, in
the absence of a detailed understanding of the inner workings of a
computer system, any substantial modification of it is very likely to
render the whole system inoperative and possibly unrestorable.
Such computer systems can therefore only grow. And their growth
and the increasing reliance placed on them is then accompanied by
an increasing legitimation of their "knowledge base." (pp. 236-237)

Weizenbaum continues:

Not only have policy makers abdicated their decision-making responsibility to a technology they do not understand . . . but responsibility
has altogether evaporated. . . . The enormous computer systems . . .
in our culture have, in a very real sense, no authors. Thus they do not
admit of any questions of right or wrong, of justice, or of any theory
with which one can agree or disagree. They provide no basis on which
"what the machine says" can be challenged. My father used to invoke
the ultimate authority by saying to me "It stands written!" But then I
read what stood written, imagine a human author, infer his values,
and finally agree or disagree with him. Computer systems do not
admit of exercises of imagination that may ultimately lead to authentic human judgment. (pp. 239-240)

Weizenbaum's is not the only expert voice expressing such concerns. More recently, Winograd and Flores (1986) write of possible
dangers in the use of computerized decision-support systems—for
example, in medical diagnosis. What I have called "perspective," they
call "commitment":

One immediate consequence of concealing commitment is an illu-
sion of objectivity. . . . Computers neither consider nor generate
facts. They manipulate symbolic representations that some person
generated on the belief that they corresponded with facts. . . . The
issue, though, is not just one of mistake or of conscious fabrication.
It is in the nature of a "fact" that it is an assertion by an individual in
a context, based on a background of (implicit) pre-understanding.
(p. 156)

In other words, my concern is that selecting and organizing perspectives are less publicly obvious in school textbooks than in other

written materials, and may be still more concealed (not deliberately but by the very nature of the medium) in computer programs. Admittedly, even if one accepts this judgment, the problem cannot be solved by education alone. But at least it reemphasizes the importance of the educational objective of critical understanding set forth by the Carnegie Forum.

I realize that this view of text—or program—as something to be questioned and critiqued is itself a culture-specific view. There are, for example, communities in the United States where such questioning would be frowned on, where texts are to be treated as sacred objects, even in the secular institution of the public school. So I am making a value judgment, and the members of Carnegie Forum were too, in calling for such education as essential in today's world.

THE PROBLEM OF TRANSFER
IN TEACHING COMPLEX COGNITIVE SKILLS

What do we know about instructional strategies that can teach complex cognitive skills, such as critical understanding?

Included in the Carnegie Forum's report is an imaginary scenario for what "schools for the twenty-first century" might be like if the educational policies they propose were enacted:

We duck into a lab room where 10 students are working, a few alone, others in small groups. Computer work stations are scattered about. A lab technician is working with some of the students.

One small group of students is developing a strategy for their full time, three-week project to assess the toxicity of the pollutants in an open sewer. They have to analyze the chemical and biological composition of the effluent, locate its source, and bring their results to the attention of the appropriate authorities. They are working on the project with the city's environmental agency, a local firm that specializes in the analysis of toxic materials, and their teachers of chemistry, biology and social studies. They know that all this work is intended to help them prepare for their statewide test in science, but they know also that their social studies teacher has designed the project so they will be well prepared for that part of the social studies examination that deals with students' grasp of conflicts in public policy.

Sarena Walsh, one of the students, does a computer search and comes up with some articles that might be used to build a candidate list of pollutants, and a second that lists standard computer-based analysis techniques for determining the presence of these pollutants in the effluent. Another student, Jim Howard, whose interests run more toward policy issues, searches the city data base to find the names of companies that have been cited over the past few years for violations of the state and local environmental laws. They know that their teachers can help them interpret the more technical language in these sources, but they want to go as far as they can on their own. Bill remembers that one of their instructors, who works part-time at the local firm that is involved in the project, offered to loan some analysis equipment that the group can use with their school computers. He calls him to arrange for the use of the equipment next week. Sarena calls an assistant director of the environmental agency who agrees to give the team a briefing on the legal procedures involved in resolving environmental issues. Together they put together a work plan, knowing that their teachers will take it apart ruthlessly when they make their presentation in two days.

We cannot help but be impressed with the mastery of subjects displayed by these students, subjects that, until only a few years ago, were not typically taught until college or even later. What is even more impressive is that these students exhibit the healthy skepticism of inquiring minds, genuine creativity, and a real understanding of the conceptual underpinning of the subjects they have studied which they are able to apply to solving real problems. (pp. 45–46)

Several features of this description are noteworthy. First, the students are using sophisticated techniques of finding and processing information. Second, the information comes from multiple sources: journal articles, city government records, and experts. The experts available for help are themselves diverse: the staff of a governmental agency and a local firm as well as a teacher. These sources of diversity may provide comparative material as useful as my three London daily newspapers. Third, a "healthy skepticism of inquiring minds" is expected by their teachers and demonstrated throughout the project. Finally, the activity as a whole has real-life usefulness in the students' own community at the same time as it provides opportunities for learning knowledge and skills that will be tested on a statewide science examination.

There is considerable evidence from psychological and educational research in the United States that complex cognitive processes—that is, complex mental transformations between the presentation of, or confrontation with, a problem and the response—are learned most easily when contextualized in a larger meaningful activity, such as this imaginary school project on toxic chemicals in the environment. For examples, I draw on a report prepared by an interdisciplinary group of social scientists for the National Research Council Commission on Behavioral and Social Sciences and Education, coordinated by the Laboratory of Comparative Human Cognition (LCHC) in San Diego. Consider just three examples (LCHC, 1985, paraphrased from pp. 20–27):

> Although children 2–3 years old have long been found poor in memory tasks in which they are asked to find an object hidden from view, DeLoache and Brown (1979) showed that when familiar toys were hidden under a piece of furniture, the children remembered where to look as long as 24 hours later.
>
> Although older children have long been found poor in ability to imagine a visual perspective other than their own, for example in identifying different views of a model of three mountains, Donaldson (1978) found that children as young as 4–5 years used this ability when the problem was transformed into a scene in which toy children were hiding from a policeman. Although learning any programming language may seem hard, Japanese adults can learn Logo easily by beginning with an analysis of the work of a well-known poet and then have their initial Logo lesson while mimicking a part of the process of juxtaposition that the poet uses in his art. (Niyake, 1984)

These are three examples of activities in which performance of a complex cognitive process occurs more successfully and more easily than would be the case if the processes were taught, or tested, in a more decontextualized manner. All three exemplify an important characteristic of the relationship between a task and its context: We cannot say that the context is what "surrounds" a task, because when the context is changed, the task is itself transformed in cognitively significant ways. In the words of the LCHC report: "Evidence indicates that changes in the context of the logical task structure changes the cognitive task itself, making available otherwise untapped cognitive resources which subjects/students can bring to researchers/educators for purposes of instruction or assessment" (p. 27).

But there is also research evidence that educational planning that has as its goal the inculcation of higher cognitive skills cannot stop with the provision of rich activities, that embedding complex cognitive processes in such activities is necessary but not sufficient for learning. If we are serious about creating schools that are not just sorting devices and credentialing bureaus, but transformation sites for developing high-level knowledge and skills (as both the Carnegie Forum and the LCHC report recommend), we still have to address the problem of how to ensure that students will transfer the skills demonstrated in one context to others in school and beyond. In the words of the LCHC report: "Re-contextualizing the task can promote the appearance of more sophisticated cognitive activity on the part of students, but the educators' responsibility to appropriate these skills for educational gain is not replaced by re-contextualization of the basic task. The trick remains to build on these enhanced basics" (pp. 102-103).

A colleague at the Harvard Graduate School of Education who is coordinator of our teaching program in interactive technology, David Perkins, has recently summarized research on transfer (Perkins, 1985). I will not repeat his review of a wide range of literature but only report his conclusions. According to Perkins, there are two kinds of mechanisms for transfer of learning, which he calls the "high road" and the "low road." The "high road" calls for deliberate and explicit abstraction; the "low road" involves more tacit generalizations from extensive and varied practice.

Perkins goes on to suggest that we do not have to choose between these roads in teaching; we can, and should, take them both. The most powerful educational environments include opportunities for traveling both roads: "direct attention to principles to foster high-road learning and transfer, and extensive varied practice to foster low-road learning and transfer" (p. 14). In the terms in which I spoke earlier, the low road of contextualized practice—as in the imaginary school scenario—provides a "context of the mind" of the learners that gives meaning to more explicit attention to particular cognitive skills and makes more likely their integration into habitual modes of response.

Again, I turn for an example to the curriculum area I know best: the language arts and, specifically, writing (in the sense of composition, not handwriting). A few people seem to learn to write clearly and effectively simply through tacit learning from extensive and varied practice in meaningful and motivating contexts—the way we all learn to speak our native language—without explicit tuition. That's what Perkins calls the low road. But for many students, it is difficult for the school alone, without help from other institutions where students spend considerable time, such as the family, to provide sufficient opportunities for rich and varied practice. And so the high road of explicit instruction—for example, in punctuation or paragraphs—is provided. That's the kind of combination Perkins recommends.

Education fails for many students, I believe, when educators try to rely on only one road or the other: either only the low road of tacit learning from richly contextualized activities, perhaps by overgeneralization from the virtually universal success of learning to speak; or only the high road of explicit tuition in decontextualized skills, often because of pressure for short-term results on short-answer, multiple-choice tests.

In the United States, where team sports are extremely popular in schools and universities as well as on television, the metaphor of teacher as coach is often used: If teachers acted more like the coaches of athletic teams, it is suggested, schools would be greatly improved. It is a useful metaphor, it seems to me, precisely because coaches operate on both the high road and the low road. They give very carefully designed and explicit out-of-the-game training in particular moves, but they also provide plenty of holistic practice.

In conclusion, I have suggested that an important educational objective in our age of information is the complex cognitive skill of critical understanding. Teaching for critical understanding poses special problems because of the nature of textbooks and computer programs. For the most effective instruction, both explicit tuition and extensive and diverse holistic practice are necessary.

Afterword. *Despite my arguments in both this and the previous chapter against the reality of autonomous texts, I agree with David Olson that some texts, especially textbooks, are written as if they were indeed explicit and autonomous statements of how some piece of the world actually is.*

This is often the case in science. Lemke (1990) has analyzed the language style (or "register") of science textbooks and oral discourse in science classrooms—a style that is marked by technical terms, passive sentences, and the absence of personification. The result, he argues, mystifies science, denies alternative interpretations, encourages a mental passivity before the seeming givenness of nature, and alienates many future citizens.

It is also often, and less defensibly, the case in social studies. In a review of research on why social studies texts are so hard for students to understand and what teachers can do to help, Beck and McKeown (1991) include the problem of their "single 'objective' perspective":

One of the most roundly criticized aspects of social studies textbooks is their single "objective" perspective and the general lack of acknowledgment that there even exists more than one lens

*through which to examine social and political events and phe-
nomena. Even when attempts are made in textbooks to bring in
multiple perspectives, they are often not very effective. (p. 488)*

To provide other perspectives and develop students' critical thinking about them, Beck and McKeown recommend—as did the Carnegie Forum on Education and the Economy—using multiple
sources, such as several trade books on a single event.

Two recent Harvard theses on social studies education contribute here. Through extensive interviews with authors and publishers, Van de Ven (1991) shows how publishing practices, including the anonymity of group authorship, influence the content of
world history textbooks. And Ajemian (1991) includes the voice of
students in her philosophical analysis. For example, one 15-year-
old student complains:

*In history, just the textbook. They talk about all the wars from
the Revolutionary War to the Vietnam War. It's all there. You
can't prove it. You can't write your opinion about it. You can't
do much about it. You just have to read it and memorize it for a
test. . . .*

*Even the teacher doesn't have an opinion. He follows the
book also. The teacher follows the book on anything. Most social
studies teachers don't speak out their opinions. They have a
lesson. And they do it. That's it. They follow it. Whatever the book
does. . . . English teachers would say, "Oh, that's wrong." English
is not the point of whether it's right or wrong. It's how you discuss
it. After reading a story, you discuss it. And there are many
different ways of discussing a story. But in social studies, there
is only one way—history. (pp. 30–31)*

De Castell asks the important question: "Why is it that so much
time is devoted to teaching students how authors of fictional texts
construct fiction, and so little to teaching students how authors of
factual texts construct fact?" (personal communication, 1990).

In writing this paper for the conference in Tokyo, I extended
the problem to computer programs and databases, even though I
had no specific example from that increasingly important medium. Recently, the Washington Post Magazine carried a long article on the Library of Congress, featuring their ambitious new project, American Memory (Weeks, 1991). This is a project to make
the library's collections in American history more accessible to the
public via videodisc. "Currently," Weeks summarizes, "among the

offerings are selected writings from the WPA Federal Writer's Project, 1936–1940; films of San Francisco before and after the 1906 earthquake; and a set of 350 African-American pamphlets from 1820 to 1920" (p. 29). And that's just the beginning.

In an interview with Weeks, Librarian of Congress James Billington is eloquent about the possibilities:

> You've got to use it [the new technology] in a way that reasserts the values of the book culture. And it reasserts—and this is what's important for this city, and for this culture—and it reasserts the value of history, of memory. . . .
>
> The great thing about the book culture was that books represented a coherent work of a human mind, bringing a universe together in a novel, in a history, in something—and they can have a distinct point of view. And a library was sort of a temple of pluralism, because it brought in all the different books, points of view. (p. 31)

Then Weeks comments on Billington's final words: "'Machines,' he says, neatly summing up the argument against the technology to which he has entrusted the library's future, 'tend to eliminate points of view'" (p. 31).

I would say, rather, that machines don't eliminate the points of view inherently involved in selecting and assembling; they just hide them behind authorless collections of seemingly raw "data" or "facts."

12

◆◆◆

Narrative Thinking
and Storytelling Rights
Differential Treatment
of Narrative Experience

Dell Hymes and Courtney Cazden

*Foreword.   This chapter and the next are complementary in deal-
ing with two large categories of nonpoetry texts: narrative and
exposition. They are different in their forms: This one, a longer
persuasive essay; Chapter 13, a shorter book review.*

*This chapter on narrative began, as my coauthor Dell Hymes
explains in his Introduction, "in instances of its own subject—use
of narratives to explore and convey knowledge." Along the way, it
contains additional narrative examples in the development of its
argument about differential treatment, including an extended In-
terlude about the Native American community where he has done
ethnolinguistic research (Hymes, 1981) on the texts of myths recorded by hand many decades earlier—including the myth about
Seal and her daughter that is retold (from Hymes, 1982) and
discussed briefly in Chapter 14. This chapter was first published
in the Keystone Quarterly, the now-defunct journal of the Pennsylvania Folklore Society, in 1978.*

*Especially now in 1992—the quincentenary of Columbus's
voyage to his, but not everyone's, new world—it is good to be
reminded that these myths from Native American communities all*

over the continent are indeed, as Hymes has called them, "America's first literature."

INTRODUCTION: DELL HYMES

This article has its origin in instances of its own subject—use of narratives to explore and convey knowledge. In the course of a conversation with Courtney Cazden, I mentioned material recorded by Joanne Bromberg-Ross. She had recorded consciousness-raising sessions of a women's group, and presented a portion to my seminar. One session in particular contained a marvelous demonstration of interdependence between two different modes of clarifying meaning. The topic was what was meant by "strength" in men and women. Discussion began with discussion of terms. An unresolved back-and-forth about terms was followed by a series of personal narratives. Suddenly definitional discussion returned, stated in a way that made it clear that there had been no break in metalinguistic focus. Narrative had solved the problem of differentiating two kinds of "strength" (one good, one bad), when direct definition had floundered. The second mode of language use continued the purpose of the first, coming successfully to its rescue.

These two foci, terms and stories, often appear to contrast, rather than to complement each other, as here. My telling of the example from Bromberg-Ross reminded Cazden of instances of contrast from her experience at Harvard, which she recounted. I urged her to write them up, for they highlighted the possibility that one form of inequality of opportunity in our society has to do with rights to use narrative, with whose narratives are admitted to have a cognitive function. Cazden's written account follows next. After it, I will cite other observations and suggest some general implications.

WAYS OF SPEAKING IN A UNIVERSITY: COURTNEY CAZDEN

We who work in universities may find contrasts in ways of speaking in our own classrooms. Two personal reports from graduate students and one case study of changes in language use over an undergraduate's four college years point to a particular contrast between narrative and non-narrative ways of clarifying meaning (exemplified, I realize, in the following account).

One fall recently I gave my class in "Child Language" to two different student groups: two mornings a week to a class of graduate students (master's and doctoral level) at the Harvard Graduate School of Education, and one evening later in the week as a double lecture to a class in the Harvard University Extension. The latter is a low-tuition, adult education program whose older-than-college-age students are either working for a college degree through part-time evening study or taking single courses for personal or professional interest. My extension class had a mixture of the two groups—degree candidates like the tuna fisherman from San Diego who works as a bartender while progressing slowly toward a B.A. and then law school, and teachers in local daycare centers, bilingual programs, and the Perkins Institute of Helen Keller fame. Each class knows of the other's existence, and students have been encouraged to switch when convenient—as an evening makeup for the morning class, or the chance to experience "real" Harvard atmosphere for the extension students.

One evening, I noted two black students from the graduate school in the extension class. Instead of sitting in a far corner, they were near the front. Instead of remaining silent, they participated frequently in the evening's discussion. Finally, the man spoke publicly about his perceptions of the difference in the two classes. I paraphrase his unrecorded comments:

> In the morning class, people who raise their hand talk
> about some article that the rest of us haven't read. That
> shuts us out. Here people talk from their personal expe-
> rience. It's a more human environment.

I remember a similar contrast described to me two years ago by a Tlingit woman graduate student from a small village in Alaska. She spoke about discussion in another course during her first semester at Harvard. Here the contrast was not only between ways of speaking, but in how these ways were differentially acknowledged by the professor. Again I paraphrase:

> When someone, even an undergraduate, raises a question
> that is based on what some authority says, Prof. X says
> "That's a great question!", expands on it, and incorporates
> it into her following comments. But when people like me
> talk from our personal experience, our ideas are not ac-
> knowledged. The professor may say, "Um-hm," and then
> proceed as if we hadn't been heard.

In Philips's (1974) sense, contributions to class discussion based on narratives of personal experience did not "get the floor."

"Michael Koff" came to Harvard College from a working-class community in Boston. Yearly interviews with him had been conducted at the Bureau of Study Council as part of a study of the impact of college experience. Some years later, for a graduate school term paper, Bissex (1968) analyzed the transcripts for linguistic indicators of what she called "the Harvardization of Michael." She found a cluster of co-occurring shifts between Michael's sophomore and junior years, including one from *for instance* to *I mean.*

In Michael's sophomore interview, there are 25 occurrences of *for instance* and other words used to introduce examples, compared with ten, three, and four in his freshman, junior, and senior years. His language as a sophomore is, as he says, "concrete": Every page of the transcript includes at least one illustrative incident, and the last half of the interview is almost entirely anecdotal. These incidents always function to clarify points. Michael does not trust the "big, vague general words that do not mean anything"; he trusts the meaning that resides in concrete experience (Bissex, 1968):

> One of the things that I developed an interest in over this past year is some young high school people who live in a housing project. . . . Somehow if I wanted to talk about life in the project, I either said, "Life is terrible!" or "Life is not too bad." It didn't mean anything. It's easier to, I mean, for instance, just talking here, it would be easier if I could think of some, something—some specific instance. (pause) For example, this family in Larchwood Heights . . .
> Michael Koff, sophomore (pp. 11–12)

Michael's junior interview is marked, in contrast, by 24 occurrences of *I mean* compared with nine, seven, and four in his freshman, sophomore, and senior years. "*I mean* has replaced *for instance* in its function of introducing an intended clarification of a previous statement. The interesting difference is in the nature of the clarification during his sophomore and junior years; the shift from concrete illustration to restatement, generally on the same level of abstraction as the original statement" (Bissex, 1968):

> I mean, you just look at things differently. I—ah—it's hard to say what. It's hard, I mean, because you can only put your finger on some of them. You feel you're growing up. I mean, certain things become less important, certain things become more important. . . .

I mean, the things that you think are important drop out and new
things take their place.

Michael Koff, junior (p. 16)

Although narratives have an honorable history as "the temporizing
of essence" (Burke, 1967, p. 430), they are often denigrated, particularly by social scientists, as "mere anecdotes." Evidently there is a press
in at least some speech situations in this university to substitute other
modes of explanation and justification.

A NARRATIVE VIEW OF THE WORLD: DELL HYMES

Let me try to generalize, or at least extend, Cazden's observations.
We tend to depreciate narrative as a form of knowledge, and personal
narrative particularly, in contrast to other forms of discourse considered scholarly, scientific, technical, or the like. This seems to me
part of a general predisposition in our culture to dichotomize forms
and functions of language use, and to treat one side of the dichotomy
as superior, the other side as something to be disdained, discouraged,
diagnosed as evidence or cause of subordinate status. Different dichotomies tend to be conflated, so that standard:nonstandard, written:
spoken, abstract:concrete, context-independent:context-free, techni-
cal/formal:narrative, tend to be equated.

When we think of differences in verbal ability, for example, many
of us think in terms of command of standard varieties of English,
command of the vocabulary, syntax, and written genres associated
with standard varieties. We tend to group standard norms and verbal
acuity together. William Labov's (1970) widely reprinted essay, "The
Logic of Nonstandard English," has done something to change that
situation, by contrasting two examples of discourse, the cogent flow of
one with the stumbling of the other—the cogent discourse being in a
nonstandard variety, the stumbling in a standard. Still, it is probably
hard for narrative to get a hearing or approval in our schools, however
apt its inner form of idea, if its outer form of pronunciation, or spelling,
or word-form and sentence-form, is not approved.

There is a connection here with Bernstein's (1971) well-known
contrast between "elaborated" and "restricted" codes. (More recently
Bernstein speaks of contrasting coding orientations, each with its
"elaborated" and "restricted" variants.) The orientation that Bernstein
calls "elaborated" is associated with such things as independence of
context, objectification of experience, analysis of experience, a kind of

metalinguistic potentiality. The orientation called "restricted" is associated, among other things, with dependence on context and a taking of preestablished meanings and values for granted. One suspects that the contrast is in some respects a version of the older contrast between "abstract" ("elaborated") and "concrete" ("restricted") modes of thought. Certainly it is Bernstein's view that an "elaborated" orientation is necessary in order to go beyond the socially given. This is part of his defense against charges of favoring the middle class and putting down the working class: An elaborated orientation is necessary for the kind of analysis that could lead to a transformation of the condition of the working class. Other sociologists have taken up the notion of a link between an "elaborated" code of orientation, and a radical social perspective, taking the one to be a condition of the other (Gouldner, 1975–76; Mueller, 1973).

Now, if one applies Bernstein's contrast to everyday genres, then one is likely to take written communication as "elaborated," as against spoken. (Various writers have done so.) A main basis is the assumption that written communication is *ipso facto* context-independent. That assumption, of course, is false. Our traditional stereotypes about the functions of writing perpetuate it, but an empirical examination of the uses and interpretation of writing would falsify it. A written document may be dependent on knowledge of nonlinguistic context for its interpretation just as speech may be. One may need to be present, or privy to a description of the scene, in order to know the referents of pronouns in spoken narratives (this kind of example is typical of work in the Bernstein vein). One may equally well need to be privy to an implicit scene to know the true referents of norms in a written narrative or document. Personal letters afford many instances. Even written documents in the most formal style may be deceptively explicit. A diplomat, a bureaucrat, a college administrator has to learn to interpret written communications as if present to a drama in which they are context-dependent utterances. In other words, it would work against adequate understanding of the cognitive uses of language to treat difference of channel as a fundamental difference. Actual uses of writing may not have the properties conventionally attributed to them. To think of spoken narrative as cognitively inferior to written statement, because less independent of context, is to rely unreflectingly on a stereotype.

Again, if one applies Bernstein's contrast to everyday genres, then one is likely to take discourse employing abstract terms, definitions, numbers, and statistics as self-evident examples of a cognitively superior ("elaborated") orientation. But the form is not a necessary evidence of the function. Abstract terms, definitions, numbers, and statistics may be present as a consequence of rote learning, rather than complex creative thought. One may find abstract, analytic forms that are bound to their immediate context, unable to transcend it, and one may find concrete narrative uses of language that leap toward alternative futures.

In sum, our cultural stereotypes predispose us to dichotomize forms and functions of language use. Bernstein's contrast of codes, distinctions between spoken and written, between narrative and non-narrative, tend to be absorbed by this predisposition. And one side of the dichotomy tends to be identified with cognitive superiority. In point of fact, however, none of the usual elements of conventional dichotomies are certain guides to level of cognitive activity. In particular, narrative may be a complementary, or alternative, mode of thinking.

Even if dichotomous prejudices were overcome, so that narrative, even oral narrative in nonstandard speech, were given its cognitive due, the greater equality that resulted would be an equality of modes and genres, not of persons. The stratification of our society, including its institutions, such as schools, would favor the telling of some stories over others because of the position of the teller. The structures of relationships and settings would discourage some displays of narrative skill, inasmuch as true performance of narrative depends on conditions of shared background, similarity of identity, and the like (cf. Wolfson, 1978). Some evidence and thinking in narrative form would not be admitted, or not counted. If reasons were to be asked, or given, very likely they would draw on the dichotomizing stereotypes just sketched. Narrative forms of evidence would be dismissed as "anecdotal," even where narrative might be the only form in which the evidence, or voice, was available. But the dismissal would be an application to others of a principle the user would not consistently apply to himself or herself—a principle, indeed, that no one could consistently apply, if I am right in thinking that narrative forms of thinking are inescapably fundamental in human life. The truth of the matter would be that only the "anecdotes" of some would count. Even if overt performance of anecdote (narrative) were to be excluded, there would still be covert appeal to narrative forms of understanding. Terms, formulae, data, statistics, would be interpreted silently in terms of "representative cases," and representative cases inevitably embody representative stories, what Burke (1967, pp. 59, 324) has called "representative anecdotes." From Burke's point of view, every pattern of thought and terms must appeal to such anecdotes. One's choice is not to exclude them, but to chose ones that are appropriate and adequate.

To exclude the anecdotes of others by a rule against anecdotes in general is in effect to privilege one's own anecdotes without seeming to do so.

In sum, if one considers that narrative may be a mode of thought, and indeed, that narrative may be an inescapable mode of thought, then its differential distribution in a society may be a clue to the distribution of other things as well—rights and privileges having to do with power and money, to be sure, but also rights and privileges having to do with fundamental functions of language itself, its cognitive and expressive uses in narrative form.

Cazden's account, and the uses to which Bernstein's categories have been put, suggest that we do indeed tend to think of our society, and our educational institutions, as stratified in ways that define certain kinds of narrative as inferior, and people to whom such kinds of narrative are natural as inferior as well. Certainly the students at Harvard that Cazden discusses are being encouraged to repress or abandon personal narrative in certain settings and roles. Very likely something similar happens in many schools at many levels of education. The student or child is told in effect that his or her own experiences do not have weight (except perhaps as diversion). Not that there is not an essential purpose to going beyond individual experiences. But if, as the Bromberg-Ross recordings indicate, narrative of individual experience is a complementary mode of solution of cognitive questions, then a pattern of discouraging it is a pattern of systematically discouraging what is at least a valid starting point, and may be an essential means of thought.

The irony, or better, contradiction, is of course that academics are not themselves like that. Consider graduate work, or teacher training. When a student is considered a candidate or initiate for a profession, he or she becomes the recipient of gossip and lore of the field, of insight and orientation passed down in narrative form, of personal experiences that were meaningful to those who tell them, that have shaped understanding of the field. What many of us know about our subject comes in part from conversations with colleagues, from the stories they have told us, not from reading and evaluating published works. And from those accepted as co-members of the profession we do not discount verbal interest and affect. Indeed, we may relish it, if the result is a good story that makes a point with which we agree. We pay it the compliment of introducing it into our lectures.

The implication of such observations is that the narrative use of language is not a property of subordinate cultures, whether folk, or working-class, or the like, but a universal function. The great restriction on its use in a society such as ours has to do with when it is considered appropriate and legitimate. Generally speaking, it is considered legitimate, a valid use of language in the service of knowledge, when it is used *among co-members of a group.*

If the narrative function is excluded in an institutional setting, such as a college or school, the implication is that the students are defined as *not* co-members of a group with those who teach them.

Perhaps some of the decline in education in the country is connected with this suppression of the narrative function. Certainly it is more and more the case that teachers come from districts outside the district in which they teach, even from outside the city. Possibly schools worked better in the past when staff and students shared more of the same world of experience, and narrative use of language was more acceptable between them. This factor could only be a partial one, but it may nevertheless be significant.

Students may come from homes in which narrative is an important way of communicating knowledge. They may take part in peer groups in which experience and insight is shared through exchange of narrative. A classroom that excludes narratives may be attempting to teach them both new subject matter and a new mode of learning, perhaps without fully realizing it. Again, difference between the culture of the teacher and the classroom, on the one hand, and the culture of the children outside the classroom, on the other, may be a problem. If so, a teacher may not be able to be an ethnographer in the community, but she or he can be an ethnographer of what is present in the classroom itself. Giving children turns at narrative may allow them to bring the outside culture inside. Finally, a teacher who permits herself or himself personal narrative, but not the children, may not be bringing children closer but underscoring the barrier (as well as being perceived perhaps as wasting time).

Consider graduate studies again. Success on the part of a graduate student, in the eyes of the faculty, is in part a matter of socialization into the profession. That socialization is a matter in part of acquiring the lore and outlook of the profession, an informal education. A student who had mastered facts and theories and methods, and who had no stories, and no interest in stories, would trouble a faculty. On the one hand, the already initiated want to be considered entertaining or at least useful sources of lore that is of interest; on the other hand, the initiates at appropriate steps should show themselves to be entertaining, or at least useful, sources of lore in turn (as when having returned from fieldwork). There is a desire on both sides perhaps for the link between generations to be more than names of documents and in bibliographies.

(Fame can be defined simply as the case in which a larger, nonprofessional circle knows some of the names and is interested in some of the stories. Others not themselves the object of interest find audiences for whatever narratives they themselves can tell that involve the names. Stories could be studied in terms of their range of distribution: departmentwide, campuswide, professionwide, general intellectual circles.)

This argument goes somewhat against the grain of a major thrust of our society that has existed for generations. That thrust has been to transcend the parochial, the local, the rural, in the interest of the opportunities and accomplishments of a general public sphere—the often-told journey to the city, or the larger city. (Though even in the city one finds the successful able to indulge their sentiment for their starting point and the events along the way, others wanting or required to listen.) But perhaps this argument also helps to point up a major dilemma of our society: Success in technical, professional fields is defined in such a way that someone cannot both stay at home, or return there, to serve and feel successful. This is a major problem for persons with strong ties to their communities of origin, such as Native Americans. One needs advanced training in order to be competent, to be able to cope with problems faced by the community of origin; but the advanced training embodies a message of on, upward, and away. Perhaps the fundamental failing of higher education in the United States is to educate for status and not for service. Or to define service without regard to considerations of locality, so that local is inevitably seen as lesser. Perhaps the treatment of personal narrative in educational settings plays a part in all this.

WARM SPRINGS INTERLUDE

Much of my sense of this problem comes from experience over the years (over the summers, mostly) at Warm Springs in Oregon. Let me try to convey something of this experience. In doing so, I draw on a letter written (August 24, 1976) to Dennis Tedlock, responding to questions about the directions of the journal he edits, *Alcheringa*, and leading into general questions about the role of language in poetry, ethnography, and social life. Just before writing, my wife, Virginia, and I had been reflecting on a quality of the use of language in the life of Indian people we know. It is a quality one comes to have a sense of through being around them over a period of time. In one way it is a sense of a *weighted quality to incident in personal lives*, as when one friend, Hazel Suppah, told us that her son had been out to look at a root cellar her family had built many years ago. He came back to say, "You know, it's still good. I think we could use it." All this in the context of a visit off the road to where an old man had lived years ago, the house now fallen in, and the barn, nothing disturbed but only gradually reassimilated to the land. Hazel had lived nearby when young; the old man had come over to their place when lonesome. One bike lay prone against a slight rise, now a magnificent red bronze, green growing around and through the lines of its structure, the lowest and nearest point, a pedal, already partly within the soil. Hazel was looking for an old-style wooden trough (resembling a canoe) that the old man had had out for watering horses; it was gone, she realized it must be the very one that the Tribe had installed in the resort at the other end of the reservation, with flowers planted in it. If she'd known the land had been sold to the Tribe, she would have come to get it herself. We rummaged all around the land, nothing to be heard but insects, the white peak of Mt. Hood just visible from certain points behind the high hills across the highway from which we had come. All those old places are vacant now and most everything in them taken, years ago, by men who built power lines across. The Indians themselves didn't take an interest then; Hazel said they all had the same things themselves then. Now these old places, the isolated homesteads allotted to families in the founding of the reservation more than a century ago, to make Christian farmers of them, are another world and time to the Indians themselves, who cluster mostly around the end of the reservation where the agency, the Tribal administration, the mill, the restaurant, the housing projects are. Places that one can go out to in order to find and pick up things, memories, like berry patches. We brought back an intact old kerosene can for Hazel; she was sure her daughter would want to go out and get the two others there. A weather-polished twin-pronged gray piece of wood, having nothing to do with the farm, was found by Ginny, and now shows between two trees just outside the window of our cabin back across the mountain. Two matching bronze sections of a broken harness, metal, a few links of chain on each, I carried about in each hand as we walked all round the rises on which the buildings half-stood, up to the fences, down to the run-off creek, and finally put in the back of the car.

Virginia pointed out that in going around with a friend from Warm Springs one often *saw* a bit of experience becoming an event to be told, being told and being retold until it took shape as a narrative, one that might become a narrative told by others. Hazel had such stories about the old man who'd had that place, Dan Walker, stories I had heard from others. Her son's remarks had the weight of a theme, a kernel, of a story, the first act perhaps. Perhaps we'll hear the rest after it has come about. My oldest friend, Hiram Smith, once did this to me. We had wandered about twenty minutes in a store in the Dalles, drifting out at last; later, to his daughter, Hiram reported, "Oh, that young guy in there, he didn't know nothin' about fishing equipment, Dell and I just turned around and walked right out." No-nonsense partners, us.

Many must have had experiences of this kind. Such experiences seem to point to something a bit beyond our current concerns. There is a current movement to go beyond collection and analysis of texts to observation and analysis of performance. That is essential, but perhaps only the second moment of three. The third is what Hazel Suppah often did, what Hiram Smith did, what members of cultures worldwide often do, I suspect. Continuous with the others, this third is the process in which performance and text live, the inner substance to which performance is the cambium, as it were, and crystallized text the bark. It is the grounding of performance and text in a narrative view of life. That is to say, a view of life as a potential source of narrative. Incidents, even apparently slight incidents, have pervasively the potentiality of an interest that is worth retelling. The quality of this is different from gossip, or the flow of talk from people who have nothing but themselves to talk about—their illnesses, their marriages, their children, their jobs, and so forth. Not that the difference is in the topics. The difference is in the silences. There is a certain focusing, a certain weighting. A certain potentiality, of shared narrative form, on the one hand, of consequentiality, on the other.

If such a view and practice are the grounding of an essential texture of certain ways of life, then it needs to be experienced and conveyed if others are to understand and appreciate the way of life. Indians do not themselves think of such a thing as their "culture." They use "culture" as we do popularly, for "high culture," dances, fabricated material objects, things that can go in a museum and on a stage. Norms for speaking and performance go further into general norms of etiquette and interaction that are at the heart of certain qualities and problems, yet not explicitly acknowledged.

Ethnography is the only way in which one can find out and know this aspect of a way of life. Of course one could ask in an interview, or on a questionnaire: "Do you ever make up little stories about things you see or do?" ("Oh, I guess so.") "Could you tell me one?" ("Well, let me see, once . . . ") Even if successful in getting little texts—texts almost certain not to be truly performed (see Wolfson, 1978)—such an approach would not discover the texture of the text, the way in which it is embodied in the rhythm of continuing life and observation and reflection of life. One has to go around and be around to come to see how the world is a world closely observed.

CONCLUSION

The narrative use of language seems universal, potentially available to everyone, and to some degree inescapable. Humanity was born telling stories, so to speak, but when we look about us, we find much of humanity mute or awkward much of the time. The right to think and express thought in narrative comes to be taken as a privilege, as a resource that is restricted, as a scarce good, so that the right to unite position and personal experience in public is a badge of status and rank. *My* account is to be listened to because I am an *x*; yours is of no interest because you are only *y*. All this in independence of narrative ability. The one who is *y* may be an excellent raconteur, *x* a bore. To be sure, the excellent raconteur may be enjoyed if he or she chooses time and topic with discretion. But very likely we hear narrative as much these days, and enjoy it less. The decline in narrative performance among ethnic groups assimilating to the mainstream of life in the United States has been deplored often enough. On the thesis of this paper, the result is not a decline in quantity, but perhaps in quality. If the Michael of Cazden's account enters the security of an established profession, and gains standing in it, probably he will find that his narrative accounts of his professionally relevant personal experiences are considered appropriate, count for something. Whether or not he tells them well. Successful people, interviewed on TV shows, are recurrently asked to tell "how they got their start." No doubt many develop a moderately interesting narrative, if only because it is needed and they have opportunity to practice it. But sheer narrative ability, apart from success, seldom finds a place. Orson Bean is a superb narrator, and sometimes Johnny Carson gives him his head, but on other shows, he has gotten short shrift from MCs looking only for short repartee, and embarrassed by the presence of small works of art.

Study of the interaction between ability and opportunity with respect to narrative experience is very much needed, and the findings have a special bearing on education.

◆ ◆ ◆

Afterword. *All of the narrative examples in this chapter are oral.
But similar differential treatment confronts students new to academic writing demands in the university, as discussed in the next
chapter. For an academic audience, supporting assertions by citation to other texts is expected (with citations to some authors
valued more than others), and support by personal experience is
acceptable only if carefully framed as a "for example" insert.*

Shortly after this article was published, I gave a copy to Lisa
Delpit, whose two recent articles (1986, 1988) were quoted in
Chapter 2 as part of my argument for the inadequacy of the conceptualization of "whole language" programs. Lisa replied as a
then beginning graduate student at Harvard:

> I want to thank you for introducing me to your and Dell
> Hymes' article. It unleashed a torrent of emotion which
> had to be unleashed. It is partially through this article
> that I am beginning to put into words the conflict of me,
> black woman from Lousiana, and now Harvard graduate student in the esoteric town of Cambridge. How true
> it is that I seek to make sense of this place by bringing
> to it my life, my "stories." And how often I am discouraged from doing so by the "expert" theoretical orientation of so many classes. It's hard to find your "self" in
> such circumstances. Yet it is a circumstance shared by
> many black students who seek each other to share their
> narratives, to "break it (the 'abstracts') down" in order to
> create a useful construct for the academic theorizing.
>
> I have often had occasion to wonder at the quest for
> "abstraction" which seems to imply a level of generality
> which purports to transcend different cultures and
> races. But who is to say if that Harvardian abstracted
> code even begins to reflect my reality? I am reminded of
> the Declaration of Independence, the authors of which
> could state so globally in such lovely abstract terms that
> "all men are created equal," while concretely enslaving
> thousands. Whose reality was that?
>
> And now, black students are brought to this institution and asked to adopt a supposed "culture-free" culture, and leave the reality of our existences (along with
> our stories) wherever it is we came from. (A poem I wrote
> soon after arriving begins, "I used to live in the world,
> and then I came to Harvard . . . "). We are therefore left,
> in an attempt to make sense of all this without benefit

of our concrete experiences, as Roberta Flack sings,
"Trying to make it real . . . but compared to what?"

    Despite lack of support from many classes/profes-
sors, I do continue to accept and internalize theories
only in relationship to my concrete experiences. (Like
my Grandma used to say, "Ain't nothin' like the real
thing, Honey.") But I do feel the pull to this culture, and
it is a pull away from my home and my commitments.
For if this place into which I have not only invested con-
siderable finances, but an extraordinary amount of time
and energy (and consequently, I realize, a great deal of
respect) refuses to validate my personal experiences, my
background, my narratives, my home and my home life,
then aren't I likely to begin to doubt the validity and
worthwhileness of that life myself? Is that why I am al-
ready beginning to question my commitment to "bring
back" my skills to my home community? Though this
understanding has been lurking wordless in the back of
my mind since my arrival, to read in your article an ex-
pression which so vividly puts the thought into form is a
true aid in my ability to assess its consequences.

    Furthermore, your article has again led me to con-
sider, as I have often before, that we black folk are "con-
crete" in our thinking—but joyously and wondrously
so—not "restricted" as some authors suggest. For it is our
concrete which we have used to explain and create our
own abstractions to describe the world. I am convinced
that there is no thought, abstract or otherwise, that we
are unable to express in concrete terms. I am daily
struck by this phenomenon—

    R.M. on her studies of Western philosophies:

> *I have visited the basement of Western thought. I have seen*
> *the foundations upon which this Western Civilization has*
> *been built.*

    H.O. on affirmative action and our responsibility as
Harvard students:

> *The white folks have been having their party for a long time,*
> *and we've been coming up knocking nicely asking to be let*
> *in. Now they didn't let anybody in until the ruckus outside*
> *started getting so loud and the voices so hostile they got*
> *scared. Then they cracked the door open and grabbed the*

first nigger they saw who was still knocking nicely and pulled him in thinking they could pacify the rest of the crowd. Now the few of us who made it in have to decide what we do. Do we just start partying or do we fight like hell to block the damn door open?

A rural black Louisiana parent at a Title 1 meeting with school administrators:

Mister, I'm from the country, and when the corn don't grow don't nobody ask what's wrong with the corn. You say, "How come it ain't rained?" or "What's wrong with the soil?" So if you tell me these kids ain't learning, don't ask me what's wrong with the kids, let me ask you what's wrong with the school and how come the teachers ain't taught them.

It goes on and on. We are the masters of metaphor. The true incorporators of abstract and concrete. For in truth there is no abstract without a concrete base, and no concrete exists without an abstract structure. It is impossible to speak of the divorce of abstract and concrete, for the two are most certainly inextricably tied together. And no one culture or class has sole ownership of either.

But that does stray from the intent of this letter. It is just that to hold on to self and roots takes a conscious effort, part of which often includes trying to put into words all those elusive feelings which are a part of the Harvard experience.

In any case, thanks for providing a spark to help me begin to put all this in order." (personal communication, October 24, 1979; used with permission)

Discussion of personal conflicts and public controversies aroused by the expectations of academic writing continue in the next two chapters.

13

◆ ◆ ◆

How to Do Academic Writing, and Why
A Beginning Account

Foreword. As writers, and as teachers of writing, we wrestle with the complex problems of composition in academia—where written texts are the most important currency for obtaining the material rewards of grades, degrees, jobs, and tenure; and where status differences are so great that it takes a very long time to feel a full-fledged member. Where, in short, "joining the club"—as Frank Smith (1988) puts it—seems especially hard.

As soon as I read Howard Becker's Writing for Social Scientists: How to Start and Finish Your Thesis, Book, or Article *(1986), I sent colleagues a memo urging them to read it for themselves and assign it to their students. This book review, published in* The Harvard Educational Review *in 1987, gave me a chance to explain why.*

There are already "how-to" books on writing, and Howard Becker is not trying to provide another. He is an ethnographic sociologist, widely respected for studies of student culture in medical school (Becker, Gear, Hughes, & Strauss, 1961), the professional lives of school teachers (1951/1980), and the worlds of art (1982). This book is an ethnography of academic writing in which Becker analyzes, as a participant-observer, "how social organization [of academia] creates the classic problems of scholarly writing" (p. xi). It accomplishes what

186

sociologist C. Wright Mills (1959) said should be the work of sociology: turning personal troubles into public issues. Throughout, the book is written in the clear, lean style that Becker recommends to others.

The book began as a paper that was itself the outgrowth of a writing seminar Becker gave for graduate sociology students at Northwestern University. The contents of that paper now comprise the first chapter, entitled "Freshman English for Graduate Students." Titles of some of the other chapters give a glimpse of both scope and style throughout the book. "Persona and Authority," "Risk," "Getting It Out the Door," "Terrorized by the Literature." The first two, written in part or in whole by former students Rosanna Hertz and Pamela Richards, are especially vivid first-person accounts.

Readers will have different favorites. "Terrorized by the Literature" should be especially useful for anyone writing a literature review as a necessary prologue to reporting original research. Because I have been trying to understand the source of stylistic norms that writers adopt, or think they should adopt, my favorite is "Persona and Authority."

As that chapter begins, then-student Rosanna Hertz is discussing a draft of her thesis with Becker. Becker had edited it extensively for style, "removing as much of the redundancy and academic flourish as I thought she would stand for" (p. 27). For example, "could afford not to have to be concerned with" in Hertz's draft became "needn't worry about" in Becker's edited version. Hertz objected: "Well, yes, that is shorter, and it certainly is clearer . . . [but] the other way is classier" (pp. 27–28). The rest of the chapter is Becker's analysis of why locutions that sound "classier" and work "ceremoniously, not semantically" (p. 31) have become one means of trying to achieve status in the academic world.

Although Becker focuses on writing in the social sciences, he suggests that readers can transfer the book's ideas to other scholarly fields. I agree, and suggest even further transfers—to precollege writing and to academic styles of speech.

Shortly after reading Becker's book, I was watching a videotape of a peer writing conference in a comprehensive secondary school class in a multiethnic section of London (Hardcastle [1985] is an account by the teacher; McLeod [1986], by an observer). Kevin (whose family comes from Montserrat) and Sunday (whose family comes from Nigeria) are discussing Sunday's composition. At one point, Sunday had written, "What I mean is . . ." And Kevin suggests two alternative phrases: "What I'm trying to say is . . ." and "What I'm trying to express in word terms . . ." When Sunday rejects both suggestions, Kevin justifies them: "Those big words could make you, right. You could look at O-level [the school-leaving exam] that way." In the end, Sunday accepts Kevin's first alternative and changes "What I mean" to "What I'm trying to say." Like graduate student Hertz, Kevin thought that sounding "classier" was the way to get ahead.

With respect to oral styles, there are striking similarities between Becker's analysis of writing and analyses of styles of speech by other researchers. The contrast in language function that he terms "ceremonious vs. semantic" is the same contrast that Douglas Barnes, James Britton, and Harold Rosen (1969) label "socio-cultural vs. conceptual" in secondary school teachers' speech; and it is also the same contrast that William Labov (1972) labels as "pretension vs. precision" in social-class differences in speech styles (see Cazden [1988] for further discussion).

Becker acknowledges that his book is not the last word on academic language style, and he calls for "a thorough analysis of the major voices in which academics and intellectuals write" (p. 37). Such an analysis requires a historical perspective as well as a sociological one to answer the question: How did these voices develop? For example, how did the requirements of plain speech and first-person accounts set forth by the Royal Society of London in the 1660s, at the beginnings of modern science (discussed in Chapter 10), become transformed into the norm of agentless sentences and passive verbs? And how do changing norms of communication reflect, and affect, different conceptions of knowledge? Becker alludes to the latter question in passing, but he does not address either issue in any detail in this book. Nor should he. Wisely, he has kept this a very readable book about academic writing for all of us who write or teach writing.

In writing instruction, two objectives are important and complementary. In the words of the literacy theorist Robert Scholes (1982), "Instruction . . . must both socialize and desocialize. That is, students need to acquire the interpretive [and expressive] codes of their culture, but they also need to see them *as* codes" (emphasis in the original) (p. 14). This book is unique in helping us to do both.

Afterword. *The last chapter, this one, and the next one are all examples—primarily from one context, the university—of how embedded writing, and responses to it, really are. Far from autonomous in any usual meaning of that term, writing is continuously being censored by our "contexts in the mind," our understandings*

of what our audience expects, and our decisions about what we are able, and willing, to say.

For some writers, this situation is further complicated by the presence of multiple audiences. Just as in oral classroom discourse junior or senior high school students may try to make their utterances acceptable to the teacher in content while spoken in a style that identifies them as still "one of the gang" (Cazden, 1988), so writers may feel caught between one part of their audience and another. This is increasingly the case as teacher as sole audience is supplemented by peer response groups.

Where these problems of multiple roles and alternative voices are not openly discussed, the result can be resistance—resistance that is unproductive in accomplishing either growth for the individual or change in the institution. The next chapter continues this discussion of both pain and promise.

14

◆ ◆ ◆

Vygotsky, Hymes and Bakhtin

From Word to Utterance and Voice

Foreword. *In* Writing from the Fringe: A Study of Modern Aboriginal Literature, *Mudrooroo Narogin (1990) describes a writer's ego:*

> *There is really no inner or outer isolation, and the tree of the ego is swayed and moved more by what is happening around, the breezes, the earth, the touching hands of a human being, than by say the sap rising from the roots and up the trunk and permeating each branch, twig and leaf. Naturally, if we did concentrate on the inner sap of the tree, its essence so to speak, we would find that it too is determined by outer things, the soil and its content, the rain, or moisture and so on. So it seems that this isolation, sometimes put out as being the abode of the writer and his ego, this spendid isolation is an illusion or, if you want, a man-made construct. (p. 181)*

This chapter is about some of the ways in which the writer is "swayed and moved by what is happening around," especially when writing on the border between cultures, or—when those cultures have unequal power—from the margin, or the fringe.

It began as a talk to a 1988 joint seminar of the American and British Associations of Applied Linguistics organized around the construct of communicative competence *that has been so influential in both countries. The term was first coined by Hymes for a talk*

to a conference on the education of "disadvantaged children" in
1966. When he could not attend the joint seminar, I decided to
compare his ideas with those of the Soviet literacy theorist Bakh-
tin. Papers from the seminar, with comment by Hymes at the end,
appeared in Applied Linguistics *in 1989.*

Then, at a set of symposia on Vygotsky's ideas presented at
the 1989 meeting of the American Educational Research Associa-
tion (Forman, Minick, & Stone, in press), I added Vygotsky, along
with additional reflections by other writers "from the fringe."

At the end of a course on "classroom discourse" at the Harvard Graduate School of Education in 1988, Martha Demientieff, a Native Alas-
kan, introduced her take-home examination with this self-reflection on
her own language use:

> As I began work on this assignment, I thought of the name
> of the course and thought I had to use the word "dis-
> course." The word felt like an intruder in my mind displac-
> ing my word "talk." I could not organize my thoughts
> around it. It was like a pebble thrown into a still pond dis-
> turbing the smooth water. It makes all the other words in
> my mind out of sync. When I realized that I was using too
> much time agonizing over how to write the paper, I sat
> down and tried to analyze my problem. I realized that in
> time I will own the word and feel comfortable using it, but
> until that time my own words were legitimate. Contrary to
> some views that exposure to the dominant culture gives one
> an advantage in learning, in my opinion it is the ownership
> of words that gives one confidence. I must want the word,
> enjoy the word and use the word to own it. When the new
> word becomes synonomous in my head as well as exter-
> nally, then I can think with it. I laugh now at my discovery
> but realize that without it, I would still be inhibited about
> my writing.

The course Demientieff had taken was primarily about one of the
ways in which mind, according to Vygotsky, is socially constituted:
through the internalization and transformation of social interactions.
The problem she faced, and analyzed so perceptively, is that mind is

also, according to Vygotsky, socially constituted in a second way: through mediation via semiotic systems, notably language, that are themselves the expressions of sociohistorical processes.

In previous work, I have focused on implications of Vygotsky's first meaning: in analyses of parent–child and teacher–child interactions (Cazden, 1979, 1988a), of peer interaction (Forman & Cazden, 1985), and most recently of one early intervention program, Reading Recovery (Chapter 9). Here I will focus on implications of Vygotsky's second meaning: the speaker or writer's relation to the semiotic system or—as I will argue—systems, in the plural.

In Vygotsky's own writings (1962, 1978, 1981), features of particular semiotic systems are left as unanalyzed as are features of the social setting and interactions within them. We know from extensive research in sociolinguistics and the ethnography of communication that all languages are spoken in many variations—variations that have a historical development, are distribued in nonrandom ways in society, and are profoundly influenced by power relationships in both the immediate setting (the context of situation) and in society at large (the context of culture).

To over simplify, language varieties can be grouped in two categories: *dialects*, which are distributed according to locale, ethnicity, or social class of speakers (e.g., dialects of English spoken in the South, or Maine, or by lower-class black speakers); and *registers*, which are distributed according to speech situations in which people occupy particular roles (the register doctors speak to patients, or judges in the courtroom).

Neither term—*dialect* or *register*—fits Vygotsky's requirement that units of analysis must be "at one and the same time units of mind and units of social interaction" (Minick, 1986, p. 122). Some sociolinguistic research shows how the two dimensions interact—for example, in Labov's (1972) analyses of pronunciation features of middle- versus lower-class black speakers in formal versus casual speech situations. But in that literature there is no term for an integrated unit of analysis. *Dialect* pertains only to the person speaking; *register*—like the construct of "role" of which it is the verbal expression—pertains only to "normatively regulated action" (Wertsch, 1991, p. 11, quoting Habermas).

One candidate term, admittedly less precise than either dialect or register but suggesting the possibility of uniting them, is the term *voice* used by Vygotsky's contemporary, Mikhail Bakhtin. *Voice* is Bakhtin's term for the "speaking consciousness": the person acting—that is, speaking or writing—in a particular time and place to known or unknown others. Voice and its utterances always express a point of view, always enact particular values. They also are social in still a third meaning: in taking account of the voices being addressed, whether in speech or in writing. This "dialogical" quality of utterances Bakhtin calls "responsivity" or "addressivity."

As part of his programmatic vision for the field of ethnography of speaking, Hymes developed the construct of communicative competence (1966, 1973, 1984, 1987). It has been widely influential in research on language in education during the last 25 years. The related ideas of Bakhtin and his circle of Soviet intellectuals are only beginning to be considered outside the world of literary criticism. Assuming readers' greater familiarity with Hymes's ideas, I will say more about Bakhtin's and then turn, with examples, to some implications for education.

The most relevant first-hand sources for Bakhtin's ideas are:

"Discourse in the Novel" (in Bakhtin [1981, pp. 259–492]; written in 1934–35 but not published in Moscow until 1975, the year of Bakhtin's death at the age of 79).

"The Problem of Speech Genres" (Bakhtin [1986] and excerpts in Morson [1986]; written in 1952 but not published in Moscow until 1978).

Clark and Holquist (1984) provide a detailed bibliography; Bakhtin (1981) includes a helpful glossary.

None of these works were available in English (and only one in Russian) in the 1960s, when Hymes began arguing for an ethnography of communication (1962) and first spoke about communicative competence (1966). Similarities between the two men's ideas are remarkable, generated as they were in such different sociohistorical environments; their differences combine to enrich our understanding.

SIMILARITIES

The fundamental similarity is that both Hymes and Bakhtin developed their ideas in explicit opposition to the Saussurian contrast between *langue* and *parole*: language versus speech, autonomous versus contingent, social versus individual, structured system versus unstructured variation in individual expression. Hymes's programmatic assertion that speech is structured and language variable was the basis of his call for an ethnography of communication and, derived from that, his development of the idea of communicative competence.

Bakhtin writes about *speech genres*:

> The single utterance, with all its individuality and creativity, can in no way be regarded as a completely free combination of forms of language, as is supposed, for example, by Saussure (and by many other linguists after him), who juxtaposed the utterance (*la parole*), as a purely individual act, to the system of language as a phenomenon that is purely social and mandatory for the individuum. (in Morson, p. 96)

In another translation, Bakhtin's term becomes *discursive genres*: "Saussure ignores the fact that outside the forms of language there exist also *forms of combination* of these forms; in other words, he ignores discursive genres" (quoted in Todorov, 1984, p. 57).

Bakhtin (1981) also writes about language variation, which he terms *heteroglossia*:

> Thus at any given moment in its historical existence, language is heteroglot from top to bottom: it represents the co-existence of socio-ideological contradictions between the present and the past, . . . between different socio-ideological groups in the present, between tendencies, schools, circles and so forth, all given a bodily form. (p. 291)

Hymes and Bakhtin also take a similar stance with respect to their more local opposition. For Hymes, this continues to be the Chomsky-ian position; for Bakhtin it was the early Russian formalists. Both acknowledge the contributions of their opponents while asserting their limitations. Both argue against essentialism—the idea of a universal essence, unaffected by the contingencies of sociocultural history. Both oppose what Hymes calls "the rhetoric of metonomy"—considering a part (e.g., grammar) as the whole. In the first sentence of *Discourse in the Novel*, Bakhtin (1981) writes, "The principal idea of this work is that the study of verbal art can and must overcome the divorce between an abstract 'formal' approach and an equally abstract 'ideological' approach" (p. 259).

The two men are more concretely related through association with an early member of the Russian formalists, Roman Jakobson. Jakobson "played a major role in bringing Bakhtin back to scholarly attention" (Clark & Holquist, 1984, pp. 331–332), starting at an international meeting in Moscow in 1956. Two years later, Hymes heard Jakobson give his "Concluding Statement: Linguistics and Poetics" (1960) that became "one of the ingredients of the answer I would reach . . . to the question of the relation between language and culture" (Hymes, 1984, English ms. pp. 1-2).

While speech is structured, for both Hymes and Bakhtin it is also emergent. There is an intrinsic tension between constraint and choice, between the *given* of tradition and the *new* of responsiveness to the moment. In Bakhtin's (1986) words:

> The generic forms in which we cast our speech, of course, differ essentially from language forms. The latter are stable and compulsory (normative) for the speaker, while generic forms are much more flexible, plastic, and free. . . .
>
> The better our command of genres, the more freely we employ them, . . . the more flexibility and precisely we reflect the unrepeatable situation of communication—in a word, the more perfectly we implement our free speech plan. (pp. 79-80)

These emergent qualities of interaction can be described in terms of the competence that produces them, yet they cannot be formulated into constitutive rules. (Mehan's [1979] analysis of anomalous sequences of classroom interaction is a case in point.)

Both Bakhtin and Hymes know literature as well as language, as did Vygotsky, who began writing about Hamlet as a schoolboy. Bakhtin's interest was in novels by Dostoevsky and Rabelais, Hymes's in the oral literature of Native Americans. All are examples of what Bakhtin calls "complex genres."

For both Bakhtin and Hymes, emergent qualities include meaning as well as form. Bakhtin contrasts the novel, where characters could act otherwise, with the epic, where they are inseparable from the plot. Hymes's (1981) book, *"In Vain I Tried to Tell You,"* takes its title from the Native American myth, "The 'Wife' Who 'Goes Out' Like a Man," whose theme is the conflict between maintenance of social norms and attentiveness to immediate experience. Hymes's analysis of this myth has multiple layers of linguistic, social, and literary significance that go beyond our concerns here. But because his writings on myth may be less familiar to readers than those on communicative competence, I detour briefly.

To the point here, the words of the book's title are the daughter's. She perceives an unusual sound when her uncle's "wife" urinates. But when she tries to tell her mother, Seal, that it sounds like a man, she is shushed. Seal later discovers her brother has been murdered, and the daughter cries, "In vain I tried to tell you." The daughter's speech preceding this remonstrance is the longest in the myth and evidently unusually long for any myth from the Clackamas tribe. It "breaks through into performance," emergent in response to the immediate situation, when the girl retells the whole incident, accusing her mother of responsibility for her uncle's death.

In Hymes's analysis, Seal and her daughter contrast in both speech style and world view (formal and ideological, to Bakhtin). Using Basil Bernstein's terms, Hymes (1982) characterizes the mother's speech as positional and restricted, the daughter's as personal and elaborated:

> The mother's speech throughout the myth is a perfect example of Bernstein's "restricted code." It is positional speech in terms of her status as a mother with a certain social position. The girl's speech is not very extensive at the beginning but the whole last part of the story is turned over to her. She retells the story metapragmatically in an elaborated code and in a burst [of] elaborated speech so that the story is, in effect, an account of her assumption of a new level of experience and understanding. (p. 133)

Thus Hymes analyzes the communicative competence both of the Native American narrator, Victoria Howard, and of the heroine.

This brings us to the final similarity: their conception of language acquisition. Briefly, according to Hymes, "in some sense difficult to specify, children learn and use, not grammar, but ways of speaking, styles that organize linguistic means, of which the formal grammar is a precipitate" (personal communication, March 1989). In similar terms, Bakhtin (1986) writes:

> We know our native language—its lexical composition and grammatical structure—not from dictionaries and grammars but from concrete utterances which we hear and which we ourselves reproduce in live speech communication with people around us. We assimilate forms of language only in forms of utterances. . . . [They] enter our experience and consciousness together. (in Morson, 1986, p. 95)

DIFFERENCES

Like Hymes, Bakhtin (1986) acknowledges the existence of differential communicative competence (though without using that term):

Many people who have an excellent command of a language often feel quite helpless in certain spheres of communication precisely because they do not have a practical command of the generic forms used in given spheres. . . . Here it is not a matter of an impoverished vocabulary or style, taken abstractly; this is entirely a matter of the inability to command a repertoire of genres. (in Morson, 1986, p. 96)

What, then, does reading Bakhtin call our attention to? First, Bakhtin asserts the intrinsic intertextuality of all utterances. The given forms we inherit include not only grammatical and speech structures but also words—not because we don't create them anew, but because we don't learn them from a dictionary. We acquire words through hearing or reading the utterances of others, and they are thereby marked with the voices of those prior contexts. Words have not only value-free denotations but value-laden connotations, and for Bakhtin (1986) denotation is not the unmarked, privileged signification:

We choose words according to their generic specifications. . . . Genres correspond to typical situations of speech communication, typical themes, and consequently also to particular contacts between the *meanings* of words and actual concrete utterances under typical circumstances.

This typical (generic) expression can be regarded as the word's "stylistic aura," but this aura belongs not to the word of language as such but to that genre in which the given word usually functions. It is an echo of the generic whole that resounds in the word.

Thus the expressiveness of individual words is not inherent in the words themselves as units of language, nor does it issue directly from the meaning of these words: it is either typical generic expression or it is an echo of another's individual expression, which makes the word, as it were, representative of another's whole utterance from a particular evaluative position. (in Morson, 1986, p. 97)

Bakhtin (1981) focuses on the consequences of this *heteroglossia* for writers: "Instead of the virginal fullness and inexhaustibility of the object itself [any referent or topic], the prose writer confronts a multitude of routes, roads and paths that have been laid down in the object by social consciousness" (pp. 278–279). But he makes it clear that this is true for all discourse.

Any speaker or writer must select among paradigmatic forms. Bakhtin (1981) is suggesting grounds for intrapersonal conflict during the process of expression because of the "auras" that accrue to those forms from awareness of their previous contextualized use:

> Language is not a neutral medium that passes freely and easily into the private property of the speaker's intentions; it is populated—overpopulated—with the intentions of others. Expropriating it, forcing it to submit to one's own intentions and accents, is a difficult and complicated process. (p. 294)

Discussion of such conflict seems stronger in Bakhtin than in Hymes. While both write of the uniting of constraint and creativity, of centripetal and contrifugal forces, Bakhtin's images suggest more intraindividual conflict among the voices internalized from a heteroglossic and stratified society. (Thus his interest in the novel as the richest expression of this heteroglossia.)

From the beginning, Hymes has argued against the Chomskyian notion of a homogeneous speech community and for recognition of diverse ways of speaking any single language. But in his portrayal of a "community as an organization of diversity," the images of coexistence seem more peaceful, and individual shifting among language varieties seems more painless unless access to the conditions necessary for their acquisition has been denied. For Bakhtin, the images are more of conflict than of coexistence, a conflict that continues beyond acquisition into moments of expression—not only because of the external positioning of any speaker in the social structure, but because of the ideological marking of speech genres and words.

Perhaps one could say that in Hymes's writings on communicative competence, the significant social problem is that of acquisition and the conditions of interaction and the attitudes of identification that influence it. Whereas for Bakhtin, who writes less of acquisition, a significant phenomenon is the intraindividual heterogeneity—and potential conflict—among whatever varieties have been acquired.

A final contrast is that such internal compositional processes are highlighted by Bakhtin, while Hymes focuses more on externalized performance. He mentions in passing that "communicative is a global term, encompassing indeed reflection and dialogue with oneself," and gives as an example his own additions to a previously typed paper, "interacting with myself over different points in time" (1984, p. 14). But his active metaphors of social life as drama are all on the external stage in which only certain parts, or certain voices, are welcome. In Bakhtin, by contrast, what Hymes calls "implicit theatre" (1984, English ms, p. 42) is internalized:

> One's own discourse and one's own voice, although born of another or dynamically stimulated by another, will sooner or later begin to

liberate themselves from the authority of another's discourse. This process is made more complex by the fact that a variety of alien voices enter into the struggle for influence within an individual's consciousness (just as they struggle with one another in surrounding social reality). (Bakhtin, 1981, p. 348)

EDUCATIONAL IMPLICATIONS

If we consider Hymes's writings about communicative competence as providing an ethnographic framework for both research and practice, then Bakhtin's writings call attention to particular speaking and writing situations within the total range, to the complexities of finding a voice, of being communicatively competent, in heteroglossic speech situations where voices (and the roles they express in the social structure) are felt by the speaker or writer to be in conflict.

Bakhtin makes it clear that he is talking about situations with both social heteroglossia and speaker/writer awareness of it. In an extended description of peasant life, Bakhtin contrasts heteroglossia alone, where speakers shift among varieties unconsciously, and heteroglossia with awareness, where decisions among alternatives have to be made:

Thus an illiterate peasant, miles away from an urban center, naively immersed in an unmoving and for him unshakable everyday world, nevertheless lived in several language systems: he prayed to God in one language (Church Slavonic), sang songs in another, spoke to his family in a third and, when he began to dictate petitions to the local authorities through a scribe, he tried speaking yet a fourth (the official literate language, "paper" language). All of these are *different* languages, even from the point of view of abstract socio-dialectological markers. But these languages were not dialogically coordinated in the linguistic consciousness of the peasant; he passed from one to the other without thinking, automatically: each was indisputably in its own place, and the place of each was indisputable. He was not yet able to regard one language (and the verbal world corresponding to it) through the eyes of another language. . . . [In a footnote, Bakhtin qualifies: We are of course deliberately simplifying; the real-life peasant could and did do this to a certain extent.]

As soon as the critical interanimation of languages began to occur in the consciousness of the peasant, as soon as it became clear that these were not only various different languages but even internally variegated languages, that the ideological systems and approaches to the world that were indissolubly connected with these languages contradicted each other and in no way could live in peace and quiet with one another—then the inviolability and predetermined quality of these languages came to an end, and the necessity of actively choosing one's orientation among them began. (1981, pp. 295-296)

To bring Bakhtin's conception of these conflict situations to life, we have a few accounts by speakers and writers. First there is the dual audience that student speakers have in most classroom discourse: the audience of teacher (usually the addressee) and of peers (as ratified auditors). One acknowledgment of awareness of this duality is a brief autobiographical comment by Roger Shuy (1981):

> There is a natural conflict between acceptability by teacher and acceptability by peers even *within* the classroom. Personally I remember very clearly my school conflicts between peer pressure and teacher expectations. One strategy to avoid this conflict is to give the right answer to the teacher but to do so in either non-standard or informal English. (pp. 170-171)

Shuy calls these dual expectations of teacher and peers "vertical" and "horizontal" acceptability, respectively. In oral lessons, his example is, "La Paz ain't the capital of Peru." And when reading aloud, the good reader reads the correct words but in an informal, peer-group style (personal communication, 1985).

Whether or not Shuy ever said, "La Paz ain't the capital of Peru," his point is clear. His communicative task was to produce what Bakhtin calls a "heteroglossic utterance"—one that expresses his dual identity as good student yet still one of the boys. Accomplishing this task was part of his communicative competence. It represents what Berlak and Berlak (1981) would call a "transformational solution" to an important dilemma, a solution that, if accepted by the teacher, may prevent for the student a forced choice between peer group and school (Cazden, 1988a).

Because writing is a more self-conscious activity than speaking, it is easier to find writers acknowledging problems in choosing words and finding a voice. In an essay on "Craftsmanship," Virginia Woolf (1942) writes about "one of the chief difficulties in writing them [English words] today—that they are so stored with meanings, with memories, that they have contracted so many famous marriages" (p. 203).

In an article on "Inarticulateness" (1988), McDermott discusses the "creative resistance" of the writers of the Irish Literary Renaissance, for whom "The English language . . . did not come . . . as a neutral medium for expressing their thoughts" (p. 54). He quotes Stephen Daedalus in his conversation with an English priest (both native speakers of English) in Joyce's *A Portrait of the Artist as a Young Man*":

> The language in which we are speaking is his before it is mine. How different are the words *home, Christ, ale, master*, on his lips and mine! I cannot speak or write these words without unrest of spirit. His language, so familiar and so foreign, will always be for me an acquired speech. I have not made or accepted its words. My voice holds them at bay. My soul frets in the shadow of his language. (quoted in McDermott, 1988, p. 56)

Woolf and Joyce are professional writers. We can also reconsider in Bakhtinian terms the problems faced by student writers who are trying, or are expected to try, to enter the academic "literacy club" (F. Smith, 1988). Demientieff's reluctance to substitute *discourse* for *talk* is a case in point. And because she reflects on the single unit of a word, which is the unit of language discussed by Vygotsky, her reluctance can be analysed to show the importance of Bakhtin's ideas as an addition to Vygotsky's.

As Vygotsky (and others) have pointed out, words have, in addition to reference, both meaning and sense. Meaning is the transsituational signification given in dictionaries. According to one dictionary (Random House, 1966), *discourse* and *talk* overlap in meaning, with some distinction at the edges. Even though one word is given as a synonym for the other, the first definition for *discourse* gives as an italicized example, "earnest and intelligent discourse," while the first meaning for *talk* (as noun) is "conversation, especially of a familiar or informal kind."

Beyond this small difference in meaning is a larger difference in what Vygotsky (1962) calls "sense"—"the sum of all the psychological events aroused in our consciousness by the word" (p. 146). Whereas meaning is stable, sense is "dynamic, fluid" (p. 146), shifting with contexts of interaction or of inner speech. And it is as a characteristic of inner speech, where sense predominates over meaning, that it assumes special importance in Vygotsky's theory.

What Vygotsky does not discuss but Bakhtin does is that connotations accrue to a word not only from the immediate context of situation, but from the general—and in its own way, stable—context of culture. That is what Bakhtin refers to as the word's "stylistic aura . . . [that] belongs to that genre in which the given word usually functions"

(1986, p. 97). It is because words are "overpopulated with the intentions of others" that "expropriating it, forcing it to submit to one's own intentions and accents, is a difficult and complicated process" (1981, p. 294) especially when those "others" occupy a more powerful place in a stratified society.

Demientieff's problem had nothing to do with comprehension of meaning, and everything to do with "expropriating" a word that came to her laden with such alien sense that she could not yet "feel comfortable using it." Whereas *talk* could function for her as an ideologically neutral "common referring expression" (Wertsch, 1985, pp. 170-171), *discourse* came to her ideologically marked by the academic contexts in which she had encountered it.

There is educational implication to this story as well. When I named my book and my course, I could have used either "Classroom Discourse" or "Classroom Talk." The referent in either case would be the same: all the talk that goes on within the classroom walls. I did not opt for *discourse* to select for attention only the more "earnest and intelligent" interactions that are more obviously related to the formal curriculum, nor to invoke the broader meaning of discourse used by Gee (1989): "a socially accepted association among ways of using language, of thinking, and of acting that can be used to identify oneself as a member of a socially meaningful group or 'social network'" (p. 18). I picked it because of the different connotations of the two words—not to make a distinction among referents, but to dignify the referent by choosing a label marked for and by use in more academic or intellectual contexts.

Barnes calls these two functions of a teacher's specialized language the cognitive and sociocultural, respectively. In his words, for the student,

> Each new item must first appear to have a socio-cultural function—
> that is, to be "the sort of thing my physics teacher says"—and then,
> in so far as the pupil is able to use the item in talking, thinking, or
> writing, it will take upon itself a conceptual function. (in Barnes,
> Britton, & Rosen, 1969, p. 58)

It will take on a conceptual function, that is, if there is one. In the case of "classroom discourse," none was intended. Reconsidering my choice of title now and acknowledging its sociocultural purpose, I realize that its effect was to make it harder for a student from outside the academic world to consider herself a member of that world in her language use.

Whereas Demientieff's problem, at least as expressed in her take-home examination, was only with an individual word, for a black teacher—Nanzetta Merriman or, in pseudonym, Zan—during his work for the same master's degree in education at Harvard, the conflict was over not only words but also syntax and style. When Zan realized he was having trouble writing papers for his courses, a white doctoral student, Judy Diamondstone, who had been a regular observer in his seventh/eighth-grade social studies class (12 to 13-year-olds) the year before, agreed to help in return for permission to document his progress for one of her own courses (Diamondstone, 1990). They did a joint presentation later in the year (Diamondstone & Merriman, 1988).

Judy writes about Zan:

> He is about to undergo a series of accommodations to the language of the academe. . . . Zan confronts one enormous hurdle . . . : to convey his dramatic communicative style, based in oral, Black tradition, and to defend Black revolutionary ideology, in an academic discourse which he believes discriminates against his culture. (Diamondstone, 1990, p. 3)

Zan writes about himself:

> During the 1950's, my time in public schools in Harlem was dotted with retentions in grades two, six and ten. My undergraduate years were clouded with failures in writing. I believe the retention and the failures are illustrative of a system which only accepts the middle caste concepts of valid knowledge and language. (Diamondstone & Merriman, 1988, p. 1)

They work together on one of Zan's papers, finally entitled "Vision of a Field Negro," for a course on "Improving Schools":

Zan: (*reads aloud the sentence from his notes*) We must realize that we are within our moral rights, when our freedom and dignity and that of others are being jeopardized, to take any means necessary.

Judy: To take any means necessary—?

Zan: Period.

Judy: To do what? To change the situation? To win our—To redress? To turn things around?

Zan: "To turn things around" is too weak, "redress" is too white. To, to (*sigh*)—to end—

Judy: *Say* it, say it, Zan.

Zan: (*seven turns later*) We will do anything that is necessary to overcome it and to stop it.

Judy: "To overcome." There you go. (Diamondstone, 1990, p. 12)

In another session, Judy asks Zan what he has learned about his writing so far. "He answers with characteristic acuity that he had first to conquer his fear, and now has to learn the language of his audience:"

Zan: I used to think writing was, as you put it, writing in a vacuum. . . . It just had to come from oneself and that's it. . . . Now I do seek out a situation of—you write with readers. You write with audiences . . . I *never* wanted to use the man's words, but I did want to let the man hear. And I wanted to do in my writing what he did to us.

Judy: You have to do it with his words.

Zen: I will use his words. I will use his words. *But!* I will use my words too. . . . So it's how to, not compromise, but how to have those co-mingle. (Diamondstone, 1990, p. 10)

Zan's struggle is not just to learn new ways of writing, hard as that is. Ways of writing, like specific words (in his case, *redress*, which is "too white"), are already saturated with the values of the context they're associated with—a context, in the case of academic discourse, about which he is deeply ambivalent. So like Shuy, he seeks the forms for creative resistance, a transformational solution in which he does not have to compromise, and in which "the man's" and his own words "co-mingle."

The problems of Tanya, a remedial community college student whose writing has also been analyzed by her tutors, Glynda Hull and Mike Rose (1989), exemplifies Bakhtin's ideas in a different way. Tanya wants to become a nurse's aide, and one of the assignments set by her tutors is to write a summary of a nurse's case study, "Handling the Difficult Patient." The result seems at first incoherent, even chaotic. Here are a few lines of the original and Tanya's summary (Hull & Rose, 1989, pp. 146, 148):

Original Text	*Student Summary*
"Oh, this is going to be a great day," I said to myself. (Paragraph 4)	Oh this is going to Be a great Day I said to myself just thinking alone.

I have pride in my profession. (Paragraph 11)	I have pride In What I Do I am going to get

But I can give the minimum, too. I can sit here most of the day and still collect my 35 bucks at the end of the shift (Paragraph 11) (reformatted from pp. 146 and 148)	pad no matter what I am still am going to collect my money no matter what happen I do Believe and I no that In my mind.

Throughout her seemingly "word salad" summary, as Hull and Rose point out, Tanya copies chunks of the original, changing the order of ideas and some of the words. When they interviewed her afterward about her composing process, they discovered her two intentions: "to display and convey knowledge . . . [so] 'a teacher'll really know what I'm talking about' and to show she's 'not . . . that kind of student that would copy'" (Hull & Rose, 1989, p. 147). Their diagnosis concludes:

> After wrestling with our own concerns about the errors in Tanya's written language, about all those markers of illiteracy, it struck us that something profoundly literate is going on here. A fundamental social and psychological reality about discourse—oral or written—is that human beings continually appropriate each other's language to establish group membership, to grow, and to define themselves. . . . Tanya is trying on the nurse's written language and, with it, the nurse's self. (p. 151)

For Hull and Rose, the educational implications are "to temporarily suspend concern about error and pursue, full tilt, her impulse to don the written language of another . . . [with a] free-wheeling pedagogy of imitation" (p. 13). Then they comment on what Tanya's "plagiarism" can teach us:

> [Our own] clearly documented writing may let us forget, or even, camouflage, how much more it is that we borrow from existing texts, how much we depend on membership in a community for our language, our voices, our very arguments. We forget that we, like Tanya, continually appropriate each other's language to establish group membership, to grow, and to define ourselves in new ways, and that such appropriation is a fundamental part of language use, even as the appearance of our texts belie it. (p. 152)

Hull and Rose do not refer to Bakhtin, but his discussion of the process by which we appropriate others' discourse fits both Tanya's "plagiarism" and our own.

As with Hymes and Vygotsky earlier, Bakhtin's writings force us to confront important issues in teaching. They remind us that no text is autonomous, and that no forms of expression in natural languages are neutral referential codes. All bring with them—for all of us as speakers and writers—both pain and promise.

At the end of a personal essay, a black woman writer, Barbara Mellix (1989), speaks to both. Like Demientieff and Merriman, she has felt the pain. And, as Hull and Rose hope for Tanya, she has realized the promise as well:

> Although as a beginning student writer I had a fairly good grasp of ordinary spoken English and was proficient at what Labov calls "code-switching," . . . when I came face to face with the demands of academic writing, I grew increasingly self-conscious, constantly aware of my status as a black and a speaker of one of the many black English vernaculars—a traditional outsider. For the first time, I experienced my sense of doubleness as something menacing, a built-in enemy. Whenever I turned inward for salvation, the balm so available in my childhood, I found instead this new fragmentation which spoke to me in many voices. It was the voice of my desire to prosper, but at the same time it spoke of what I had relinquished and could not regain: a safe way of being, a state of powerlessness which exempted me from responsibility for who I was and might be. And it accused me of betrayal, of turning away from blackness. To recover balance, I had to take on the language of the academy, the language of "others." And to do that, I had to learn to imagine myself a part of the culture of that language, and therefore someone free to manage that language, to take liberties with it. Writing and rewriting, practicing, experimenting, I came to comprehend more fully the generative power of language. I discovered—with the help of some especially sensitive teachers—that through writing one can continually bring new selves into being, each with new responsibilities and difficulties, but also with new possibilities. Remarkable power, indeed. I write and continually give birth to myself. (p. 52)

◆ ◆ ◆

Afterword. *After reading* Lives on the Boundary, *Mike Rose's (1989) autobiography of his life as a writer and writing teacher, and finding that students at both the Bread Loaf School of English* *and Harvard loved it as much as I did, I wrote Rose a fan letter and sent him a copy of the manuscript for this chapter. In his reply, Rose admitted that using the language of current literary or cultural theorists sometimes made him feel the way Martha did about discourse. The he went on:*

> *"Special thanks for the quotations from Martha Dementieff and Zan: they really capture the feeling, but the complexity too, of facing a new, power-laden language. What I like about both—and the use you make of them—is that Martha and Zan admit to the strangeness of this language, to their reluctance to use it, and the connection of that reluctance to the sense of who they are. Zan admits, finally, to the fear behind his reluctance/resistance—and that's powerfully honest. Then we see both working to make the language their own: through changing it, playing with it, incorporating it, stripping it bare of its oppressive ghosts. I'm worried about a position I'm hearing increasingly at conferences that goes something like this: academic language (whatever that is, exactly) is generated by an oppressive, hegemonic, patriarchical class, and, thus, in some* philosophically necessary *way, will determine the mind, consciousness, politics of any oppressed group who tries to learn it. The end result, pedagogically, of this position is to oppose, abandon, overturn such language and embrace alternative discourses, or to value only those discourses that the students already bring with them. I certainly applaud the attempt to enrich traditional academic prose and to honor students' own language—I hope my work does both—but there's something about the position as I hear it that bothers me very much: it relies on a simple linguistic determinism and essentialism, and is, finally, patronizing; and it gives over to the elite a linguistic way of doing things that should be made available to the kinds of incorporations and appropriations and revisions that Martha and Zan are engaging in." (personal communication, January 12, 1991, by permission)*

That says, better than I could say it, and from more first-hand experience as a writing teacher, what our goals should be.

Part IV

◆ ◆ ◆

Equity in
New Zealand Education

15

♦♦♦

Differential Treatment
in New Zealand Classrooms

Foreword. *All four chapters in this section come from my seven trips to New Zealand between 1983 and 1991. These trips began with the First South Pacific Conference on Reading in 1983, at which the oral version of Chapter 4 was presented. After the conference, I stayed in New Zealand for four months as a visiting professor at the University of Auckland.*

During that stay, I heard for the first time about Reading Recovery (Chapter 9) and also about the observational research that Marie Clay was then conducting on interactions between teachers and their "new entrants" (5-year-old) children. Because of my long-standing interest in classroom interaction (now in Cazden, 1988a), we discussed the possibility of my returning to New Zealand in 1987, when I could again take leave from Harvard, to follow-up her research. These plans worked out, and I returned to New Zealand for a quick week of planning in 1986 and then for a six-months Fulbright research fellowship in 1987.

The first report of this research was written for New Zealand teachers and (still is) distributed in pamphlet form by the Auckland Reading Association (Cazden, 1988b). The version in this chapter, including "further reflections" added after a later visit, was published in the international journal Teaching and Teacher Education *in 1990.*

Both versions start, unconventionally for a research report, with a very short piece of fiction by a New Zealand writer.

A New Zealand Maori writer, Patricia Grace (1987), includes in her recent collection a very short story about a teacher's response to a Maori child's writing. The teacher is presumably white—"Pakeha," as Maori refer to New Zealanders of European (mostly British) descent:

Butterflies
by Patricia Grace

The grandmother plaited her granddaughter's hair and then she said, "Get your lunch. Put it in your bag. Get your apple. You come straight back from school, straight home here. Listen to the teacher," she said. "Do what she say."

Her grandfather was out on the step. He walked down the path with her and out on the footpath. He said to a neighbor, "Our granddaughter goes to school. She lives with us now."

"She's fine," the neighbor said. "She's terrific with her two plaits in her hair."

"And clever," the grandfather said. "Writes every day in her book."

"She's fine," the neighbor said.

The grandfather waited with his granddaughter by the crossing and then he said, "Go to school. Listen to the teacher. Do what she say."

When the granddaughter came home from school her grandfather was hoeing round the cabbages. Her grandmother was picking beans. They stopped their work.

"You bring your book home?" the grandmother asked.

"Yes."

"You write your story?"

"Yes."

"What's your story?"

"About the butterflies."

"Get your book, then. Read your story."

The granddaughter took her book from her schoolbag and opened it.

"I killed all the butterflies," she read. "This is me and this is all the butterflies."

"And your teacher like your story, did she?"

"I don't know."

"What your teacher say?"

"She said butterflies are beautiful creatures. They hatch out and fly in the sun. The butterflies visit all the pretty flowers, she said. They lay their eggs and then they die. You don't kill butterflies, that's what she said."

The grandmother and grandfather were quiet for a long time, and their granddaughter, holding the book, stood quite still in the warm garden.

"'Because you see,' the grandfather said, "your teacher, she buy all her cabbages from the supermarket and that's why."

"Butterflies" is a fictional story, not a transcript of an actual event. But when the back cover of the book prepares the reader for stories in which "sunlight, childhood and nature are set against conflict and misunderstanding," we should assume that Grace is writing about what she perceives to be a typical event in the lives of Maori children in mainstream New Zealand schools.

The Maori are the indigenous people of New Zealand—now some 10 percent of the population but closer to 20 percent of primary school students (*National Education*, 1989, p. 131). They share a single language, with only minor tribal/regional dialect differences (in contrast to the many languages of Native Americans in the United States and Aborigines in Australia). That language is now endangered by television, the fragmentation of intergenerational families with movement into cities, and educational policies and practices that, until recently, were at best unsupportive and at worst punitive. And, as with minority students (especially indigenous minorities) in so many countries, the rates of low achievement, dropouts, and incarceration are abnormally high.

Grace's story is an appropriate introduction to this report of attempts to improve the education of Maori children. I read it on the plane returning home to the United States after six months in New Zealand on a Fulbright research fellowship. The story about one teacher's response to a Maori child's words seemed to epitomize the problem I had gone to New Zealand to work on: the general problem of differential treatment in one specific sociocultural setting.

This is not a typical research report. Discussion of the construct of differential treatment is followed by presentation of existing New Zealand research and of my inservice work with New Zealand teachers. Then, following a brief reference to one New Zealand primary school that embodies features of learning environments advocated in the inservice work (more fully described in Chapter 17), it ends with reflections on two issues concerning the process and substance of research on minority education.

DIFFERENTIAL TREATMENT

"Differential treatment" labels one fact of institutional life: Opportunities for participation, and response to that participation, are not distributed equally or randomly. Within schools, the quantity and quality of participation correlates with variables of gender, race, and/or social class.

Such patterns result from within-school tracking (or streaming; e.g., Oakes [1985]) and from more subtle influences within seemingly undifferentiated classroom lessons and discussions (summarized in Cazden [1986, 1988a]). While "differential experience" would be a more neutral label, "differential treatment" suggests the special responsibility of educators—teachers, and those above them who shape the contexts within which teachers and children work.

Contexts for learning are nested—from those most immediate to the act of speaking and listening through the more distant (school, school system, community, etc.). Differential treatment in teacher-student interaction is one important site of inequalities. As the most proximal context for learning, classroom talk constitutes a critical part, and the most exposed edge, of the enacted curriculum.

EXISTING NEW ZEALAND RESEARCH

Research on differential treatment in New Zealand classrooms by Clay (1985b) and Kerin (1987) predated and prompted my inservice work. Together, their studies document both the existence of differential treatment of Maori children and patterns of its distribution during children's first year in school.

Clay (1985b) wanted to look closely "at the first term of school and in particular at the New Entrants' (5-year-olds) engagement with the programme of instruction" (p. 20) and at how teachers "provide appropriately for cultural difference in the classroom" (p. 22). She and her assistant spent six mornings during both the first and second terms of the 1983 school year in each of six new entrants' classrooms taught by European teachers.

In each classroom they selected for observation two European, two

Maori, and two Pacific Island children whose birthdays were nearest to the beginning of the term. Rotating attention among these six children, they recorded by hand whether the children were engaged with whatever tasks the teacher had assigned, and wrote down (as close to verbatim as possible) the interactions between each child and the teacher. Because all observations were made in the morning, they document what was happening during the three activities that fill the morning in many junior classes: news and other whole-group talk, beginning reading, and some combination of drawing/dictating/writing appropriate to the individual child.

In these situations, Clay found that most children—new to school though they were—were on task more than 90 percent of the time, and that there were no ethnic differences in this surprisingly high rate of engagement. She also concluded that the individual teacher-child interactions "were the most novel and interesting aspect of this project. . . . It was possible to locate many episodes in which the teacher sat alongside a child and did some teaching. . . . It was usual to obtain five or six episodes of teacher-child interaction *for each child* on each of the five or six observation mornings" (pp. 28-30; emphasis in the original).

It was in these individualized teacher-child interactions that the children's differential experience occurred:

> The teacher's attention fell unequally across ethnic groups. . . . In one-to-one teaching the teacher used her opportunities to work in similar ways with each ethnic group in the teaching moves which were labelled *restates, models, supports, links, shapes,* and *adds.* There was one category only which accounted for most of the [ethnic] differences. Teachers started as many contacts with Maori children as with European or Pacific Island children but they asked less often for verbal elaboration [which Clay labelled *talk more*]. These results were consistent across the two samples [Terms 1 and 2]. (Clay, 1985b, p. 31)

Here are some transcribed interactions that show what *talk more* (abbreviated TM) sounds like. The first four examples are from Kerin's research. The fifth is from the examples given by Clay at the end of the manuscript version of her report. In the first three positive examples, the teacher's turn that was considered by the researcher as an invitation to the child to "talk more" is marked with > in the left margin. All child names have been changed to pseudonyms.

Examples 1 and 2 are from reading episodes:

Example 1. Child: Maria

Teacher: What else is this story about?
Child: A ball and pictures.
Teacher: Yes, that's at the end. (Teacher asks what the coach did.)
   Maria?
Child: He taught them how to scramble.
Teacher: How to?
Child: Scramble.
>*Teacher*: What do you do when you scramble?
Child: Get them on the ground.
Teacher: Scramble, yes.

Example 2. Child: Rose

Teacher: Where's Bill going? [in the story]
Child: To bed.
Teacher: Good.
>How do you know he's going to bed, Rose?
Child: Because he's got his pajamas on.
Teacher: You're clever. You're clever. You're thinking hard. He has
   got his pajamas on.

Examples 3, 4, and 5 are from teacher–child conversations during
writing. In Example 3, the teacher does ask the child to Talk More; in
Examples 4 and 5 she does not:

Example 3. Child: Julia

Teacher: I'm writing your story, aren't I, Julia.
Child: (nods.)
Teacher: Right. Right, who's this?
Child: (Points to picture.) My sister.
>*Teacher*: And what's her name?
Child: Mary.
Teacher: Mary.
>And what's Mary doing?
Child: Putting the plant up.
Teacher: Mary is putting the plant up. Standing the plant up?
Child: Yeah.
Teacher: Is she?
Child: Yeah.

Teacher: Right. (Teacher writes.) "Mary is standing the—" You
watching, Julia? "—plant up."
Child: I help her.
Teacher: Do you? You copy it onto your book. You read it.
Child: Mary is standing the plant up.

Example 4. Child: Sharon

Teacher: Sharon, come and tell me your story.
Child: I wanted to mow the lawns.
Teacher: Mmm (Teacher writes.)
Child: Just for you.
Teacher: Mmm (Teacher writes.) Good girl. Read it to me.
Child: But I was too little.
Teacher: Oh! (Teacher writes.) Good girl. Read it to me.
Child: "I wanted to mow the lawns. Just for you. But I was too lit-
tle."
Teacher: Good girl.

Sharon takes the initiative in adding an important idea that completely changes the point of the story—"But I was too little"—even
though the teacher does not invite any such additions and had evidently considered the story complete.

Example 5

Child: Can I choose? (Shows a picture.)
Teacher: Right. Read it back to me.
Child: I can't.
Child: (Reads with help and teacher support.)
Teacher: Good boy. Now put it on the pile and choose.

All of the teachers' TM responses in these particular interactions
are questions, including a metacognitive question that asks the child to
reflect on the grounds of her own reasoning in Example 2. Sometimes
teachers accomplished the same TM function by comments rather
than questions.

Table 15.1 shows the number of times Clay's European teachers
asked the focal children for elaboration (TM) as an average per child
morning, reported separately for Term 1 and Term 2:

To put the first column of this table into words, during Clay's
observations in the first term, teachers asked European and Pacific

Table 15.1 Average number of Talk More invitations
per child-morning[a]

Children	Term 1	Term 2
European	5.37	3.81
Pacific Islands	5.20	3.53
Maori	3.80	1.92

[a]Source: Clay, 1985, P. 31, table 6.

Island children to talk more about whatever was the topic of conversation more than five times per morning. but made the same request of the Maori children less than four times. As Clay (1985b) summarized these results:

> While the differences are small in the research tables, the sampling arithmetic [that is, considering the time observed in relation to the total morning] suggests that Maori pupils missed four teaching opportunities each per morning, six per day. 30 per week and 300 per term. That could make a difference. (p. 31)

Note that this differential experience for the Maori children is true both for Term 1 and Term 2, even though different children—those who had just turned 5 and entered school—were being observed in the two terms. The absolute numbers decrease for all children from Term 1 to Term 2, but the Maori children's relative disadvantage actually increases as the year goes on.

In Table 15.1, the observations for all six teachers are combined, and no report of the individual classrooms is given in Clay's published report. But Clay made the original tabulations available for further analysis. Table 15.2 displays the averages of Talk More per child morning for each individual classroom for Terms 1 and 2 combined. The first column gives the average for all six children together; the second column for non-Maori (European and Pacific island) children, who were similar to each other in Table 15.1 and therefore combined here; and the third column for the Maori children. The numbers in parentheses show the absolute number of child mornings counted in each average. To put the first row into words: During 50 child mornings of observations, Teacher A spoke a daily average of nearly six TM invitations to each child. Her average for the non-Maori children considered separately was about six and one-third invitations in 40 child mornings, while her average for Maori children was just under four and one-half in 10 child mornings.

Table 15.2 Incidence of Talk More, by classrooms

	All children	Non-Maori	Maori
Teacher A	5.96 (50)	6.30 (40)	4.40 (10)
Teacher B	5.00 (58)	5.53 (51)	1.14 (7)
Teacher C	4.74 (53)	5.13 (32)	4.14 (21)
Teacher D	2.88 (56)	3.46 (28)	2.29 (28)
Teacher E	2.76 (55)	2.77 (31)	2.50 (24)
Teacher F	2.07 (55)	1.97 (36)	2.37 (19)

Two important patterns are evident in this table: First, there is a large difference among teachers in their overall use of TM invitations. Teachers A, B, and C do it more than twice as often as teachers D, E, and F. Second, the ethnic differences that result in differential treatment for the Maori children are a pervasive pattern across the classrooms. Thus the combined results in Table 15.1 can not be explained by idiosyncratic features of one or two teachers or one or two classroom groups.

Specifically, four of the six classrooms (A, C, D, and E) fit the composite picture given in Table 15.1. In Teacher B's case, the ethnic differences are exaggerated, but the number of Maori child mornings is so low (only seven, presumably because of low attendance of the focal children) that the average of these particular observations may not give a true picture. In Teacher F's case, the Maori children receive more TM invitations than do their European and Pacific Island classmates, but the numbers are so low for all children that it would be hard to consider any children advantaged in this respect. Displayed as in Table 15.2, Clay's data are particularly valuable in showing both within-teacher and among-teacher variation on a single variable.

Because all of Clay's teachers were themselves European, we cannot tell from her research whether the teacher's ethnicity is somehow an important influence. In 1986, Kerin—a primary school teacher who is herself Maori—replicated Clay's study as a master's thesis (1987) under Clay's direction. Because this was a student project with no outside funding, it was smaller in scale: observations in another six classrooms, but only two mornings spent in each one; her results should therefore be considered more tentative than Clay's.

Two of the teachers Kerin observed were Maori and four were European. In each classroom the focal children were three Maori and three immigrant children from one or another Pacific Island. (In these classrooms, in a different part of Auckland from those observed by

Clay, there were not enough European children to be included in the study.) Kerin's observations were made during Terms 2 and 3 of the 1986 school year, and data for the two terms have not been analyzed separately (as Clay's were) because of the smaller absolute numbers.

Table 15.3 presents the averages per child morning for all of Kerin's observations. Overall, the absolute frequency of Talk More is lower in these classrooms than in those observed by Clay; and the pattern of ethnic differences is quite different. The highest frequency is when Maori teachers are talking with Maori children (nearly three per child morning); and the Maori teachers issue more TM invitations to both groups of children than do the European teachers.

Considering together the results from Clay and Kerin's research, we have three significant patterns in the distribution of Talk More requests:

1. *There was an overall decrease in TM invitations as the school year went on.* This is evident primarily from the comparison of Term 1 and Term 2 for the same teachers within Clay's study, since the Clay/Kerin difference could be due not to time in school year but to differences among teachers and schools. The decrease may happen because New Zealand children enter school the day they are 5, and so the new entrants class gets larger as the school year goes on, and the teacher simply cannot spend as much time with each child. And/or, as one teacher looking at Table 15.1 suggested, it may be that talk among the children may be replacing some of the talk with the teacher, and only the latter was tracked in these studies.
2. *There were marked differences among classrooms in teachers' interactional styles.* Some teachers issued TM invitations twice as often as others. And in the one smaller study that compared teachers by ethnicity, Maori teachers were more apt to ask their children to "talk more" than were Pakeha teachers.

Table 15.3 Averages of Talk More per child-morning

Teachers	Maori children	Pacific Island children
Maori (2)	2.92	2.34
European (4)	1.58	1.50

[a]Source: Kerin, 1987.

3. *There were marked differences within classrooms such that some children received more TM invitations than others.* The most significant aspect of the children's differential experience was that Pakeha teachers were more apt to ask their Pakeha children and their recent immigrant children to "talk more" than their Maori children. Of all the aspects of teacher–child interaction that Clay and Kerin examined, this was the one in which they found the largest ethnic differences.

There are at least four reasons for considering these patterns a cause for concern. First, Clay emphasized the importance of teacher–child conversation for children's continuing language development, in vocabulary and complex syntax, during the school years. Research studies on the language development of preschool children in the United States, Britain, and Australia (reviewed in Cazden, 1988c) have converged on the finding that a particularly beneficial kind of talk occurs when an adult follows up on the topic of the young child with a topically related (semantically contingent) comment or question. Teachers will never be able to spend as much time with each child as parents can do at home, but Table 15.3 shows that improvement is possible—for all children in some classrooms, and Maori children in all.

Second, Vygotsky (1962) calls our attention to the value of children's talk about events and ideas for their understanding of the world, and for their growing ability to articulate that understanding orally and in writing. Third, in addition to benefiting directly in these ways, children will also gain indirectly from such conversations through the teacher's increased understanding of their ideas.

Fourth, there is some evidence from one study in the United States (reported in Cazden, 1972a, pp. 189–196) that children differ, individually and/or culturally, in how much of what they know they will offer in answer to any one adult question. Without teacher requests to children to "say more," some children's knowledge will be seriously underestimated.

INSERVICE WORK WITH TEACHERS

At the end of her report, Clay called for further research that considers cultural differences in communicative style and tries to identify classroom situations that maximize opportunities for more extended interactions. Despite my own longstanding interest in social class and cultural differences in patterns of communication (Cazden, 1988a), the work with New Zealand teachers followed Clay's second direction—focusing on classroom situations rather than cultural differences among children.

The decision to focus on the classroom became an important part of negotiations with members of the Maori educational community in Auckland before, and during, the work. And concern on this point continued to be expressed by other Maori educators who were not part of those planning discussions. For example, at one university elsewhere in New Zealand, a Maori faculty member whom I had not yet met sent a memo of concern to my Pakeha faculty host:

> It seems crucial to the success of this project that she be able to identify that behavior which is culturally different if she is then to identify the classroom situations that maximize opportunities for extended interaction and learning opportunities. This kind of research would not be unproblematical for a Maori academic fully bilingual and bicultural, such is the diversity of experience and identity-related issues displayed amongst Maori children today. How will she, an American, presumably with only limited skills in bilingual/ bicultural contexts which are Maori, pursue this aspect of the research? (personal communication, August 31, 1987)

To all such comments, I explained that I was not studying Maori culture or Maori children; rather I was focusing on social and interactional events in a primarily Pakeha institution for which the teacher bears special responsibility.

Keeping within these limits, we focused on characteristics of structures for interaction within the New Zealand classrooms, and only mentioned in passing any converging evidence from Maori culture. If teachers felt that "Maori children were harder to talk to," as Clay reported from her postresearch discussions with the teachers she had observed, then what could teachers do to make that talking more fluent and more informative for both children and teacher? Could teachers' attention be shifted from characteristics of the children to characteristics of the settings for interaction in school? Could both patterns in Table 15.2 be changed—so that teachers would invite all children to "talk more" and the gap in frequency of such opportunities between Maori and Pakeha children be eliminated?

I was joined in this work by a Maori colleague, Marie-Anne Selkirk, seconded from the Maori and Pacific Island Advisory Service, and we consulted with an informal group of Maori advisors. Together, we initiated direct discussions with volunteer teachers, individually and in small groups. Because these were not teachers who had been subjects in Clay and Kerin's research, we also visited their classrooms but did not do any systematic observations.

During these discussions, we presented the Clay and Kerin research as a statement of a significant problem, gave the teachers transcripts of both positive and negative instances of Talk More, and explored with them possible reasons for these patterns and possible alternatives. We also encouraged the teachers to tape interactions in their own classrooms and listen for ways in which they did, or did not, encourage children to express their ideas about the topic of the moment—whether chosen by the teacher as in discussion of teacher-selected books, or chosen by the child as in much of the dictation and writing.

In these discussions with teachers, and in later presentations in New Zealand (at universities, reading conferences, etc.), I drew on existing research—primarily in the United States—to suggest that four aspects of the New Zealand classroom and school environment might be important influences on classroom interaction for which alternatives should be explored.

Individualization versus Small Groups

One can think of each classroom as a particular instance of an educational philosophy and a social organization in which to carry it out. In New Zealand primary classrooms (Ashton-Warner, 1963/1986; Richardson, 1964), instruction is more individualized than in the United States. In most of the classrooms for young children that Clay and Kerin observed, and that Selkirk and I visited, teachers typically moved around the room helping children as they worked individually at reading and writing activities. Some teachers worked with small groups, but primary school advisors told us that individualization was preferred.

Each intersection of philosophy and social organization is presumably vulnerable to particular forms of differential treatment; that is, while differential treatment is a universal phenomenon, it will have different manifestations in different educational environments. In New Zealand–style individualization, it is not surprising that differential treatment occurs in the patterns of teachers' individualized conversations with children as they read, write, draw, and so forth.

While some of these conversations were extended in length, many were short: giving help with a word, then the ritualized praise—"Good boy" or "Good girl"—and moving on (as Resnick [1972] found in earlier research in infant schools in England). Such interactions probably help to sustain the high level of engagement with school tasks that Clay reports, but they are less likely to stimulate a child's thinking or language development.

We therefore suggested that the New Zealand ideal of individualization might be reconsidered, that it might be more a part of Pakeha culture than an essential feature of successful junior classes. Examples 1 and 2 presented earlier come from small reading groups, showing that a teacher can personalize teachings and extend conversations in such a setting. And it seems possible that teachers would be more apt to ask a metacognitive question—"How did you know . . . ?"—when they are sitting down with three or four children and know they are going to stay there for a few minutes, than when they are stopping momentarily on their individualized rounds.

There is also converging research evidence that, with respect to cultural differences, individualization may fail to take advantage of the abilities, or interactional preferences, of Maori (or more generally, Polynesian) children (Graves & Graves, 1974; Metge, 1984; Thomas, 1975). But we did not stress this cultural argument.

Pace

The interactional feature of pace is better known as "wait-time." Rowe (1986) summarized research on wait-time in classrooms from elementary school through college: When teachers wait for three seconds or more before responding to a student utterance, students speak at greater length and with greater complexity, and teachers become more adept at using student responses in their next turn. (See also reviews of this research by Tobin [1986, 1987].)

From this research base, we suggested that a slower pace of teacher questioning might make it more likely for Maori children to say more, and thereby give teachers more information on which to construct their next response. Here too, we found converging suggestions that silence is perceived positively in Maori culture, but with the teachers we stressed only the potential value of wait-time in contrast to the fast pace of their individualized classroom rounds.

Topic

From Clay and Kerin's transcripts and our classroom observations, it seemed that three kinds of topics posed problems for Pakeha teachers. First are topics specific to Maori culture—for example, the events at a Maori funeral. These were rare and only came up in classrooms taught by Maori teachers. Second are topics specific to individual children—the details of personal family life. We heard teachers, Pakeha as well as Maori, responding to children in ways that showed considerable familiarity. But in a more random sample of teachers, it is likely that Maori teachers would have easier access to relationships with Maori families and community.

Third are those topics that are familiar to both child and teacher but that have different means and/or different values to child and teacher. Butterflies, from Grace's story, is one example. Another appeared on a videotape of morning "news" (the equivalent of U.S. "sharing time" or "show and tell"): When a Pakeha girl showed her doll, the teacher asked several appreciative questions for more information; but when a Polynesian boy (either Maori or an immigrant child from another Pacific island) showed a new scrapbook with a rock-and-roll singer on the cover, the same teacher acknowledged it with a very brief comment.

Research on sharing time (morning news) in the United States (Cazden, 1988a) yields many additional examples. We therefore spent a lot of time in the inservice workshops talking about how to select and develop curriculum topics, drawing on positive examples from research of another New Zealand educator (Simon, 1986).

Ethnic Diversity of the School Staff

One of our Maori advisors often cautioned against the reductionism of focusing only on within-classroom sources of inequality, and there is U.S. research to support that concern. Cohen (1986) conducted a series of experimental studies of how children's status characteristics affect the rate of peer interaction and influence in collective tasks. In one study, she and her colleagues discovered that unless an ethnically diverse staff modeled equal-status relationships, change in children's behavior was unlikely.

Therefore the report written for the New Zealand educational community (Cazden, 1988b) included, in addition to classroom social organization, pace, and topic, the additional influence—at a higher level of nested contexts—of the composition of the school staff.

By the end of this inservice work, there was no evidence of whether these suggestions made any difference. We could only hope that the suggestions might be picked up, developed, and tested by other New Zealand teachers and researchers.

A POSITIVE MODEL: RICHMOND ROAD SCHOOL

In May/June 1989, almost two years later, I returned to New Zealand for a brief three weeks with a new purpose: to document—via teacher interviews—one Auckland primary school, Richmond Road, that embodied at least three of the four alternatives we had suggested in the inservice work.

The Maori principal of the school, Jim Laughton, an exceptional educational leader who had built the school over 16 years, had died suddenly nine months before, and a Maori colleague hoped to edit a book about the school to substitute for the book he and Laughton had not had time to write. My interview study (in Chapter 17) was intended as a contribution to that end. To give a glimpse of the school's philosophy and practices, here are Laughton's own words from the introduction to a videotape about the school produced for inservice workshops for New Zealand principals and teachers:

> Richmond Road School is a multiethnic primary school in Auckland's inner city. Seventy percent of the students are of Polynesian extraction: from Samoa, the Cook Islands, Nuea, Tonga, and the Tokelaus. Another 12 percent are Maori, and 10 percent are Pakehas. The rest are of exotic origin: from Fiji, India, Afghanistan, China, and Zambia. The ethnic diversity of the student body is reflected to a significant extent in the staff. Of the 20 teachers: 5 Maori, 3 Samoans, 1 Nuean, and 1 Maori-Samoan make up a 50 percent Polynesian component. Seven New Zealand Pakehas, a Scot, and an Australian comprise 45 percent of the total; and there is one Chinese teacher.
>
> Throughout the school, family grouping provides both an organizational frame and an educational model. The emphasis is on shared experience by children of different ages, abilities, and backgrounds, [and] the promotion of family-type concepts and obligations across boundaries of ethnic and cultural difference. Teachers are expected to recognize such obligations in their professional relationships with colleagues, and to model appropriate behavior in the teaching role.
>
> Within the family framework, the key value is unity. It derives from mutual respect, and is not to be confused with uniformity. Indeed, dimensions of difference provide both the context and the sources of learning. The object is to

learn *from* each other, to learn *about* each other, and thus to enrich our experience and to begin to understand the world.

Educational diversification to meet special needs began in 1976 with the establishment of an ESL unit. The two teachers in the Language Unit continue to provide for this need. Then, at the end of 1984, a bilingual Maori/English class was opened. From 1986, it too is a two-teacher unit. To avoid separation from the parent body, both of these units are integrated into the life of the school. They, like other branches of the extended family, must be seen to belong, must feel just as valued. [By 1989, a Samoan/English class has been added.]

For the recognition of equal status is fundamental to the promotion of unity. Various expressions of that recognition articulate terms of respect. Equality in this sense is essential to multicultural development. It must be part of the process, or it won't be part of the outcome. As Ghandi had it, "There is no *way* to equality. Equality *is* the way."

Richmond Road, as Laughton reorganized it, embodied—throughout the school—interaction in many group contexts; systematic inclusion of non-Pakeha curriculum topics—for example, the life of immigrants from the Cook Islands and refugees from Southeast Asia in May 1989—each drawing on the authentic knowledge of particular children and staff and making their knowledge important in the total school community; and a staff as multiethnic as the students.

Despite the myriad of visitors, local and foreign, to the school in recent years, there is no systematic description of teacher–student interactions in Richmond Road classrooms. But it seems likely that Laughton created some of the necessary conditions for more equal participation of Maori (and other minority) children.

FURTHER REFLECTIONS

In computer software, the "default option" is what a program is set to do "naturally," without user intervention—like printing single space. With respect to differential treatment, "default option" applies to what is called, in more political circles, institutional or structural racism. Although there is much talk of structural racism in New Zealand, we did not talk in those terms with teachers, believing that they were more apt to close minds than open them. But we did draw on Giddens's (1979) integration of interpretive and structural sociology to suggest that our actions have sources we are not aware of and consequences we do not intend.

The practices uncovered in Clay's research were not intended to disadvantage Maori children, but they had that effect. In any society where groups have differential power, if teachers from the dominant group "do what comes naturally," the result is apt to advantage children from their own group and disadvantage others. As New Zealand antiracist activists put it, the most useful Pakeha response is not guilt for the past but responsibility for the present and future. Thus the argument for "affirmative interaction."

Attempts to change deep-seated cognitive and behavioral default options fall into two overlapping categories: Think people into new ways of acting or act people into new ways of thinking. Controversies continue over the most effective strategies, but most evidence seems to support the second: changing attitudes by changing the contexts of action (Kelman, 1980, and in education, Elliott, 1991). In the terminology of behavioral analysis, one powerful way to change behavior is to change the "setting events" in which it occurs (e.g., Glynn, 1982). Both our short-term inservice work with teachers and Laughton's long-term reconstruction of Richmond Road followed that principle, but within different levels of setting event, or context. Within the classroom, we focused on the setting event of groups versus individualized interaction, pace, and topic. In Richmond Road, Laughton gradually reorganized the settings throughout the school—architectural as well as social and curricular—in which teachers and children work.

While in the country to interview Richmond Road teachers, I also listened for any reactions to my earlier report, still being distributed by the Auckland Reading Association. It did not seem to have been picked up by local educators, Pakeha or Maori.

Retrospectively, two reasons seem important. With respect to Pakeha educators, the initiating problem of differential treatment was not theirs. It had been discovered by a New Zealand researcher and pursued by an American visitor; it never had priority for the teachers themselves. As the then New Zealand Director General of Education put it:

> Unless teachers and other practitioners are able to take part in defining the reality that the researchers are inquiring into, there is little chance that they will recognize the outcome as a useful contribution to their daily work. (Renwick, 1986a, p. 78)

With respect to Maori educators, the problem was not theirs either, but for different reasons. Yes, they are concerned about the treatment of Maori children in mainstream schools taught by Pakeha teachers. But, as a group, their priorities are elsewhere—on schools like Richmond Road and beyond. Their priority is the revitalization of Maori language and culture, with the schools as one important site for struggle (Irwin, 1989; Spolsky, 1989).

Starting in 1982, the National Department of Maori Affairs initiated a network of Maori language immersion preschools—Te Kohanaga Reo, the "language nests"—which now number more than 500 across the country. By 1989, there were only about a dozen bilingual primary schools, plus bilingual classes within schools as in Richmond Road, in which graduates of the Kohanga can continue their bilingual/bicultural development.

This revitalization movement is racing against time: trying to educate a critical mass of new speakers before the older generation of native speakers dies. Now, with a 1989 administrative reorganization of the entire New Zealand school system providing new openings for local control, Maori efforts concentrate on separate structures, including separate schools operating with government funds but under Maori control (anticipated in Renwick [1986b]; outlined concretely in Penetito [1989]; argued for by L. Smith & G. Smith [1989]).

In some ways, our inservice work had been planned well—that is, planned in consideration of recommendations for research on minority education formulated separately in New Zealand (Stokes, 1985) and the United States (Weiss, 1977). Maori educators were consulted during a planning trip in 1986, and their approval and continuing advice were then formally solicited at a *hui* (meeting held according to Maori protocol) during the first week of my 1987 stay. The research was designed to intervene on behalf of Maori children, not just describe the status quo; and we reported back fully and frequently.

So far, so good. But the agenda—the problem of differential treatment in mainstream primary classes—was mine. It had not been initiated by either the Pakeha teachers who would have to carry it out or the Maori educators who represented the children it was intended to benefit. It is easy to agree, in principle, with the importance of involving both those groups in shaping the research or staff development focus. It is harder to see, in action, how the perspectives of these sometimes conflicting groups can easily be integrated. That is the issue of process.

The issue of substance concerns the benefits or dangers of calling teachers' attention, via the words of oral or written texts, to cultural features of groups other than their own. Research on differential treatment and on cultural differences represents complementary perspectives on how teachers adapt to differences among their students. The differential treatment perspective asserts that teachers now differentiate among their students in ways that may reinforce, even increase, inequalities of knowledge and skills that are present when students start school. The cultural differences perspective asserts that students would be better served if teachers took differences into account more, or in different ways, than they now do.

It is of considerable symbolic importance that *National Education*, the professional journal of the union of New Zealand primary teachers, devotes half of the 50 pages of its final issue to "the Maori experience," with all Maori authors. (Presumably, "this abrupt end to a tradition going back 90 years" is somehow related to the current restructuring of the national educational system.) One of the articles in this section is "a guide for teachers" by a Maori executive officer of the union:

> This guide is intended to begin to build understanding and knowledge about aspects of Maori lifestyle and aspirations, with the purpose of helping teachers to affirm more positively the "maori-ness" of Maori children. (Hamilton, 1989, p. 129)

Children's "Maoriness" is then described under such headings as time orientations, group orientation, learning styles, body language, and so forth.

While information such as this may be helpful, it also risks creating and reinforcing stereotypes. One incident that occurred in the United States in the fall of 1987 exemplifies these dangers. In a widely circulated working paper on dropout prevention, the New York State Board of Regents (University of the State of New York, 1987) recommended that "instructional techniques . . . must be tailored to meet students' particular needs and effectively deal with the different cultural styles and backgrounds of students" (p. 15). The paper then went on to list "qualities noted in Afro-Americans" (p. 15). Specifically because of this section, the paper was soon under attack from many quarters and was finally withdrawn for revision (*New York Times*, October 2 and November 16, 1987).

Perhaps out of some such concern, Hamilton (1989) included a cautionary note in his introduction: "Members are asked to discuss [these statements] with Maori teachers, parents and community groups before making final decisions" (p. 129). But texts develop a life of their own and are recontextualized in settings far from control by their original writers (discussed in Chapter 10). No matter how ethnographically or experientially valid texts may be in the context of writing, pedagogical validity depends on their effects in all those subsequent new contexts. At the very least, we need research that documents what happens when reports on cultural differences are disseminated into mainstream schools and become part of mainstream teachers' thinking.

A second concern is simply that information on children's home culture still leaves teachers with the problem of how to use that information to benefit children (Cazden, 1983). A Navajo-Anglo couple, Agnes and Wayne Holm, have documented the history and philosophy of another positive model—Rock Point, a bilingual K-12 school on the Navajo (American Indian) reservation that they helped develop over more than 20 years. About pedagogy they write:

> [S]ome Anglocentric educators seem to have assumed that education is education: that teaching in Navajo would involve using Navajo in the same ways and for the same purposes Anglo teachers use English in teaching middle-class Anglo students. Others, who might be termed anthropological romantics, seem to have assumed that there is a Navajo style of teaching, which would-be Navajo teachers need only discover and apply. Unfortunately, almost all their examples came from the less verbal performance of traditional skills.
>
> The Rock Point experience would suggest that while there are certainly Navajo ways of interacting with others and of transmitting verbal knowledge, these are not just waiting to be discovered and applied. They must be integrated with new ways and used with new content. Rock Point teachers created, over time and by a combination of theory and trial and error, not the only Navajo but a contemporary Navajo way to go to school, a Rock Point way. (Holm & Holm, 1990, p. 179)

Rock Point has a bilingual and bicultural staff. To ensure that the Anglo staff members do not dominate the Navajos, the two groups are organized in parallel, and equal, structures—Navajo language teachers and English language teachers, Navajo principal and Anglo principal, Navajo evaluators and Anglo evaluators, and so forth.

In both schools, Richmond Road and Rock Point, curriculum and pedagogy evolved from a combination of theoretical knowledge and discussions based in the lived experience of the multicultural or bicultural staff. That constitutes the best possible setting, albeit one all too rare in most countries, for successfully working through the complex issues involved in successful minority education.

Afterword. Although the observations in this "talk more" research all come from primary classrooms, differential treatment in teacher-student interactions can occur at all grade levels. While in New Zealand for a week in 1991 to participate in a symposium honoring Marie Clay, I spent a day with some of the educators who work for the Education Review Office, the national government agency that since 1989 has been charged with evaluating all New Zealand schools. One criterion on which all schools are evaluated is equity for Maori students. To initiate a discussion of what to look for and ask about in this part of the evaluation task, the senior Maori educator present, Pera Riki, reported a recent visit to a secondary school.

In one social studies classroom, students who had been studying Neanderthal man were then assigned to do some related writing: Compare your life with that of a Neanderthal man. Two Polynesian students—one Maori and one Samoan, as it turned out—were seen whispering to each other after the assignment was given. Then the Maori boy raised his hand: "Which of my lives should I write about?" One can easily imagine a curt teacher reply: "What do you mean, 'Which of your lives?' Get on with it." But instead, the following conversation took place between the teacher (T) and the student (S):

T: How many lives do you have?
S: Two
T: Two?
S: Yes, my country life with grandma, and my city life here.
T: Well, you chose the one you'd like most to write about.

Then the Samoan boy explained that he had three lives: his island life (when he visits family in Samoa), his city life in Auckland, and his church life—which to him is quite separate from the other two. Again, the teacher accepted with interest his qualification on what turned out, for some students, to be not such a simple assignment.

The problem posed for all teachers by Patricia Grace's story, "Butterflies," is how to attend to our students' inner meanings instead of their surface behaviors. Scheffler (1968), quoting John Dewey, puts the challenge this way:

> It is important to stress the subtlety and delicacy of the teacher's interchange with the student. A crude demand for effectiveness easily translates itself into a disastrous emphasis on externals simply because they are easier to get hold of than the central phenomena of insight and the growth of understanding. In an important essay of 1904, John Dewey distinguished between the inner and outer attention of children, the inner attention involving the "first-hand and personal play of mental powers" and the external "manifested in certain conventional postures and physical attitudes rather than in the movement of thought." . . . The "supreme mark and criterion of a teacher," according to Dewey, is the ability to bypass externals and to "keep track of the child's mental play." . . . Effective classroom performance surely needs to be judged in relation to the subtle engagement of this inner mode, difficult as it may be to do so. (p. 9)

16

◆ ◆ ◆

Butterflies
and Origami Birds
Teachers, Actors, and Subtext

Foreword. In 1987, in the midst of the New Zealand work described in the last chapter, I returned to the United States for two months to teach in the Program in Writing at the Bread Loaf School of English, a program that is enriched by connections with the work of an ensemble of professional actors and their director, Alan Mokler.

While at Bread Loaf, I drew on the writing/theater connection to explore further the teaching problem that I returned to in the Afterword of the last chapter: how to attend to our students' inner meanings, specifically, the meanings that lie behind their written texts, and how to raise teachers' consciousness of the importance of trying to do so. Can drama have value—at least as a metaphor and perhaps as a medium—for such consciousness-raising?

This chapter was originally written for a conference on "The Creating Word" in Calgary, Alberta, and published only in shortened form in the Bread Loaf and the Schools *magazine in 1988. Both versions began with "Butterflies," but that little story and other overlaps with the last chapter have been omitted from this otherwise longer version.*

DRAMA AS METAPHOR

At Bread Loaf last summer, the major drama production was *Macbeth*. All rehearsals were open and could even be taped for further analysis. One high school teacher, Elizabeth Marshall, taped a rehearsal of Act II, scene ii, in which Macbeth lurches downstairs after murdering the king and reports almost incoherently to his wife. Part of his report has come to be called "the sleep speech":

> Macbeth: Methought I heard a voice cry "Sleep no more!/Macbeth does murder sleep"—the innocent sleep,/Sleep that knits up the ravelled sleave of care,/The death of each day's life, sore labor's bath,/Balm of hurt minds, great nature's second course,/Chief nourisher in life's feast—

At which point, Lady Macbeth interrupts to ask, "What do you mean?"

Marshall, experienced in doing a literary analysis of *Macbeth* first as student and now as high school teacher, was surprised to hear how director Alan Mokler talked to the professional actor, Jonathan Fried, about this speech:

> When you do the sleep speech this time, Jonathan, it can move to your own considerations. You're doing, "Sleep that knits up the ravelled sleave of care." Now what is that? So you get an image in your mind of being unravelled the night before, for some very specific reason, a bad rehearsal or, ah, you couldn't get a paper done or whatever, and you are just unravelled, and you go to sleep and the next morning you can deal with that paper. . . . Yeah, that "knits up." Now why do you say it in those terms? "That knits up the ravelled sleave of care." Why those words and not some other? Same problem, finding something that will make you say it that way. Maybe it's not a paper, maybe it has something to do with [long pause]—something to do with clothing, how you, how you put, how you protect yourself from the day, from everything.

Here are excerpts from the paper Marshall wrote about the differences she saw between two methods of interpretation:

As an English major and an English teacher, the process of literary analysis is very familiar to me. But what I saw going on in front of me was something quite different. Reading *Macbeth* in a classroom was, for me, a lot like reading a poem. The language was in many respects poetic and not immediately accessible; the questions we asked of the text were those we would ask of a poem, and the words themselves were more important than the characters speaking them. [As] I began to recreate the method of analysis used in the classroom, the central question I found myself trying to answer was: how did the characters get left out of the interpretation?

If I use the tools of literary analysis as they've been taught to me, my first impulse is to go to the text. Word choice is critical. Perhaps the most difficult line in this passage is "Sleep that knits up the ravelled sleave of care." To understand what Shakespeare might have meant by this in 1623, I have to use the *Oxford English Dictionary.* According to OED, a sleave is "a slender filament of silk obtained by separating a thicker thread." Even with this knowledge, meaning is elusive. Perhaps the image refers to a frayed strand of silk knit back into wholeness, as sleep regenerates the tired soul. Each image in this passage echoes major themes in the play as a whole. In the process of analyzing this speech I search out key words—"sleep," "nature," "innocence"—and look for the places where they connect to other parts of the text. I consider the passage in particular, but analyze its meaning in terms of the themes that exist throughout the play. This process of creating meaning is very different from that which an actor uses in preparing a scene for performance. For the actor and director, a play is an unfinished text, completed only in the process of rehearsal and performance. In theatre-director Mokler's words, analysis of a play for dramatic purposes uses the text as a "blueprint for performance." Much of the creation of a role—for that is what an actor is doing in interpreting the text—relies on the creation of a subtext—a context in which [the actor] can understand his or her motivations and emotions. The process of making the play come alive involves bringing personal experiences directly to bear on the words themselves.

The connection between actor and role is extremely intimate and this, I think, is the source of the greatest difference between the two methods of interpretation. In literary analysis we take the text apart, down to each separate word, and then build meaning. In some cases that may require research into the history of a word, as in the case of "sleave." Actors break down scenes to the individual moment—not the word—and create meaning through experimentation, shaping, and discovery. The job of an actor is to close the distance between text and speaker so the two become one. In the process, meaning is not found, it is created.

The term "subtext" comes from the still influential teaching of Konstantin Stanislavsky, director of the Moscow Art Theatre until his death in 1938. In *An Actor's Handbook*, Stanislavsky (1963) defines subtext as what the actor supplies at the moment of performance. And in his fictionalized book, *An Actor Prepares* (1948), he explains:

> The fundamental aim of our art is the creation of this inner life of a human spirit. . . . You must live it by actually experiencing feelings that are analogous to it. . . . To reproduce feelings you must be able to identify them out of your own experience. . . . The essence of art is not in its external form but in its spiritual content. (pp. 14, 23, 34)

(Stanislavsky died in 1938 at the age of 75. Psychologist L. S. Vygotsky, who died in 1934 at the much younger age of 38, was interested in the theater throughout his life, included a chapter on *Hamlet* in his dissertation on the psychology of art, used Stanislavsky's notes for actors in developing his own ideas on relationships between thought and language, and wrote about subtext in the final chapter of *Thought and Language* [1962].)

Before leaving the world of the theater, I want to mention a more contemporary and more cross-cultural account: Arthur Miller's (1984) book *Salesman in Beijing*, about his recent experience directing a Chinese translation of *Death of a Salesman* in the People's Republic of China. Working with the Chinese cast, Stanislavsky-trained Miller found the contrast between outer actions and inner spirit to be extreme; traditional Chinese acting seemed to him overacting to the point of melodrama. At the first rehearsal, he addressed the cast:

> The first thing I want to discuss with you is the problem of how to act like Americans. The answer is very simple and I urge you to try as hard as you can to believe what I say—you must not attempt to act

like Americans at all. . . . The way to make this play most American is to make it most Chinese. . . . [If] you are emotionally true to your characters and the story . . . I am betting that the cultural surface will somehow take care of itself." (p. 5)

Miller knew that just saying so would not make it happen. And it took long discussions with members of the cast to discover underlying similarities between the United States of 1949 and Beijing in 1983: No, there were no traveling salesmen in China, but "we must all sell ourselves, convince the world of a persona that perhaps we only wish we really possess" (p. 44). Yes, it is hard to understand how Willie could be deaf to his son Biff's bad news that no businessman would loan him money, but during the Cultural Revolution, in the face of surrounding catastrophe, people were still always "finding some hope" (p. 61).

At the end of six weeks of rehearsal, waiting for the curtain to go up on opening night and knowing he would leave for home the next day, Miller reflects on the larger significance of what he and the cast have done:

> We do not meet defensively in the theatre, quite the opposite—here we have to search each other out. If I fail to understand them or they me, we have a mutual catastrophe. Thus we dispense with culture, hammer away at the opacity of our languages, strive to penetrate rather than justify ourselves or defend the long past. Indeed, our whole objective has been to unearth our common images and analogous—if superficially different—histories. If they are making the Lomans intimately comprehensible to their fellow Chinese, it is because they have found the Lomans in themselves. . . . The job of culture, I have always thought, is not to further fortify people against contamination by other cultures but to mediate between them from the heart's common ground. (p. 249)

These quotes from the theater at Bread Loaf and Beijing have caught the process by which an actor finds an inner life of his or her own part. Just as important at any moment, in the directions of both Mokler and Miller, is really listening for that inner life in the fellow members of this imaginary world.

Is the metaphor of classroom as acting ensemble a useful one? At the moment I can only say that my class at Bread Loaf was enriched by exploring this question. Thanks to the frequent presence of Jim Lobdell—a member of the faculty group of professional actors who is also, during the school year, a high school English teacher—we explored many acting/teaching/writing connections:

Dramatic renditions, whether of fiction or of a transcription of actual classroom talk, may help to accomplish two contrasting processes. By framing the ordinary and all-too-familiar events of the classroom as if on stage, dramatization may help to make the familiar strange and therefore worth serious reflection. And by focusing the attention of actors/readers and audience on the underlying thoughts and feelings—the subtext—behind the words of the characters, it can help us to understand someone else's understanding and thereby help to make the strange, especially the culturally strange, more familiar— to make us, in short, more like the grandfather in "Butterflies" than like the teacher.

Afterword.   *Understanding the thought of another person is never simple, and I have continued to mull over the problems it poses for teachers. Here's another way of thinking about it, from Morson's (1986) writing on Bakhtin, whose ideas were presented in Chapter 14:*

> *By making others a version of ourselves, we transform them so that we learn nothing. It is no less impoverishing to empathize with others so much that we silence our own voice. (p. 177)*

Instead, Morson suggests, we learn most when we engage in dialogue.

17

◆◆◆

Richmond Road
A Multilingual/Multicultural
Primary School in Auckland

*Foreword. In Chapter 15, Richmond Road Primary School is sug-
gested as a positive model of multiculturalism, and the vision of its
principal of 16 years, James Laughton, is given in his own words.
This chapter gives a more detailed picture of that school through
the words of teachers and other adults in the school community
spoken in interviews nine months after his death.*

*Together, they indicate how an educational leader communi-
cated his vision to the staff, and embodied that vision in organizational structures and thereby in patterns of interaction—among
staff, children, and the community.*

This report was published in Language and Education: An
International Journal *in 1989.*

This is the story of one multilingual, multicultural primary school as
told through the words of present and former adult members of the
school community.

Their words come from 45-minute interviews held at the school
(except for two former teachers who were interviewed in their homes)
between May 30 and June 15, 1989. I made this trip to New Zealand to
do this work. Originally, I had one purpose; later, another was added.

Shortly after the death of the school's Maori principal of 16 years,
James (Jim) Laughton, in September 1988, his friend and colleague in

the national Education Department, Wally Penetito, wrote to explore ideas about a possible book about the school that might substitute for the book that he and Jim hadn't had time to write. I offered to help in any way I could and promised to come to New Zealand in May 1989.

By the time I explained my purpose to the Richmond Road teachers at their staff meeting on May 30, I realized that more than this particular school was in a period of transition. The entire national school system of New Zealand was being reorganized (Lange, 1988), and I heard expressions of both hopes and fears about what the future would bring, especially for Maori education. (For one statement of these hopes by a Maori university educator, see Irwin [1989].) Perhaps, I thought, a description of one unusually successful inner-city multilingual and multicultural school as it still was, when only one teacher had left in the nine months since the principal's death, would be locally useful, whatever the future of a possible book.

So I had 24 45-minute interviews, primarily with present members of the staff. I talked only with those who volunteered. In the end, I talked with 18 of the present teaching staff plus the caretaker, three former teachers, and two parents active in school affairs. In ethnicity, there were nine Maori; five Pakeha (the Maori name for New Zealanders of European, primarily British, descent), and one Chinese New Zealander; three Samoan; and one each from Australia, England, and four South Pacific island countries: Cook Islands, Fiji, Niue, and Tokelau.

Most of the teachers I had known from previous trips when I had spent time in the classrooms and regularly attended staff meetings; some had become personal friends; a few I met for the first time on this visit. I would like to have interviewed some students and many more parents, but there wasn't time. Thus this report speaks well only for the staff (and has been read by all those interviewed).

After returning to the United States, I interviewed another American educator, Mary Snow, who had been at Richmond Road on a study tour in July 1988, two months before Jim's death. The tour had been led by Don Holdaway, who had developed some of his now-influential ideas about "shared book" reading (Holdaway, 1979) at Richmond Road. Because of Holdaway's past association with the school, the group spent a week there, more time than usual visitors did. The Richmond Road staff spoke to the group at their Teacher-Only Day; the Americans then spent time in the classrooms; and Mary had a chance for a good talk with Jim.

As I explained at the staff meeting, I was especially interested in what made Richmond Road a different, or special, or significant school to the people who knew it best. And because several people insisted that I tell an honest picture and not idealize or romanticize the school, I asked everyone about aspects of the school that they thought needed discussion and further evolution. Beyond these two preplanned questions, the conversations were just that—conversations, varying in each individual case.

Of course, some of each conversation was about Jim Laughton: his powerful vision that came from in-depth reading and thinking about education and society; his understanding of "how children thought, and how they saw the world"; his integrity—"Jim wouldn't even take home a school pencil." And his "passion."

Those personal qualities died with the man. But the school he built did not. To an extent unusual in any country, Jim figured out how to put his ideas and beliefs into practice. The ideas in themselves may seem simple: for example, a deep belief that "all people can go *somewhere*." The importance of Richmond Road is its embodiment of a set of such ideas in organizational structures and thereby in patterns of interaction—among staff, children, and the community.

Jim's underlying theories are included only as they appeared in our conversations. New Zealand colleagues will have to write more about the philosophical base of the school, or edit whatever writings Jim himself left. Some of his ideas came from reading; for example, several people mentioned British philosopher R. S. Peters's distinction between ascribed and provisional authority. Some came from his own experience: "His first statement always was, 'I don't know what's right in education. But over the years, these things have proved to me that at least for minority people, they haven't been successful. So what is the point of pursuing those same things?' He never changed from that."

The school in practice nine months after his death is what I have tried to capture in these pages. Indented text, or words in quotation marks within the main text, are from the interviews. To preserve the confidentiality that was promised to everyone, no speakers (except American Mary Snow, to keep her words separate) are identified by name. Within sections, spaces between paragraphs indicate a change of speaker, and nobody is quoted more than once. Responsibility for selection, categorizing, editing, and commenting on the quotations is mine.

"THE KIDS ALWAYS COME FIRST"

The children at Richmond Road are as multicultural as the staff. On May 5, 1989, the 269 students were 21 percent Samoan, 20 percent

Pakeha, 18 percent Maori, 34 percent other Polynesian, and 7 percent Indian and others.

> The thing that's special about Richmond Road is that it's a school for children. It's something that I always wished was around when I was a child, because it's a place where children are made to feel—not *overly* important—but important. They've got a place there. I know from being a Maori how I felt the odd one out. My being Maori was just a nothing, a minus sort of thing.
>
> There was quite a lot of the staff brought their children to the school. I started my daughter here, at 5, because of all the opportunities that it offers. Then when the bilingual classes were set up, she went in there right from the start. I knew what was going on, and I *liked* what was being done for the children.
>
> My two big girls didn't have as long at Richmond Road as the others. We moved around a lot when they were small. But they've become much stronger with their time here. What helped them? I think the Polynesian Club, and the family grouping, and the paired teaching. They talk about that a lot at home, who they're working with. And everybody seems to *know* everybody. Like Tu, the caretaker, knows *every* child in the school. He spends his lunchtime playing sport with them out there. Everybody just seems like a big family.
>
> One of the first things I noticed when I came here was the acceptance of children's cultures within the classroom. Like setting up the ESL [English as a second language] unit and allowing children to speak in their own language, and accepting that—not forcing them to speak English.

Mary Snow commented on differences between Richmond Road teachers and the group of American visitors in goals for their children:

> All the American teachers kept asking, "Well, how do the children do when they go to the intermediate school?" And the teachers at Richmond Road sort of said, "I guess they do OK." They hadn't really worried about it! We always have thought of education for some goal in the future. What

they're interested in—and Jim keeps talking about that—
education should be for the *present*. You had to start by
making *everyone* feel that they had access to what was important, to be a learner, and the rest would sort itself out.
The *most* important gift that could be given a child would
be this growing sense of who he or she *is*, with a sense of
pride and self-confidence about that.

When I asked Mary if she noticed any expressions of this pride in
the classrooms, she told a story from her last day in the school: "I had
been observing in the class, and there was a wonderful-looking child
with a long pigtail down the back, wearing a teeshirt and shorts. I had
been assuming, for some reason, that this child was a girl, and said
something at the end of class that betrayed my assumption. And the
child just put his head back and roared. 'No, I'm Niuean! We don't cut
our hair.' The way he stood there with such pride and delight and
humor gave me a sense of how sturdy his self-image was."

"WE HAVE AN AGENDA FOR CHILDREN, BUT IT'S ACTUALLY AN AGENDA FOR EVERYONE"

Although Richmond Road is first and foremost a school for children, it is also—and more remarkably—a learning community for
adults. Many of the staff spoke with pleasure and pride at what they
individually and personally had gained. Some expressed gratitude to
Jim for his personal encouragement, and for the "systems" he established in which they were helped—even pushed—to grow. Others paid
tribute to the professionalism of their colleagues: their high energy,
their belief in what they're doing; and the continual sharing of knowledge and support within the group.

The adult learning is about teaching, about other cultures, and
about oneself.

Learning About Teaching

I'm always learning in the staff meetings. Reading: That's been
a relearning here. All the tests [running records] you have
to do for monitoring reading; dictated texts and all that.
They always go over it for new staff. It's a good learning context.

Jim always pushed me to do things. He asked me, "Do
you want to do Reading Recovery?" (see Chapter 9). I've

learned a lot from it. I'm not a good reader. But after—it's true—after joining Reading Recovery [being trained as a tutor], I really appreciate reading—for myself, and for my resources for the children.

I got really angry with him [Jim] about the topic maths, because it [organizing the materials] was quite hard for me. But in the end, he would always say, "You're lucky to have made those reorganizations, because you *know*. You were part of creating this system, and you *know*. You're lucky because you have *knowledge*." I remember telling a friend—he says, "Why'd you come back here [to Richmond Road]?"—"Purely and simply to learn."

In my second set of resources, our topic was Buddhism and Kampuchea. I was looking at two social studies areas—determination and survival: leaving one place and moving on to another, with the idea that we have refugees in this country, in this school; and culturally symbolic behavior: people couldn't carry a lot of things with them, but they could carry their Buddhist faith. In the end of the resource work, there's not just the product that you create, there's the fact that you realize how much knowledge you actually own yourself, and then how much you can share with others.

You were always feeling at Richmond Road that *teachers* were learning all the time. I was better prepared for going to the university by what we'd done. A lot of people who go to the university at my age, they go to this New Start program [but I didn't]. Having been at Richmond Road has kept my mind active. When we had to do talks [at workshops and conferences], that prepares you— you've got to do some reading. We had the latest of everything that was out. If there was an article that Jim thought we should have, it was discussed at staff meeting. He'd say, "Right. You two people can prepare this." I remember this Gay thing about mathematics [an anthropologist's report of mathematics learning in Africa]. It made us look at all sorts of culturally different ways children could have mathematics. . . .

And making resources: Whenever I finished one of them, I had learnt. I had learnt something that I would *never* have looked into deeply, if I hadn't been made to do it. [I remember] the topic we did on China. "I don't really want to know about China." [But] if you made resources, you really had to know what you're making them about. I did medicines. I'm quite sure people didn't use them [with children]; I got them back pristine clean. [But] I learned an *awful* lot about natural healing. You see, there's medicine and natural healing in *all* cultures. The Maori had certain ways of doing things, so perhaps you might bring it up in other ways. And don't you think *all* learning makes you a *much* more interesting teacher?

Learning About Other People and Other Cultures

Something that Richmond Road has taught me is to be (pause) humble, to respect differences. People aren't like me, and I have to work with this group of people. The hardest thing is not working with the kids; it's working with your colleagues.

I think on the whole that recognizing differences does carry through [to staff as well as children]. To me, this is a safe school to be in. A lot of schools I couldn't be as out and free of who and what I am as I can be here. We've got so many different people here, and there's no tightness in the staff.

We, as teachers, share our various ethnic backgrounds with each other. This helps to enrich us as a group of people working together. And not only that—the children also share their backgrounds with each other and with the teachers. The whole basis of the subject-content matter of the school is who we are in *this* school.

I'm learning from the kids—their cultures, and not only that, their languages as well.

I'm learning different ethnic cultures, like the Maori one. It comes from working on the resources, and just *using* those things, and the language, in the classroom.

Learning About Oneself

There are things that I've been made to do that I didn't want to do, that I've actually been enriched by. If you put me in a public-speaking situation, I freeze. Last year, a group of American visitors came for our Teacher-Only Day. Each member of the staff had to pick something about the school and speak to it. You *had* to participate; there was no other way. I didn't think it was going to be much of a learning situation for me. So I thought, "I'm going to do something that I don't really know much about." We were given a list of possible topics, and I picked the school's organization for change. When I was researching it, I found I was looking at values and all sorts of things. I wrote something, and I remember reading those notes out. I was just shaking in my shoes. But anyway, what made me feel good was when Jim asked me for my notes. He wasn't there [because of illness], but he read them; and it was brought to my attention that he thought they were bloody good. I had gone into it thinking, "Oh, what a load of rubbish. We were going to put on a show for the visitors." But in hindsight, I can say for me that was a very important Teacher-Only Day.

We grew up in a very strict Samoan way and always found it hard to remember that we didn't do this, and we didn't do that, outside. Like, even in the staff room. I *finally* learnt to have eye contact, coming to this school. That was the most difficult thing. We were always taught you must show respect, and right up to training college days, it was a nightmare. But I finally mastered it by coming here, because I had the support. It didn't happen overnight. The first time I presented my curriculum resources, I presented this way [looking away from the group]. And by the time I put the book down, I was *bawling*. They were all sitting there, and one person just cracked a joke and said, "Have a good cry and then get going." And over an 18-month period, I've got a lot better.

If I hadn't gone there, I don't think I would be fluent in Maori now, which is a real *gift*. When I went to Richmond Road, I was starting to look around, to look for my taha Maori [the Maori side of life], because I had really lived as a brown Pakeha most of my life. It was just the right place for me, because I felt being a Maori was a good thing there. I was like the children; I learnt to value what I had. Then after I came back [from the Maori language course in Wellington], Jim started the bilingual class. That year, teaching the children, I really became fluent—just having to speak in

Maori, and not a word of anything else, from 9 to 10:30—
the language all sort of came together. I really think that's
the most valuable thing that *I* got from Richmond Road.

It's taken a long time, but for me—like many people
before—I think of Richmond Road now as my
turangawaiwai [a place to stand]. It's the place, and what
it represents to me, in my mind and my heart. I left Fiji
with a chip on my shoulder, and I had nothing to do with
Fijian people for 10 years. It's only by being involved with
the philosophy here: We're constantly telling people not to
be sucked up in the system that says you have to speak English and be like an English person before you succeed.
And I realized that here *I* was, telling them to do these
things, and *I* wasn't even doing them myself. I had never
spoken to *my* children in Fijian. That was a big discovery to
me. I felt good about myself before, but as a *New Zealand*
person. Whereas now, because of the experiences that I had
here, I feel totally different.

In a community as ethically mixed as Richmond Road, ways to
learn are not always obvious. One teacher, used to learning by asking
questions, remembered a time when questions about a culturally sensitive situation went unanswered. Another teacher spoke, as if in answer,
about the importance—and yet the difficulties—of learning:

For me, the *most* important thing is that it [Richmond
Road] really is a place for (pause) all sorts of people. I'm
not just talking about children. I'm talking about people in
teaching; I'm talking about community. But along with that
goes a real responsibility to learn. And when I say *learn*, I
mean step back and not always want control, not want to
be the powerful one. What happens with teachers—we've
been trained to think that we're knowledgeable people, that
we should control situations and always contribute and always participate and take the lead. There are people who
may *lead* things who may not have the qualifications that
we have as teachers. But to *learn*, there are times when you
can't contribute, when you can't participate—because listening to other people and having their experience *first* is
more of a learning situation.

This philosophy of deferring to, and learning from, the authentic knowledge of others applies throughout the Richmond Road community. As one teacher suggested, collaborative relationships among teachers are a model for the children: "I think that's why the children work together here, because they can *see* us working together."

"IT'S A HIGHLY ORGANIZED SCHOOL"

In contrast to the isolation of teachers in single-cell-classroom schools, Richmond Road teachers work in a setting of intense collectivity. Children and staff interact in complex organizational "systems," as they are always referred to: vertical/family groupings of children; nonhierarchical relationships among the staff; curriculum materials that are created by teacher teams at the school and rotate around the school for use by all; and monitoring systems for continuous updating of information on children's progress. They are interrelated, although described separately here.

Vertical Groupings of Children

When Jim Laughton came to Richmond Road in 1972, the school was organized in the usual single-cell classrooms. Over the years, he changed the organization to vertical groups, on the model of the family and the nongraded country school. These are called *ropu* (group) to keep the term *whanau* (extended family) for the school as a whole. The change was gradual, as architectural renovations and teacher acceptance permitted. Now there are four *ropu* in "shared spaces" (SS), and one includes the Samoan bilingual group.

Two *ropu* are still in separate "teaching spaces" (TS): the Maori bilingual *ropu* and the ESL language unit for non-English-speaking newcomers to New Zealand. (The latter is always referred to within the school as "TS 15 and 16" to avoid a possibly stigmatizing label.) Each *ropu* has the entire age range, new entrants (5-year-olds) through Standard 4 (11-year-olds). Also part of the school, although with separate funding, are the Maori and Samoan immersion language preschools: *Te Kohanga Reo* and *A'oga Fa'a Samoa* (the Maori and Samoan language nests).

Children stay in the same *ropu*, with the same teachers, for their entire primary schooling. But within each *ropu*, each teacher has his or her own "home group" of 16 to 20 children. These groups, which still include the full age and achievement range, are re-formed twice a year through a consultation between the principal and each *ropu* staff. The home groups are the basic teaching groups for part of each day. And these are the children each teacher monitors regularly and reports on to parents.

> What are the features of the ideal family? Nurture, and love, and support, and accepting the good and bad things about our brothers and sisters and mothers and fathers. Jim said there are many things from the family that can't be replicated in the school; but there are many things that can be. That was his urgent drive: to see what *could* be replicated. Out of this arose peer tutoring, and the wide spread of babies with big kids, the one caring for the other, nurturing and disciplining.

> I like vertical grouping; I think it's excellent. I would *not* like ever to go back to a straight class. I like the way the children can fit in. I think of Maori in particular. In a regular school, they start school as 5-year olds, probably with no preschool education. So, straightaway, they're on a sort of back foot, compared with all the others. Whereas here, they could gain confidence. They fitted in perhaps way down here. But then in their own time, they could work up, without this feeling of always not making it. For me that was great—not only for Maori children, but for *all* children.

> [This way of organizing a school] is the way for me. I come from the islands, and I spent my primary school there. It had that closeness, and open spaces. We haven't got spaces like single cells. Plus my family background too: I was told by my family to look after little kids. It's just natural for me to like the atmosphere here, once I've understood and feel more confident. As Jim said, it's no different from when you've got a country school class. Most people *love* country schools. It's one of the best teaching experiences most people have. People who've attended country schools have always enjoyed them too. I think in a lot of ways it takes pressure off the teacher too, because you're able to do a bit of pairing to teach younger children. You can't help 20 children all at the same time, you know. I like the way the kids are grouped, that there is no pressure on

them, in terms of grading—in terms of kids having to be in low groups or high groups, particularly in reading and math.

It makes the teacher realize that "I'm going to have this child for quite some time!" The teacher has to keep on her toes and watch the development of each child. We do a lot of paired situations—like paired reading, paired maths, and paired writing—where the child, whoever has the knowledge, has the chance to *be* a teacher.

As positively as teachers described the vertical grouping—as a structure for their work as teachers as well as for children's learning—some remembered how hard it had been to adjust to in the beginning; and how Jim had supported them as they are expected to support children:

When I first started working with different levels of children, I just thought that I couldn't fit in. "Oh, no! I don't belong." I was feeling quite down about it. I talked to Jim—I think we were talking two *hours*—and he said, "Look, things like that don't happen overnight. Take it one step at a time. We're right here beside you. Don't expect to be the same as everyone else who's been here a *long* time. You settle in at your *own* pace. As long as you put your heart and soul into things and just *do* it, things will work out." [Now] I wouldn't leave here, not unless I *had* to, not unless somebody *pushed* me out.

Nonhierarchical, Provisional Authority

Several teachers mentioned the important contrast between ascribed and provisional authority. A principal or senior teacher has ascribed, or formal, authority by virtue of the role. But anyone can have provisional authority by virtue of greater or more authentic knowledge on a particular topic at a particular moment. Jim Laughton clearly had both.

The antihierarchical notion of "provisional authority" has wide applicability throughout Richmond Road:

Whoever has knowledge teaches. Sometimes this would be a teacher; other times it can be a child; other times it can be a parent from the community. I particularly like that. Although we have a principal, assistant principal, senior teachers, and then we ordinary plebs, it has never really worked that way. It's always been a case of who has the greater knowledge. My strength was in social studies, and particularly in the early days I helped strongly in that area.

It's a school where, if you want to, they allow you to come forward and utilize their strengths—like art, for instance, is something that I've always been interested in. Even though I'm just—not *just*—even though I'm a scale-A teacher [the lowest step on the certified teacher ladder], I have as much power and influence as any senior teacher.

The major responsibility of senior teachers is that we have to go to a meeting on a Monday. And if something goes wrong in your area or reports are not in on time—you're in the can. Otherwise we all share responsibilities—scale-A teachers, the language assistant. Look at the DPs [deputy principals]: they do exactly the same work we do; they're presenting their resources; they're on the curriculum areas. Otherwise, it ends up more like a business. You have your chairman, your manager, and the workers. And it goes against what you're teaching. You're trying to teach the kids equality; everybody does the same work load. So it works well. [But there is a difference:] To the kids, we say, in simple terms, "Do your best." To the teachers, "You're going to *make* these resources; you're going to do them *this* way; they're going to be done by this *date*." So, in a way, we're told what to do, and I think we should be too.

The extent of this nonhierarchical principle among the staff is seen dramatically in the work of the *kiarahi reo*, the "language leader" (translation) or "language assistant" (formal title in the New Zealand system). He's the one member of the teaching staff who has had no formal professional training, and yet he functions at Richmond Road as a full teacher by virtue of on-the-job training via released time to observe other teachers, staff meeting discussions, and the general help that's always available from colleagues.

I asked him whether he was glad that Jim had insisted that he take on full teaching responsibilities. "In the short term I was cursing. But in the long term, I'm glad. I know the stuff now. And it's helped make the rest of the staff accept me, I suppose." As Jim had explained to him later, his insistence on a full teaching role was also based on the benefits of professional knowledge for a young Maori adult, should he want later to acquire formal credentials. "He was being mean to help me, really."

In different ways, the principle extends to the caretaker too (whom I was reminded to be sure to include in my interviews).

> When Jim was alive, we used to talk sometimes—about the school and the kids and the staff and everybody in the community. He always used to say, "You don't have to feel low because you're only a caretaker. In a school like this, whether you're a caretaker or cleaner or staff or whatever, principal or deputy principal, you're all the same." I think that's one of the most important things about Richmond Road; you don't just work *as* a caretaker; you have to get involved with the staff and the kids.

The caretaker said that he joins in trips, welcomes visiting groups, and coaches rugby and other sports. Others added to this description the deep mutual respect between him and the children, and how often he speaks for the school on formal occasions. At Jim's *tangi* (his funeral, which was held at the school), it was the caretaker who gave the final farewell for the school before the coffin was taken to the cemetery.

The Development of Curriculum

For work on curriculum development, teachers are organized into curriculum groups that deliberately cut across the *ropu* teaching teams. The most extensive work is making "focus resources" for social studies twice each year. The staff is divided into five teams—led (in June 1989) by the two associate principals, two scale-A teachers, and one acting senior teacher. The schoolwide topic follows from a multi-year plan that ensures inclusion in the curriculum of all ethnic groups in the school community; subtopics for each team are agreed on in staff meeting discussions.

During the first half of the 1989 school year, the teams were making materials on people from the Cook Islands and Buddhist groups from southeast Asia, both at home and as immigrants or refugees in New Zealand, for use during the second half of the year. Then, during the second half, materials on a Maori topic will be developed for the first term of 1990. Every year, the first term focus involves some aspect of Maori culture—one indication of the special status it has in multicultural Richmond Road (and arguably should have in New Zealand generally—see Irwin [1989]).

Because 1990 will be the 150th anniversary of the Treaty of Waitangi between Maori chiefs and representatives of the British crown, the group decided that would be the focus:

> a consideration of the rights (and obligations) of firstly the
> two groups party to the signing of the treaty, and by impli-
> cation the wider aspects of rights (and obligations) of all
> groups of people living in New Zealand today.

Whatever the topic, each team must make materials on 10 reading levels and for use in four learning modes:

- *Superior/inferior*—where one person, whether teacher or child, has special knowledge or competence and conveys it to others, as in reading a book to a group
- *Cooperative*—where all members of the group share the same information and work together to complete a task, such as a mural
- *Collaborative*—where each member has access to different information, and the pair or small group must achieve shared understanding through negotiation
- *Independent*—where a child works alone at his or her own level and speed

Each teacher is responsible for making at least 18 different items. At the end of the preparation period, each team presents their materials to colleagues during a staff meeting. Once in use, the materials rotate through the school, staying in each *ropu* area for four weeks.

Reading and math materials are also organized, but in ways that require only maintenance and occasional additions rather than continual creation. "Box books" contain books at all reading levels from 5 to 11 years; they rotate through the school, a fortnight in each *ropu.* "Fluency kits" have high-interest books at the lower reading levels and stay in the rooms. (In addition, there is a much-used school library, and a teacher–librarian.)

Math materials are also provided in two categories: "Topic math" (into which materials from the national mathematics curriculum have been redistributed) were organized by the math curriculum group into topics such as "movement" and "symmetry" but are undifferentiated by level; they rotate around the school every two weeks. "Number math" kits were made by the entire staff. They are organized by competency levels and stay in each room.

Curriculum teams, which teachers serve on according to their interests and expertise, supervise these materials and provide leadership in the school and support to individual colleagues in other areas, such as art and sports.

The primary function of all these curriculum systems is to resource children's learning. But because they each are organized on a schoolwide basis, with the participation of the whole teaching staff, they produce an unusual coherence and consistency across the school. "You can go to another room and just take up what they're doing. I can go into the Samoan bilingual unit and assume that we can still do the same—except that I can't speak Samoan. And they could come into *my* unit the same way." This also contributes to the remarkable degree of solidarity among the teachers; it's easy to request and give help because basic materials and expectations are the same for all.

Monitoring Children's Progress

Finally, there are the systems for monitoring individual children's progress, making sure that all children grow in their "personal standards of excellence," in the words of one of the charter documents for the national school reorganization. Each Richmond Road teacher is expected to monitor, on the average, three children each week from his or her home group and record the results of schoolwide forms. The monitoring includes running records in reading, observations during maths, and taking time to reflect on the child's development as a whole. Regular training and retraining in both observing and recording takes place in staff meetings.

Some of these monitoring systems, notably the running records for keeping track of children's progress in reading (Clay, 1985) are a feature of New Zealand primary education generally. At Richmond Road they are an important part of the philosophy of noncompetitiveness and of belief in the potentiality of each individual child.

> Jim believed all people can go *somewhere.* When children leave this school, he hasn't put expectations on them that they would disappoint him with. The only time Jim says you will ever *fail* is somebody saying, "This is the benchmark that makes you a success or failure." And you have to have

failure as soon as you say, "Well, at age 7, you've got to be here; at 10 you've got to be here." We don't have that. And it doesn't happen.

I couldn't turn to you and say, "Look, Johnny is Standard 3." I couldn't tell you how old that child is. But I can tell you exactly where he is working in math and where he's working in reading. And that's what's important for the child. And not, "He's stupid; he can't do his alphabet" sort of thing. For me, that's one of the most important things about this place.

More attention is devoted [now than some years ago] to helping children step by step with their reading and their math, and the children are quite aware that the teachers monitor this regularly. I don't think the children *mind* it; in fact, they quite enjoy being monitored. And there doesn't seem to be any fear or worry about it. The children are aware that the teachers are helping them and watching their progress, and are pleased because of that.

I think children are [challenged to do as well as they can]. If they see other children around, "Oh, man, he's going up! Can I get tested now, Miss?" I'll test one today and the kid might go up.

"Oh, I've gone up a level."

"What level are you on?"

"Level 6."

"Is that all? I'm on level such-and-such."

And I blow them up. I say, "Yeah, that's cause you're *there*. She's not ready for that yet." And the kid goes, "Oh, OK."

The levels children are working on in reading and math are public knowledge, displayed on a wall chart in each classroom. But the purpose and meaning of these displays is entirely different from, really the opposite of, what such displays would signify in many other countries (as Jim was surprised to learn when he talked about Richmond Road at the International Association of Applied Linguistics in Sydney in August 1987). At Richmond Road, the public information on individual achievement is not used competitively or threateningly. Instead, it reports who can be turned to for help, and who has the responsibility to provide it.

For example, resource materials are marked for the reading level needed to do the activity. If children pick an activity at a reading level higher than their own, they can turn to the wall chart to find a classmate who can help. A fundamental Richmond Road principle is that knowledge is power and must be shared. So greater knowledge brings not higher status but increased responsibility to others, among the children as among the staff.

Richmond Road is known, and rightly so, for empowering minority students, teachers, and parents. I realized in the course of these conversations that it is also contributing toward a complementary task essential in both our countries: creating structures in which those who have power now are expected to share it in various forms of partnerships.

This does not always happen easily. One teacher described how hard it sometimes is to get competent, articulate children who are used to being leaders to "tone down" and learn from their peers. In education generally, this challenge has been termed by two Americans with experience in liberation theology movements in South America "pedagogies for the nonpoor."

"THE POINT OF DUAL IMMERSION IS TO OFFER THAT VARIETY"

Richmond Road includes two dual immersion bilingual units that now provide continuous bilingual education for graduates of the Maori and Samoan preschools. The Maori-English class was set up first and has now expanded into a separate *ropu* that is still divided between two teaching spaces. The Samoan-English class is newer and smaller and is a part of SS3. Any parent may choose one of the bilingual units for their child, and no child is placed there without parental choice.

Both units are based on Jim's dual immersion philosophy and on the basic timetables that he established: during half of each morning and every other afternoon, the teachers speak only Maori or Samoan, and children are encouraged to respond in the same language.

All of the teachers expressed commitment to the dual immersion principle. But some raised questions, as I would, about the wisdom of child language choice, once a family has decided to place the child in one of the bilingual units.

Jim and I used to have arguments about the Maori bilingual unit, about him letting *other* groups in, other ethnic groups. We didn't have the resources, teaching resources— that was my argument. At one stage we had 80 kids, and the resources were so spread out that not much Maori was getting into them. But I never won. He said, "No, that's not our philosophy. We're not excluding anyone."

The bilingual unit works on a *choice* basis. Parents have the option of putting their children into the bilingual unit. In the morning I speak only Samoan, and the children have the choice. They're encouraged to speak Samoan. The fluent ones do, and the little ones sort of copy. When I first came in, Jim said, "The parents do not *have* to put the children in, and the children do not *have* to try and make a sentence in Samoan." He said, "*You* have that responsibility, because you have that expertise, but the children don't. The most *important* idea is their identity, and to value what they've got." At first, I thought, "Well, now that's a bit silly. Shouldn't you say to them, 'Try it out'?" But when he put it like that: "Isn't it important to make them *feel* comfortable with who they are? Language is important for participating. But you can *be* that person in other ways, by believing in the values that they have, and participating in other ways." It really does work, and I've got a totally different outlook now.

From a professional point of view, I *like* the fact that children are exposed to *good* Maori and *good* English. When I'm working in both languages, there is an overlap. The children see that overlap, and I actually think that's good. I think the children ought to see me struggling with mathematical concepts that are *essentially* Western, struggling to find a concept similar to that in Maori. That struggle is a sign to *me* that our language is growing. For children to see that, I value that. Because then they'll take up the challenge themselves to fit the language to a new environment. I'd like my children to come to this school. The *best* thing about the Maori bilingual unit is that the quality of time, of resources, and of personnel is excellent. It's excellent—in both English and Maori.

I actually thought it was very difficult to teach children Maori in a dual immersion, because you can't do justice to the one that you wanted them to learn *most*, which for me was Maori. So I went to see Jim. I said, "I can't see the point of this dual immersion." He said, "The point of dual immersion was that if you put children into just one area, one language, then you forget about all the good things that other as to offer." He said to me, "How many books are written for children in Maori that are as rich as the literature in English? Sure, they might read those afterwards, after school. But this is the point of school: to offer that variety." I thought about it for *months*, not just a day or two, and I believe it now. You spend so much time looking for material that isn't there. Your objects are there. You've got your math equipment, and you've got things outside. But you haven't got the written documents. . . .

I know Jim said, "Don't force them to speak Maori." But I couldn't hear what they were saying, and I didn't know how to gauge their success. So I made it a rule in *my* area that "When it's Maori time, then you speak Maori. If you don't know a word, use whatever word—make it up, or use an English word—that's fine by me." And we make exceptions, like for new entrants, if they've not been in the *Kohanga Reo*. We introduce it slowly, and they just look and follow.

Of course it is true, as the second teacher says, that identity and values are separable from language competence. Jim himself exemplified that separation: He firmly identified himself as a Maori and yet did not speak the language because he had grown up in an era when Maori parents were convinced that speaking English was the way to success for their children. Yet that personal biography makes me wonder if his recommendation about child language choice in the bilingual program might have reflected his own personal situation more than any theory or research on language learning and language loss. (On every other language issue, his knowledge was very sophisticated—dating, I now realize, to his year in the ESL Diploma course at Victoria University in 1976.)

In practical terms, there may seem a fine line between encouraging children to speak the non-English language but giving them the choice, versus establishing a firm expectation that at certain times of the day "we all speak only Maori" or "only Samoan." Experience in other countries suggests that, especially for languages that have low status in society, the latter is what "immersion" should mean. Such languages need all the support they can get to avoid being swamped—

in New Zealand as in the United States—by English. This is even more true for Maori than for Samoan, because of more limited opportunities to hear and speak it outside school.

"THE PARENTS HAVE A PLACE HERE TOO; THE DOOR'S ALWAYS OPEN"

After the last Teacher-Only Day before Jim's death, when the staff talked about the school to the group of Americans led by Don Holdaway, the parents hosted a *hangi* (traditional feast) for staff and visitors. American Mary Snow remembered: "At the end of a *long* day, parents began to drift in, and children who lived in the neighborhood began to drift in; and it turned into a feast, and dancing. Parents were teaching American teachers how to dance! It was *very* clear that they felt much at home in that great room."

This experience is the rule, not the exception. The front door is indeed always open, even on a chilly fall day in June. Many of the teachers described the involvement of "the community"—especially the parents. They come in large numbers to special events: fundraising fairs, concerts, and dances; the school's centennial in 1984; the blessing of the deck for *Te Kohanga Reo*; and for Jim's *tangi*.

Twice a year, they *must* come on a special afternoon and evening to discuss their child's report card with the teacher. No reports go home without discussion. During trip week at the end of the year, family members are welcome to go along with their children. They stop in individually at other times—to contribute to a social studies discussion, for example, or just to chat.

> It's surprising how many of the parents you get to recognize, how many of the parents know quite a lot of the teachers, how much personal interaction goes on. I'm sure if you talked to teachers, there wouldn't be many of the children's parents that they don't know. Just in this area alone [one of the *ropu*], we'll have 4 to 5 parents wandering in and out during the day, or after school, just for an impromptu chat about their children. The door's always open. It's that feeling that parents *can* come in, and parents *can* ask why certain things are happening. And the report system here, where parents have to come into the school to get the reports: It makes the parents feel involved,

that their input is valuable [instead of] a them-and-us situation with the child in between.

When I was a child, my mother never came near the school, because she felt she didn't have a place in it. Here people come and feel they're *helping*, and I think that's what's important—that everybody's got something they can *do* for the school. If parents and children feel that school is a special place for them, then the child benefits from this liaison. When you, as a teacher, have the support of the parents who feel good about the place, then there's nothing that can't be done for that child. That's special about Richmond Road. And, of course, it's happening for *each* ethnic group.

"PEOPLE WHO WANT TO LEARN OFFER YOU HEAPS"

The solidarity of relationships among teachers and the unanimity of their views raises the question of how a staff gets that way. Many kinds of inservice education take place within the school. But what about the selection, or self-selection, of new staff? Self-selection certainly plays a part, because Richmond Road is known—through visits to the school and through presentations by members of the staff at workshops and conferences. But what about selection?

I asked the teachers what qualities they would look for, if they had the power to help select among applicants for a position at the school. Part of the answer would be specific to the particular opening at the time, so that each appointment increases the diversity within the staff group:

For example, if in that room there, you had a male teacher of 50 or so, then one of the first things I would be looking for would be a female teacher of about 20.

Certainly, if it's somebody who brings a different viewpoint—either through ethnicity or gender or anything else—that's good, not bad. The more differences we've got, the better. If it's somebody who will add to our adult community something we're lacking—for instance, we don't have ready access to Tongan teachers—and everything else was equivalent, then I would choose the one who would give us that extra dimension.

Beyond that, the important criteria mentioned are not knowledge but attitudes:

> A person who's prepared to work with *other* people; who respects other peoples' views; who respects other peoples' ways, other languages, other cultures. A person who's not set in their ways. You have to be prepared to take responsibility for things. It's not a school where you can sit back and let everybody else do the work. And that's good.

> [In answer to a question about why some teachers didn't work out and left] People who were not prepared to share, say, the giving *up* of some of their authority [the ascribed authority of formal roles]. I remember one STJC [senior teacher junior class] who got released from the two-year clause and left; she found the job confusing because there were no clearly identified roles, or boundaries.

> I would write off—it's easier to start at that end—anybody who came in here and straightaway said, "Right. Here's what I'm good at." Basically, I'd hire a person who said, "I want to come because I want to learn." People who want to learn offer you *heaps*.

An attitude of wanting to learn is essential at Richmond Road in part because so many of the "systems" are different from most schools and have to be learned on the job. And it is essential on a deeper level because of the importance of an attitude of humility, of listening as much as contributing, of giving up the control that may seem inherent in the usual role of "teacher."

Selection on this criterion works because of the help that is available: "The first year is hard. But there's always support. If you're puzzled, or you're stuck, anyone, *anyone*, will drop what they're doing and help you out with it. That's the brilliant thing about this place."

A few teachers added that teachers "have to be prepared to work very hard." Part of the extra load comes from the conditions of work within the school: "It's tiring working here. The expectations on you are heightened by peer group pressure. Because everything you do at this school isn't individual; it's actually as a member of a team. 'Don't let the side down' *really* carries a lot of weight here." And part of the extra load is the work done after hours: staying at Tuesday staff meetings regularly until 6:00 o'clock, and making resources outside of school.

But opinions differed on whether, in the long run, this makes teaching at Richmond Road a harder job than at other schools. The hours for staff meetings and resource-making are indeed long. "I guess *our* school has the longest staff meetings of any primary or secondary school in the whole of New Zealand, maybe in the whole world!" Nobody calculated the hours spent making resources twice a year, but between planning meetings and time for individual production, they take hours and hours for everyone. "I find myself staying up till very early hours of the morning to meet those [resource] requirements for the team."

Differences of opinion arise over trade-offs with the time that would be spent in other ways at other schools, especially if a teacher tried individually to plan a curriculum and then prepare materials of equivalently high quality:

> Although it seems a long time, think if you'd prepared that quality of work all by yourself for your class, for weeks, how much time it would—well, it'd be impossible to do that, for the amount of quality you get back. You get a greater range of ideas too, because here the whole staff is contributing.

Some people suggested that the "systems" also help lighten the load by providing clear and consistent expectations throughout the school: "The routines are established. You know exactly what you've got to do. You have freedom within the system, but you can't really fall behind before you'd be caught up and helped."

"WE'RE ABOUT CHANGE, REMEMBER?

In thinking about the future, nobody spoke simply for trying to preserve Richmond Road as it is. Everyone acknowledged that the story of Richmond Road in the 16 years of Jim's leadership has been a story of continuous change and that further change is both inevitable and right. Many expressed the hope that changes would continue to be based on the same underlying philosophy.

> I do have a fear that because Jim is no longer with us, that we're going to stop; and instead of looking forward and moving forward, that we keep looking back. This school's been a moving force in education in Auckland for quite a while. It's got to keep doing that. It's got to keep growing.

Everything's going really well. We just lost Jim, that's all. The thing is—Jim's still here, because of the way things are being maintained and moving on.

I like this school, and I know it's different from other schools. And to keep the school running the way it is at the moment, the structure of it, you need to have somebody who wants to do that. If somebody came in and started to change it, I think that would be a real loss. There'd have to be good reason—a reason that I would understand and go along with. Whatever happens, I just hope that family grouping, plus teachers being encouraged to share their knowledge, and to work together, will carry on.

One thing I'm sure of is that everybody has got this aim: to not let it have been something for nothing. We're about change, remember? But *our* change. We'll change, but *our* change.

As one person put it, since Jim's death the school has demonstrated the capacity to be a "self-sustaining system: when you look around this place, it's all still going on here nine months later. If it were based on a person, a personality, it could have collapsed, easily." Now the task is to help the school become not just self-sustaining but a "self-improving" system, and to figure out what "our change" should be.

Without Jim's guiding vision, decisions about change fall—at least for now—to the collective group. This report is offered as a small contribution to that end.

As I had promised the teachers in the May staff meeting, I asked in each conversation for suggestions for change, or at least for aspects of the school that needed rethinking and rediscussion. Three aspects were each mentioned by several people: how *ropu* teaching schedules could become more flexible, thus making possible some activities that are now hard to fit in; how the resource-making process could be made even more valuable; and how teachers could participate even more in decisions about the school. I cannot say how many people share any of these concerns, only that all were mentioned in more than one conversation.

Schedules and Flexibility

The only thing I don't like about the program is its strict timing.

Possibly the most difficult thing is you haven't got much leeway. If you're doing something great, it's very difficult to continue on because you've got other classes dependent on your changing. That's always been a disadvantage, and it's very hard to get around.

I do feel the timetable has become too rigid. If you're really into a piece of work involving drama, or expression with poetry and prose writing, it's always breaking, and putting away, and coming back to. The afternoons are freer, but the morning programs are very compartmentalized. I think the *main* reason is that we've put such things as sustained silent reading, paired reading, paired writing, topic maths, number math—all have to be scheduled. And although these things are very admirable, I think the adverse effect is that they've made the timetable very rigid.

Any form of school organization involves trade-offs between advantages and disadvantages. Team teaching inevitably involves more firm scheduling than single-cell classrooms. As several teachers mentioned, the resulting predictability of daily life is efficient: children become familiar with the routines, and direction-giving by teachers is minimized. But the rigidity of timetables that several teachers complained about is a resulting disadvantage.

Creative writing, which one person said should be "the number one growth point in the curriculum," was the activity most often mentioned as difficult within the present timetables. More than other school subjects, it's hard to turn on and off according to strict schedules.

Some people created more flexibility for their groups in various ways: by using language-oriented resources during morning language time, doing math through art activities, or occasionally opting out of resource activities to finish a project like a newspaper.

Consider, just as an illuminating contrast, a possible alternative: Each home group could function as a single-cell class—retaining the vertical grouping but allowing each teacher more flexibility in planning the day. Although this would indeed give more flexibility in planning, the costs would escalate: decreasing the opportunities for children to learn from a larger group of their peers and from a more diverse group of teachers, and eliminating some of the need for teachers to work together and learn from each other.

Can ideas for achieving more flexibility be shared among the staff, so that, within each *ropu*, the benefits of team teaching are maximized and the costs reduced?

Focus Resources

Because of the amount of teacher time devoted to making the focus resources, and their importance to the multicultural content of the entire Richmond Road curriculum, it is not surprising that many teachers commented on them. Everyone agreed that they were incredibly beautifully made.

Several people described resource activities with their children. For example:

> At the moment we're looking at the concept of change through looking at fishing and the Kaipara tribe, a coastal tribe. But we've actually gone off on a tangent, because this is the interest of the children, and we've gone more into a study of fish. And because of a Maori student teacher, not only have we been learning about the Kaipara, we're actually learning about this woman's *iwi* [tribe]. She's brought along things that have enriched us through song and dance—not necessarily about the Kaipara people, but to do with fishing.

One teacher felt, from experience as a reliever, that the resources were used well throughout the school. But some teachers, in answer to my question about change, suggested that the resources deserve rethinking:

> Personally, the thing that comes to mind is the resources. It's *very* time-consuming for teachers. We've done it long enough along the same sort of lines, and now we've got to the stage where we're just doing the same resources with different content. There's so much stuff there that the kids don't get full use of it. The kids are tired too, tired of the same activities being reproduced. I'd be more willing to carry on the way things are if I felt that the time I put in, and the understanding that I wanted the kids to get—not only through the resources but from the whole study—that they would be getting that. But I'm not sure that they are.

Sometimes when the resources come to our area, some children don't really do them, because in those resources are the same ideas as the last ones [that is, different content, but the activities are the same]. Plus, after reading the science syllabus, it seems to me that we're not really going deep into the aim of things. We divide those resources into different groups, and we have groups doing conservation, science, health. But we're not really going *deep* into it. The children are not trying to *find* out things, discovering things for themselves. I find it very hard to keep the kids *interested* in the resources. It makes me cry, because I know how much time went *into* them, and some of them are fabulous. The kids, we found, tend to go for the *game*-type stuff, and they weren't necessarily *reading* what was in the games, what you're supposed to be doing. Like "You have to find firewood, so go back three spaces" and then more things about the focus. But they just read "go back three spaces" and not whatever the game is about.

I'd be interested to see if we could do some type of research on the resources work. For example, before they got the resources, "What do you know about Buddhism now?" And go back six weeks later: "What do you know now?" On all levels too. Go to the 5-year old; go to the 7-year old; go to the 10-year old. A lot of time goes in—you saw the resources yesterday (whistles). Beautiful!

It seems to me a lot of energy is going into making things that we can't actually use with kids; that we're taking on ideas that are not really at a kid's level. I think we're taking a university subject and trying to bring it down, rather than taking something basic and trying to widen it. You've got five people's sets of 18 resources, and you've only got four weeks, so there's a hell of a lot of stuff you don't use. The next class might use what you don't. But a lot of it is not for children at the age group we're working with. We almost need a time line: from when they [focus resources] were first brought in—What was the idea behind them? What were they and how were they made?—to looking at them now. I think what's happened is that we've got away from the basics into the intellectualization of them. We should start right back at the beginning and look through to where did it start getting almost out of control.

I think we need more evaluation in our focus resources. I believe a number of changes are necessary there,
and I believe this can only be done through using demo-
cratic principles, where *all* of us are able to discuss such
things.

These thoughtful comments raise important questions:

- What are the most important learnings expected from the resources
  activities—for children? for teachers? Is it learning specific content—about peoples and cultures (like the Maori tribes that settled
  in what is now Auckland; or Kampuchea and Buddhism) or concepts
  like refugees and historical change? Or is it the process of respecting
  others' knowledge and sharing—cooperatively and collaboratively—
  within the child and teacher groups?
- If the kind of monitoring of specific learnings that works so well in
  reading and number math seems inappropriate for social studies, are
  there ways of observing—more like what is done for topic math—that
  could provide information on the effectiveness of the activities?
  Would one only observe during focus resource time, or more generally? For example, several teachers (and Mary Snow) mentioned the
  absence of discipline problems in the classrooms and on the play-
  ground; does the social studies curriculum contribute here?
- And then more practically, is teachers' resource-making time used to
  the best advantage? And can children's use of the materials be made
  even more valuable?

I assume that the focus resources are basic to Richmond Road's
philosophy in many ways. But one teacher's suggestion of rediscussing
the basic purposes may be a useful idea—either in full staff meetings
(as monitoring techniques are periodically reexplained) or first by the
social studies curriculum group that would then present their ideas to
the whole staff. Such rethinking could include some of the writings that
guided Jim's original conception. The goal of such discussions would
not be preservation, but the strongest possible base from which to plan
for change.

Participation in Decision Making

How decisions get made at Richmond Road was discussed in many
of our conversations—in part because of my interest in what seemed a
paradoxical process, and in part because we happened to be talking

during the days in May-June 1989 when the timing of the advertisement for the Richmond Road principalship became a public issue.

One paradox, it seems to me, is a seeming conflict between an ideal of discussion versus what some staff perceive as decisions handed down from the top. Here are contrasting comments:

> I remember Jim always said you talk through things at great length, and you just keep feeding in ideas, keep playing with ideas, keep talking, talking, talking.

> It seems that things that happen at this school are the things that happen according to our Samoan way of life. Anything that happened at home, big or small thing, we always get together and talk it out. That's why I said on that day [the Teacher-Only Day] that this is a *family* too, because what is happening out there in our family is happening in *this* school.

> I think, over the years, decision making has been at the top. It has been discussed with various people who have been considered to have the knowledge about the particular decision. But where I feel we haven't gone far enough is that it hasn't been discussed further down.

Several people expressed appreciation for recent changes toward fuller discussion—for example, about the formation of home groups, and the concepts to be developed through resources about the Treaty of Waitangi—and hoped that trend would continue.

Hearing these comments as a New Englander, I was reminded of the difference between two forms of town governance in my part of the United States: "town meeting," where the entire voting citizenry gathers to debate and decide; and "representative town meeting," where a few are delegated to decide for the whole. In the New England case, the shift to representatives comes with growing size: 200 people can come together in one room and discuss, but 2,000 cannot. At Richmond Road, there seemed general agreement that decision-making power was based not on formal hierarchy or ethnicity, but on special knowledge on a given issue. Although that criterion fits the general school philosophy, when it is not based on public status like "senior teacher" or head of a particular curriculum team, the way is opened to perceptions of private decisions and hidden power.

As another paradox, these complaints about governance can be considered a tribute to Jim rather than criticism. As one of the teachers explained his sometimes "autocratic" leadership, "*Now* his ideas are being seen to be very innovative, and in lots of ways how education should be. But they weren't seen like that ten years ago. And maybe he had these ideas in his head and wanted to get these things *done*." In the process of getting them done, Jim constructed "systems" that have resulted in the high quality professional staff in which everyone expressed pride. It seems natural that members of such a staff should want to have more of a say in what happens from now on.

A FINAL IMAGE: JIM'S TREE

The newly blessed deck of *Te Kohango Reo* was built around an oak tree that Jim had planted years before. He loved the *Kohanga*, especially as it was the last year or so before he died. He often walked over for lunch, or just sat on the deck and watched the children.

And he loved that tree. In the last two weeks before he died, he gave the caretaker special orders to trim the tree and keep it tidy, and trim the deck around its trunk as it grows. At his *tangi* last September, one of the tree's first spring shoots was placed on his coffin.

More than one staff member thought of that tree as Jim. "Now he can look down and see all the roots growing and spreading." "The roots growing and spreading" are Richmond Road's children. They can be Jim's ideas too: spreading by being taken by former Richmond Road teachers to other schools and to other areas of New Zealand life (for example, empowering factory workers in their communications with management, as one former teacher is now doing); and growing deeper in the understanding of those who now can't rely on Jim but have to understand and act for themselves.

Afterword. *Richmond Road was, under Laughton's leadership, a school uniquely designed for particular purposes in a particular community. But the ideas about education that it embodied are more general. One such idea is the importance of a sense of community—values felt, believed, and lived—by students, staff, and parents alike.*

In the United States, schools infused with such a pervasive sense of community are hard to find, especially within the public system. Sheer size plays a part. New Zealand schools are small by our standards: Richmond Road has fewer than 300 students, and that is not atypical. But whether or not small size is necessary, it certainly is not sufficient.

A picture of positive possibilities in the United States is given in Bryk and Lee's (in press) analysis of Catholic high schools, combining a qualitative field study of seven very different schools (single-sex and co-ed, multiethnic and mostly white) with a quantitative survey of a large national sample.

Bryk and Lee find unusually high engagement among both students and staff, and decreased disparity in academic achievement between initially advantaged versus disadvantaged students (in contrast to increased disparity as students go through public schools). Their "lessons" for public education come from analyses of how the Catholic schools achieve such effects, over and above any selectivity of their student bodies.

Prominent among the characteristics singled out is a "caring community." In these Catholic schools, that ethos of caring comes from a religious moral philosophy. But Bryk and Lee see no reason why secular schools can't be based on an equivalently powerful humanistic vision. Richmond Road stands as one positive example of exactly that possibility.

18

◆◆◆

The Case of
the English Syllabus
for Forms 6 and 7

Foreword. This chapter is about the English curriculum in New Zealand secondary schools. As Raymond Williams (1961) reminds us:

> *The content of education, which is subject to great historical variation . . . expresses, . . . both consciously and unconsciously, certain basic elements in the culture, what is thought of as "an education" being in fact a particular selection, a particular set of emphases and omissions. (p. 125)*

The controversy over the New Zealand English syllabus for the oldest secondary school students is one example of a public and political struggle over what that "particular set of emphases and ommissions" should be.

This brief report was written for the journal Educational Perspectives, *published in Hawaii, to be included in a 1992 theme issue on multicultural literacies in the Pacific.*

From 1984 to 1990, New Zealand had its fourth Labour government. In the United States, we heard mostly about its antinuclear foreign policy. Domestically, the government was an unusual combination of an economic policy colloquially called "Rogernomics," to signify a hybrid of its local designer and Reaganomics, and a social policy responsive to demands for honoring the Treaty of Waitangi (1840) by a more equal partnership between the dominant Pakeha (European) majority and the indigenous Maori *tangata whenua* ("people of the land"), who are one-tenth of the population with a single culture and language. (Codd [1991] gives a brief history of curriculum reform during this period.)

Education came to assume a position of unusual importance in this government when Prime Minister David Lange kept the education portfolio for himself after winning reelection in 1987. Under his leadership, a reorganization of educational administration in the entire country was put into effect in October 1989. In the words of one New Zealand researcher:

> In New Zealand social policy, debates about 'race-relations' have recently assumed increasing importance. This was particularly true of the brief period in which Labour was designing and putting into place its restructured system of educational administration—the years between 1987 and the 1990 general elections. (Middleton, 1991, p. 5)

In this restructuring, decision making over appointments, budgets, and programs was decentralized into the hands of newly elected boards of trustees in each individual school. These boards were made up of parents of enrolled pupils, the principal, one or more staff representatives, and (in the case of secondary schools only) a student representative. Each board wrote its own "charter," but within the constraints of an obligatory commitment to "equity."

The charter guidelines contained the statement that "equity objectives" were to "underpin all school activities."

> *These requirements were particularly* strong with respect to gender and biculturalism. With respect to biculturalism, each board of trustees was required to accept 'an obligation to develop policies and practices which reflect New Zealand's dual cultural heritage.' (Middleton, 1991, p. 9)

In October 1990, just one year after the new boards took office, Labour lost a national election to the National party. One month later, the new National minister of education, Lockwood Smith, announced that "equity requirements" in the school charters were to become optional rather than mandatory. Middleton concludes:

The equity clauses in school charters have, at the time of writing (January, 1991), become foci for both local and nation-wide political struggles. . . . The restructuring policies of New Zealand's Fourth Labour Government both localised and intensified educational debates within institutional and private spaces. . . . Formerly sensitive and often 'silenced' debates about race-relations in education were brought into public visibility. (p. 23)

One instance of this enhanced public visibility and debate about the implications of "equity" arose during this period in response to a longstanding process for curriculum change in New Zealand (which, like Hawaii, is a single educational system). In that country, a new syllabus in any subject is formulated by a broadly representative committee that solicits responses to its drafts from the teaching profession and the public. This has been happening over the past five years with a proposed English syllabus for forms 6 and 7, the oldest secondary school students.

THE DEVELOPMENT OF THE SYLLABUS

The original curriculum committee appointed in 1986 by the minister of education included "representatives of the Department, the secondary teaching profession, the universities, the teachers' colleges, the polytechnics, employer and employee organizations, Boards of Governors, the young people themselves, the media and the community" (Department of Education, 1988). Of the 22 persons, three were Maori and one Samoan. After a highly consultative process, the committee issued its report in the form of a draft syllabus (referred to as Draft 4) in August 1988, with a request for responses by June 30, 1989.

This draft was then rewritten within what had been the Department and became the Ministry of Education after the reorganization in October 1989, and Draft 5 was issued by the ministry before the end of that year (Ministry of Education, 1989), with requests for further comments from teachers and other community groups; 150 responses were received, representing 749 people, mostly secondary or tertiary teachers (Rathgen, n.d.).

The ministry then contracted with Elody Rathgen, head of English at Christchurch College of Education and president of the New Zealand Association for the Teaching of English (NZATE), to prepare yet another draft of the syllabus, to be submitted in December 1990.

DIFFERENCES BETWEEN DRAFTS 4 AND 5

My focus here is on differences between draft 4, prepared by the representative curriculum committee, and draft 5, rewritten within the government. Those differences were the subject of a panel presentation by members of the original committee at the International Federation of Teachers of English (IFTE) meeting in Auckland in August 1990, and were clearly of great concern to Maori educators at that conference. The two sections in which the changes were of greatest concern were the Introduction and the section on Language itself.

Changes in the Introduction

The Introductions of both drafts are reproduced at the end of this chapter (Appendix, Drafts 4 and 5), with paragraph numbers added for easier citation. Significant differences in how the curriculum is framed with respect to "equity" will be evident to any reader. Five changes epitomize the rest.

First, Draft 4 begins (1) with an eloquent and personal statement in Maori about the importance of "my language," and two paragraphs later (3) reminds us that both "Maori and English are official languages." Draft 5 begins (1) with statements about the importance of language "within a New Zealand context and the wider world community" and its contribution to "the wider aims of education." Maori is mentioned for the first time in paragraph (9) as one of the "two major traditions [that] have shaped . . . New Zealand language and identity," and no words in Maori are included anywhere in this Introduction.

Second, in Draft 4, the name of the country is introduced first (3) as "Aotearoa" (the Maori name for New Zealand, meaning "land of the long white cloud") and then shifts to "New Zealand." Draft 5 uses "New Zealand" throughout, except for one shift (5) to the increasingly common combined form, "Aotearoa/New Zealand."

Third, paragraph (4) of Draft 4 asserts: "The treaty of Waitangi is a cornerstone for educational policy, including English. We work in partnership but we speak with our own voices." The term *partnership* has become a symbol for Maori demands for equity under the Treaty in all domains of social life. This Introduction uses it again between the sexes (14) and at the end (22) among "students, teachers, families, and the community." Draft 5 does not mention the Treaty, and the word *partnership* refers only to "between the sexes" (14).

Fourth, and most illuminating of all, Draft 4 says (5), "In the past, the Pakeha looked to Britain for language standards and literature." Draft 5 speaks in direct response (7), but with a critical shift in the referent for the pronoun *we* and therefore in the self-identity of the authors of the entire document: "While it is true that in the past we looked to Britain . . ." Whereas "*we* work in partnership" (Draft 4) has an inclusive reference to all New Zealanders, "*we* looked to Britain" (draft 5) can refer only to the Pakeha; no one should claim that the Maori "looked to Britain."

Fifth and last, the Draft 4 Introduction as a whole moves from early statements about the unique language situation in this country at this time to later statements about the general importance of English for personal, vocational, and lifelong growth. Draft 5, in reverse, places earlier emphasis on English as an international language and the universality and timelessness of Shakespeare (6), and only later contextualizes language and language study in New Zealand. Then, having eliminated all mention of partnership under the treaty, Draft 5 ends with a very general sentence about "equity objectives." (Shakespeare appears in the Literature section of both drafts and is the only author so mentioned by name.)

Changes in the Section on Language

Significant changes in the Language section are more easily summarized. Draft 4 states: "The descriptive study of language . . . will include a simple comparison of English and Maori." And "issues relating to language" include "the state and status of the Maori language in New Zealand and the meaning of the Treaty of Waitangi." In Draft 5, an English/Maori comparison is one of "several approaches" to descriptive study; and there is no mention of Maori and the Treaty as issues.

While the Introduction presents a framework and point of view, the later sections, including the one on Language, set down the experiences that students are expected to have and teachers therefore obliged to provide. So, whereas I have spent more space on the Introduction, it is not surprising that the requirement of Maori/English language comparison should have prompted more controversy in New Zealand. In an excellent half-page newspaper article on the 1990 IFTE conference, Peter Calder (1990) (identified as "himself a former English teacher") devotes half his space to the panel on this syllabus and most of that to a discussion of the proposed requirement of a Maori/English language comparison:

[The] draft syllabus raised howls of outrage among educational conservatives for its prescription of a comparative study of English and Maori.

The idea has been widely portrayed as requiring English students to "learn" Maori—although there is no such statement explicit or implicit in the syllabus. Rather the syllabus used a comparative linguistic model to illuminate the study of a native language by reference to another—preferably unrelated—language. . . .

[The syllabus's] critics saw the sinister hand of social engineering in a proposed syllabus that quite simply reflected the most up-to-date research about how language was best taught.

DISCUSSION

What happened in the little over a year between the two drafts to account for these changes? During this period, I was only in New Zealand for three weeks, in June 1989 (for the research reported in Chapter 17). What I could learn then has been supplemented by generous mailings from New Zealand colleagues, but it is still only a partial picture.

Certainly the media played a role. With the exception of a few articles like Calder's that reported accurately and contributed positively to public understanding, many simply broadcast and magnified whatever negative comments Draft 4 elicited. One of the most influential pieces (Du Chateau, 1989) appeared in the June 1989 *Metro*, a glossy magazine published montly in Auckland that seems opportunistically to take any side of any issue that will increase sales.

The article begins innocuously. A full-page picture of one of the members of the Draft 4 committee quotes her as saying,

We've got obligations under the Treaty of Waitangi and we should be using our cultural heritage in the teaching of English. . . . It won't dilute English, it will give it strength. (p. 74)

And on the title page, a senior school inspector in Auckland is also pictured and quoted about the controversy already underway:

One group has grabbed the high moral ground of anti-sexism and anti-racism and run with it, and the other group has taken over the similarly high moral ground of Shakespeare and latin roots. (p. 75)

Then the article's slant and purpose is exposed in its title:

TE ENGLISH?

The big news in education isn't *Tomorrow's Schools* [the blueprint for school reorganization] but the attempt by a little-known committee to alter radically the English curriculum taught in the country's sixth and seventh forms. (p. 75)

"TE ENGLISH" says it all: combining Maori *te* with the name of the most beloved legacy from Britain. As the article says in so many words eight pages later, "the English language is suffering, is being debased." The cause of that crime is the Maori language; its perpetrators the "little-known committee."

Implications of a subversive conspiracy recur throughout the article: identifying the committee as a "small and secretive group of educationists" and describing its work as "changes so radical that they will make the late and now largely lamented 'new maths' look like a stroke of inspiration" and "social engineering on a scale that has never been seen before in this country."

Several committee members are discredited by their associations. The two Maori women members both teach at Auckland Girls Grammar School, "undoubtedly the leader [among Auckland schools] in the politics of biculturalism" and "a hotbed of new ideas." The head of English at Auckland University is identified as husband of the head of the English department at Auckland Girls Grammar and as himself claiming "a Maori great-grandmother."

And the whole effort to institutionalize "Te English" is ominously likened to other "failed educational reforms" like "the new maths . . . and other radical changes introduced in the later 60's and early 70's."

So what are the morals for "multicultural literacies?" First, whatever the final version of this syllabus, in the struggle for equity in New Zealand as I have observed it between my first visit in 1983 and now, progress has been impressive. The work of Maori and Pakeha to "honour the Treaty" can be slowed by the efforts of some politicians and some media commentators, but not stopped.

Second, for both our countries, this controversy is a reminder that—for better and worse—currents of both progress and reaction flow internationally. Positively, the movement for equity in New Zealand has been strengthened by struggles elsewhere, notably, the civil rights movement in the United States and the anti-apartheid movement in South Africa. (The latter became a source of internal radicalization through protests against visits to New Zealand of the South African rugby team in the early 1980s.)

Negatively, at least one newspaper article attack on the syllabus, entitled "A Folly of Shallow Thinking" (Moses, 1990) begins with a quote from Allan Bloom's *The Closing of the American Mind* (1987). Reading it, one wonders whether the term *political correctness* (or just *PC*) has also been imported into the New Zealand debate from the United States.

As Raymond Williams reminds us, education always involves "a selective tradition": "an intentionally selective version of a shaping past and a pre-shaped present, which is then powerfully operative in the process of social and cultural definition and identification" (1977, p. 115). Public discussions over what that selection should be are both inevitable and healthy in a democracy. But, as Gerald Graff points out, different views are not treated equally in the debate: "There's a double standard here: criticizing the status quo is political, while accepting it isn't (quoted in the *New York Times*, December 9, 1990).

A POSTSCRIPT

As of July 1991, this syllabus controversy continues, now as much about the process of curriculum change as about its content. Briefly, Rathgen completed her review of the comments on Draft 5 with the help of a "national reference group of 12 teachers and lecturers throughout the country" (Rathgen, 1991, p. 31) and submitted Draft 6 to the minister. But evidently he was still not satisfied. Rathgen reports:

> In December 1990, the Minister invited a group of people to discuss the completed text of the 1990 *Draft*. The group represented some of those who had been most outspoken in their criticism of the syllabus development. . . . Although I had been responsible for presentation of the 1990 *Draft*, I was not invited to the meeting. . . .
> (M)y main concern is over the huge change the Minister has brought to the process of syllabus development. The New Zealand tradition which has been so successful in the past has been representative of the educational sector, as well as of those beyond it. It has been public, consultative, developmental and accessible to teachers. . . . We need to be cautious of moves which remove these safeguards, and result in a Minister being able to call his selection of "experienced practitioners" together to gain opinions on professional work. (1991, pp. 33-34)

At last report, "in May this year the Minister picked six teachers, very unrepresentative of the profession and totally inexperienced with

syllabus writing, to continue the work" (Rathgen, personal communication, July 12, 1991).

In many discussions of United States curricula today, whether at
the school level or the university, it is implied that those who argue for
"multicultural literacies" are trying to use the schools to impose their
minority views. In the case of the New Zealand syllabus controversy, it
is very clear which side is negotiating democratically through a representative and consultative process, and which side is using governmental power to dictate curriculum in a nation's schools.

APPENDIX

Draft 4:   English syllabus for forms 6 and 7 (1988)

INTRODUCTION

1) Ko taku nui   My greatness
   Taku Whei   My inspiration
   Taku whakatiketike   My elevation
   Ko taku reo   Is my language

2) "Language is fundamental to learning, communication, personal
   and cultural identity, and relationships." (The *Curriculum Review*, p. 12)

3) We live in Aotearoa. We recognize this country is not monocultural
   and monolingual. Maori and English are official languages.

4) The treaty of Waitangi is a cornerstone for educational policy,
   including English. We work in a partnership but we speak with our
   own voices.

5) In the past, the Pakeha looked to Britain for language standards and
   literature. In the present global context, English is a major international language. The cultural influence of the English language,
   spoken and written in other parts of the world, especially in the
   United States and the Pacific, has become increasingly important
   for Maori and Pakeha.

6) Pakeha are evolving a distinctive identity, shaped by their historical
   origins, by the language and culture of the tangata whenua, and by
   the continuing development of the English language overseas.

7) The Maori voice has long been clear and is increasingly heard by
   the Pakeha. But the forces for socio-linguistic change are such that,
   without urgent and active commitment on the part of all New

Zealanders, the voice of the tangata whenua will be lost. If education is to be just and equitable, a bicultural approach is necessary.

8) Both cultures have a rich heritage and vigorous contemporary voice. An English syllabus with a bicultural approach offers the opportunity and challenge to weave together this dual heritage.

9) English programmes should therefore give a central place to the language and literary resources unique to New Zealand. There is a substantial body of literature written in English by New Zealand writers, both men and women, Pakeha and Maori. This writing speaks to New Zealand students as it springs from our cultural roots.

10) The programmes should incorporate Maori language examples and comparisons as well as Maori literature written in English and in translation—thus encouraging a respect and love for the Maori voice as well as the Pakeha.

11) The syllabus in similar ways should aim to foster the other languages and cultures in New Zealand—Pacific and other voices need to be heard.

12) Linguistic diversity represents challenges to English teaching which this syllabus attempts to address. The biggest shift is from seeing linguistic diversity as a problem for English teaching to recognition that it is a normal and desirable state. English programmes which address linguistic diversity will develop students' competence in English and equip them to live in a linguistically diverse community.

13) Ko te kumara te wai-u   As the kumera is mother's milk
    Ko te reo te (wairua) mauri ora! So language is the essence of
                                      being!

14) The voices of women and girls need recognition in a new and equal partnership with those of men and boys.

15) Women's past, women's literature, women's language, women's skills need to be valued. It is important that men and boys respect the values of women, learn from them and adopt a new role in an equal partnership.

16) If education is to be just and equitable, it must be non-sexist. Sexism exists in New Zealand society. This is reflected in language, in much of the literature, and in the different ways girls and boys are treated in schools. Language plays an important part in determining male and female roles. English programmes need to sensitize teachers and students to uses of language which shape negative sex roles and stereotypes, and promote non-sexist uses of language

which affirm the contribution to society of women as well as men. Changes in language will be a necessary part of changes in attitude.

17) A non-sexist perspective should be taken to apply not only to the representation of girls and women in literature but also to the portrayal of boys and men. All New Zealanders need to know and learn from women's literature. In New Zealand we are fortunate to have a particularly strong women's literary tradition, both Maori and Pakeha.

18) Teachers of English have an important role in education and must address these issues, develop their programmes accordingly and create a classroom environment in which the aims of the syllabus can be achieved.

19) A course of English at sixth and seventh form must be flexible and balanced, acknowledge the individual needs and interests of students, their aspirations, their different levels of achievement and the diversity of their social and cultural backgrounds.

20) Programmes in English should promote personal growth; students should learn that through language people can communicate effectively with others, express their feelings, thoughts and ideas lucidly, deepen their understanding, initiate action, order their world.

21) Sixth and seventh form programmes provide the last opportunity for formal study of English for many students. Therefore it is very important that the students be given the opportunity to achieve standards of excellence in all aspects of the English course available to them. It must provide for a quality of learning which enables students to continue to develop their language skills. The course must be wide-ranging enough to accommodate not only the vocational needs but also the lifelong needs of students.

22) "Learning happens when there is an active partnership of students, teachers, families and the community." (*The Curriculum Review*, p. 8)

Draft 5: English syllabus for forms 6 and 7 (1989)

INTRODUCTION

(1) Language is fundamental to learning, communication, personal and cultural identity, and relationships. This syllabus affirms the

vital importance of language for helping students to communicate effectively and develop as people, both within a New Zealand context and the wider world community. People need competence in language in order to participate effectively in society. Language makes a unique contribution to the wider aims of education, which are concerned with promoting the development of students' intellectual, personal, social, and aesthetic qualities.

(2) Sixth and seventh form programmes provide the last opportunity for formal study of English for many students. Therefore, it is important that they be given the opportunity to achieve standards of excellence in all aspects of the English course available to them. The programmes must provide for a quality of learning which enables students to develop their language skills and their individual language strengths and interests.

(3) A programme in English should also enable students to develop their thinking and reasoning, and their ability to discriminate and evaluate material, so that they become independent learners who can operate effectively in the world beyond school. Students should learn that through language people can express their feelings, thoughts, and ideas, deepen their understanding, initiate action, affirm their identity, and order their world.

(4) This syllabus builds on the understandings about language that are central to the statement of aims for English, Forms 3-5, and acknowledges the importance of language and literature in the English curriculum. The term "language" includes verbal, visual, and non-verbal forms of communication. English programmes should therefore encourage the development of students' competence in reading, writing, speaking, listening, the media, drama, and research. The aims of the syllabus provide a framework for the development of students' knowledge, skills, and attitudes in the English curriculum.

(5) English programmes must be wide-ranging enough to accommodate not only vocational needs and further education, but also the lifelong needs of students and the language demands that are placed on them in the wider community. The programmes should encourage an enjoyment and love of language and literature for their own sake, in order to enhance the lives of young people, and to enhance their leisure activities. They should be flexible and enable students to cope with change. In a world that is changing rapidly through the advances of technology and information systems, students need to develop skills in English to function effectively. This syllabus addresses the present and developing needs of

students in Aotearoa/New Zealand—students, who as a group, are increasingly diverse: socially, academically, culturally, and linguistically.

(6) This is a New Zealand English syllabus shaped specifically for the needs of all Form 6 and 7 students in New Zealand. English is an international language. New Zealand students in the senior secondary school need skills and competence in English to provide a means of communicating with other people around the world. In studying literature, students need to read and respond to literature of the past, as well as to contemporary writing. The plays of Shakespeare, for instance, speak powerfully to the students of today because their message is universal and timeless.

(7) While it is true that in the past we looked to Britain for sources of English language and literature, today students also need access to the language and literature of English as it is in every part of the globe.

(8) New Zealanders now have their own distinctive variety of English— New Zealand English. New Zealand students are able to benefit doubly, having access to both the heritage of a unique New Zealand literature and the riches of literature written in English throughout the world.

(9) This country has many cultures. Two major traditions, Maori and British, have shaped the development of our distinctive New Zealand language and identity, and have influenced the literature produced by our writers. Both cultures have a rich heritage from past centuries and a vigorous contemporary voice—an English syllabus with a bicultural approach offers the opportunity and challenge to weave together this dual heritage.

(10) Other languages and cultures have contributed to our development. We live in the Pacific, and, as a Pacific nation, we need to hear Pacific voices from within this country, as well as from the surrounding nations. In addition, our language and culture is being strengthened by interaction with other cultural groups.

(11) English programmes should therefore give an important place to the language and literary resources unique to New Zealand. There is a substantial body of literature written in English by New Zealand writers, both men and women, Pakeha and Maori. This writing speaks to New Zealand students, as it springs from our cultural roots.

(12) Programmes in English should encourage a respect for the Maori voice as well as the Pakeha by including Maori literature, written in English and in translation. Maori language examples and compar-

isons could be used to illustrate how New Zealand English has evolved its unique linguistic identity.

(13) In New Zealand we have a particularly strong womens' literary tradition, both Maori and Pakeha. Women's past, women's literature, women's language, and women's skill need to be valued and respected. This syllabus affirms the voices of women and girls alongside those of men and boys.

(14) Programmes in English, and the resources used in them, should draw upon the experiences, concerns, and attitudes of both genders. Development of an equal partnership between the sexes will require recognition of the voices of girls and women, and fresh approaches within the classroom to ensure that young men and women learn mutual respect.

(15) Language plays an important part in determining male and female roles. English programmes need to alert students to uses of language which shape negative sex roles and stereotypes. Sexism is reflected in language, in much of the literature, and in the different ways students are treated in schools. Courses should promote non-sexist uses of language which affirm the contribution to society of women as well as men. A non-sexist perspective should be taken to apply not only to the representation of girls and women in literature but also to the portrayal of boys and men.

(16) Equity objectives underpin all the aims of this syllabus. Teachers will enhance students' learning and language development by helping to ensure that the English curriculum is non-racist and non-sexist, and by helping to ensure that programmes provide equitable outcomes for students and positive role models for young women and men.

Afterword. *Curriculum controversies continue in the United States too. The advent of 1992, the quincentenary of Columbus's voyage, has stimulated these controversies, as 1990, the 150th anniversary of the Treaty of Waitangi between Maori chiefs and Queen Victoria, did in New Zealand.*

In English, what counts as "literature"? In social studies, what knowledge about which "civilizations" is of most worth? How, in a nation's schools, can we combine due attention to the history and culture of each local community with appreciation for that of peo-

ples more distant? And all the while, how can we create some common subjectivity, some shared contexts in the mind, for our citizenry as a whole?

Whatever one's answer to these questions, Graff's statement quoted in this chapter holds true: defending any status quo is just as "political" as working to change it.

References

Adams, M. J., Anderson, R. C., & Durkin, D. (1978). Beginning reading: Theory and practice. *Language Arts, 55,* 19–25.

Ajemian, G. L. (1991). *Perspectives on the teaching of history from the philosophy of history.* Unpublished doctoral dissertation, Harvard Graduate School of Education, Cambridge, MA.

Allington, R. L. (1980). Teacher interruption in behaviors during primary grade oral reading. *Journal of Educational Psychology, 72,* 371–377.

Anderson, P. S. (1964). *Language skills in elementary education.* New York: Macmillan.

Anderson, R. C., Hiebert, E. H., Scott, J. A., & Wilkinson, I. A. G. (1985). *Becoming a nation of readers.* Washington, DC: National Institute of Education.

Ashton-Warner, S. (1986). *Teacher.* New York: Simon & Schuster. (Original work published 1963)

Atkinson, P. (1985). *Language, structure and reproduction: An introduction to the sociology of Basil Bernstein.* London: Methuen.

Au, K. H. (1979). Using the experience-text-relationship method with minority children. *The Reading Teacher, 32,* 677–679.

Bakhtin, M. (1981). *The dialogic imagination.* Austin: University of Texas Press.

Bakhtin, M. (1986). *Speech genres and other late essays.* Austin: University of Texas Press.

Barnes, D., Britton, J., & Rosen, H. (1969). *Language, the learner and the school.* Baltimore: Penguin.

Bartlett, E. J. (1981). *Learning to write: Some cognitive and linguistic components.* Washington, DC: Center for Applied Linguistics.

Bazerman, C. (1981). What written knowledge does: Three examples of academic discourse. *Philosophy of the Social Sciences, 11,* 361–387.

Beck, I. L., & McKeown, M. G. (1991). Social studies texts are hard to understand: Mediating some of the difficulties. *Language Arts, 68,* 482–490.

Becker, H. S. (1980). *Role and career problems of the Chicago school teacher.* New York: Arno. (Original work published 1951)

Becker, H. S. (1982). *Art worlds.* Berkeley: University of California Press.

Becker, H. S. (1986). *Writing for social scientists: How to start and finish your thesis, book, or article.* Chicago: University of Chicago Press.

Becker, H. S., Gear, B., Hughes, E. C., & Strauss, A. L. (1961). *Boys in white: Student culture in medical school.* Chicago: University of Chicago Press.

Berlak, A., & Berlak, H. (1981). *Dilemmas of schooling: Teaching and social change.* London: Methuen.

Bernstein, B. (1960). Review of *The Lore and language of school children. British Journal of Sociology, 11,* 178-181. (Also in Bernstein, 1971.)

Bernstein, Basil (Ed.) (1971). *Class, codes and control Vol. 1.* London: Routledge and Kegan Paul.

Bissex, G. (1968). *The Harvardization of Michael.* Unpublished term paper, Harvard University, Cambridge, MA.

Bissex, G. (1980). *GNYS at work: A child learns to write and read.* Cambridge, MA: Harvard University Press.

Bloom, A. (1987). *The closing of the American mind: How higher education has failed democracy and impoverished the souls of today's students.* New York: Simon & Schuster.

Bloom, B. (1971). Mastery learning. In J. H. Block (Ed.), *Mastery learning: Theory and practice* (pp. 47-63). New York: Holt, Rinehart & Winston.

Bowerman, M. (1985). What shapes children's grammars? In D. I. Slobin (Ed.), *The crosslinguistic study of language acquisition* (Vol. 2) (pp. 1257-1319). Hillsdale, NJ: Erlbaum.

Brennan, W. J., Jr. (1985, October). *The constitution of the United States: Contemporary ratification.* Paper presented at the Text and Teaching Symposium, Georgetown University, Washington, DC.

Britton, J., Burgess, T., Martin, N., McLeod, A., & Rosen, H. (1975). *The development of writing abilities* (11-18). London: Macmillan.

Brown, R. (1958). *Words and things.* Glencoe, IL: Free Press.

Brown, R. (1973). *A first language: The early stages.* Cambridge, MA: Harvard University Press.

Brown, R. & Ferrara, R. A. (1985). Diagnosing zones of proximal development. In J. V. Wertsch (Ed.), *Culture, communication, and cognition* (pp. 273-305). New York: Cambridge University Press.

Brown, R., & Gilman, A. (1972). The pronouns of power and solidarity. In P. P. Giglioli (Ed.), *Language and social context* (pp. 252-282). Baltimore: Penguin.

Bruner, J. S. (1972). Nature and uses of immaturity. *American Psychologist, 27,* 687-708.

Bruner, J. S. (1985). Vygotsky: A historical and conceptual perspective. In J. V. Wertsch (Ed.), *Culture, communication and cognition* (pp. 21-34). New York: Cambridge University Press.

Bryk, A. S., & Lee, V. E. (in press). *Renewing the common school: Some Catholic lessons.* Cambridge, MA: Harvard University Press.

Burgess, T. (1985). Curriculum process and the role of writing. In M. Chorny (Ed.), *Teacher as learner: Language in the classroom project* (pp. 49-64). Alberta, Canada: University of Calgary.

Burke, K. (1967). *The grammar of motives*. Cleveland: World. (Original work published 1945)

Burke, K. (1973). *Philosophy of literary form*. Berkeley: University of California Press. (Original work published 1941)

Calder, P. (1990, September). It's as simple as anger bluster confusion. *New Zealand Herald*. (Exact date and page number not available)

Calkins, L. (1980). When children want to punctuate: Basic skills belong in context. *Language Arts, 57,* 567-573.

Cambourne, B., & Turbill, J. (1987). *Coping with chaos*. (Australian) Primary English Teaching Association. (Distributed by Heinemann in U.S.A.)

Cardenal, F., & Miller, V. (1981). Nicaragua 1980: The battle of the ABCs. *Harvard Educational Review, 51,* 1-26.

Carnegie Forum on Education and the Economy. (1986). *A nation prepared: Teachers for the 21st century*. New York: Carnegie Corporation.

Carroll, J. B. (1966). Some neglected relationships in reading and language. *Elementary English, 43,* 577-582.

Carter, R. (Ed.). (1990). *Knowledge about language and the curriculum: The LINC reader*. London: Hodder & Stoughton.

Cazden, C. B. (1968). The acquisition of noun and verb inflections. *Child Development, 39,* 433-448.

Cazden, C. B. (1972). *Child language and education*. New York: Holt, Rinehart, & Winston.

Cazden, C. B. (1973a). Problems for education: Language as curriculum content and learning environment. In E. Haugen & M. Bloomfield (Eds.), *Language as a human problem* (pp. 137-150). New York: Norton.

Cazden, C. B. (1973b). *Watching children watch* The Electric Company: *An observational study in classrooms*. Final report to Children's Television Workshop.

Cazden, C. B. (1975a). Hypercorrection in test responses. *Theory into Practice, 14,* 343-346.

Cazden, C. B. (1975b). Concentrated versus contrived encounters: Suggestions for language assessment in early childhood education. *The Urban Review, 8,* 28-34. [Longer version in A. Davies (Ed.), *Language and learning in early childhood* (pp. 40-54). London: Heinemann, 1977.]

Cazden, C. B. (1979). Peekaboo as an instructional model: Discourse development at school and at home. In *Papers and reports on child language development*, No. 17 (pp. 1-29). Stanford, CA: Stanford University, Department of Linguistics. [Revised version in B. Bain (Ed.), *The sociogenesis of language and human conduct: A multi-disciplinary book of readings* (pp. 330-358). New York: Plenum, 1983.]

Cazden, C. B. (1983). Can ethnographic research go beyond the status quo? *Anthropology and Education Quarterly, 14,* 33-41.

Cazden, C. B. (1986). Classroom discourse. In M. E. Wittrock (Ed.), *Handbook of research on teaching* (3rd ed.) (pp. 432-463). New York: Macmillan.

Cazden, C. B. (1988a). *Classroom discourse: The language of teaching and learning.* Portsmouth, NH: Heinemann.

Cazden, C. B. (1988b). *Interactions between Maori children and Pakeha teachers: Observations of an American visitor.* Auckland, New Zealand: Auckland Reading Association.

Cazden, C. B. (1988c). Environmental assistance revisited: Variation and functional equivalence. In F. Kessel (Ed.), *The development of language and language researchers* (pp. 281-297). Hillsdale, NJ: Erlbaum.

Cazden, C. B. (1992). Performing expository texts in the foreign language classroom. In C. Kramsch & S. McConnell-Ginet (Eds.), *Text and context: Cross-disciplinary perspectives on language study* (pp. 67-78). Lexington, MA: D. C. Heath.

Cazden, C. B., & Bartlett, E. J. (1973). Review of *Talk Reform: Explorations in language for infant school children. Language in Society, 2,* 147-160.

Cazden, C. B., John, V. P., & Hymes, D. (Eds.). (1972). *Functions of language in the classroom.* New York: Teachers College Press.

Chall, J. S. (1979). The great debate: Ten years later, with a modest proposal for reading stages. In L. B. Resnick & P. A. Weaver (Eds.), *Theory and practice of early reading* (Vol. 1) (pp. 29-55). Hillsdale, NJ: Erlbaum.

Chall, J. S. (1982). Rich and sharp memories of reading [Commentary on *Hunger of memory*]. *Change, 36,* 39-40.

Children's Television Workshop. (1971). *The electric company.* New York: Author.

Chomsky, C. (1972). Stages in language development and reading exposure. *Harvard Educational Review, 42,* 1-33.

Chomsky, C., & Schwartz, J. L. (1983). *M__ss__ng L__nks* [Computer program]. Pleasantville, NY: Sunburst Communications.

Chukovsky, K. (1963). *From two to five.* Berkeley: University of California Press.

Clark, K., & Holquist, M. (1984). *Mikhail Bakhtin.* Cambridge, MA: Harvard University Press.

Clay, M. M. (1983). Getting a theory of writing. In B. Kroll & C. G. Wells (Eds.), *Exploration in the development of writing* (pp. 259-284). London: Wiley.

Clay, M. M. (1985a). *The early detection of reading difficulties* (3rd ed.). Portsmouth, NH: Heinemann.

Clay, M. M. (1985b). Engaging with the school system: A study of interactions in New Entrant classrooms. *New Zealand Journal of Educational Studies, 20*(1), 20-38.

Clay, M. M. (1987). Learning to be learning disabled. *New Zealand Journal of Educational Studies, 22,* 155-173.

Clay, M. M. (1991). *Becoming literate: The construction of inner control.* Portsmouth, NH: Heinemann.

Clay, M. M., & Watson, B. (1982). *The success of Maori children in the Reading Recovery programme.* Report prepared on research contract for the Director-General of Education, Department of Education, Wellington, New Zealand.

Codd, J. (1991). Curriculum reform in New Zealand. *Journal of Curriculum Studies, 23*, 177–180.

Cohen, E. G. (1986). *Designing group-work strategies for the heterogeneous classroom*. New York: Teachers College Press.

Coles, R. (1973). *The old ones of New Mexico*. Alburquerque: University of New Mexico Press.

Coles, R. (1975, March 6). The politics of middle-class children. *The New York Review*, pp. 13–16.

Cordeiro, P. (1988). Children's punctuation: An analysis of errors in period placement. *Research in the Teaching of English, 22*, 62–74.

Cronnell, B. (1980). *Punctuation and capitalization: A review of the literature* (Technical Note 2-80/27 [ED 208404]). Los Alamitos, CA: Southwest Regional Laboratory.

Culler, J. (1976). Presuppositions and intertextuality. *Modern Language Notes, 91*, 1380–1396.

Davidson, J. L. (1988). *Counterpoint and beyond: A response to* Becoming a Nation of Readers. Urbana, IL: National Council of Teachers of English.

Dear, P. (1985). Totius in verba: Rhetoric and authority in the early Royal Society. *ISIS, 76*, 145–161.

DeFord, D. E., Lyons, C. A., & Pinnell, G. S. (1991). *Bridges to literacy: Learning from Reading Recovery*. Portsmouth, NH: Heinemann.

DeLoache, J. S., & Brown, A. L. 1979). Looking for Big Bird: Studies of memory in very young children. *The Quarterly Newsletter of the Laboratory of Comparative Human Cognition, 1*(4), 53–57.

Delpit, L. (1986). Skills and other dilemmas of a progressive black educator. *Harvard Educational Review, 56*, 379–385.

Delpit, L. (1988). The silenced dialogue: Power and pedagogy in educating other people's children. *Harvard Educational Review, 58*, 280–298.

Demuth, K. (1989). Maturation and the acquisition of the Sesotho passive. *Language, 65*, 56–80.

Department of Education (1988). *Forms 6 and 7 English syllabus* (Draft). Wellington, New Zealand: Author.

Derewianka, B. (1991). *Exploring how texts work*. (Australian) Primary English Teaching Association. (Distributed by Heinemann in U.S.A.)

de Villiers, P. A., & de Villiers, J. G. (1972). Early judgments of semantic and syntactic acceptability by children. *Journal of Psycholinguistic Research, 1*, 299–310.

Diamondstone, J. (1990). Doing the do at a tete a tete: Struggles over academic discourse. Technical Report No. 4A. Newton, Massachusetts: The Literacies Institute. Revised version in N. A. Branscombe, D. Goswami, & J. Schwartz (Eds.), (1992), *Students teaching, teachers learning* (pp. 179–197). Portsmouth NH: Boynton/Cook.

Diamondstone, J., & Merriman, N. (1988, February). *To be heard, to be understood, to be believed: Unpacking unpackables.* Paper presented at the annual Ethnography in Education Forum, University of Pennsylvania Graduate School of Education, Philadelphia.

Dolhinow, P. J., & Bishop, N. (1970). The development of motor skills and social relationships among primates through play. In P. J. Hill (Ed.), *Minnesota Symposium on Child Psychology,* Vol. 4 (pp. 141–148). Minneapolis: University of Minnesota Press.

Donaldson, M. (1978). *Children's minds.* New York: Norton.

Donaldson, M. (n.d.) *Sense and sensibility: Some thoughts on the teaching of literacy.* Unpublished manuscript, University of Reading, Reading and Language Information Center, Reading, UK.

Du Chateau, C. (1989, June). TE ENGLISH. *Metro,* pp. 74–84.

Edelsky, C. (1983). SEGMENTATIONANDPUNC.TU.A.TION: Developmental data from young writers in a bilingual program. *Research in the Teaching of English, 17,* 135–156.

Elkonin, D. B. (1971). Development of speech. In A. V. Zaporozhets & D. B. Elkonin (Eds.), *The psychology of children* (pp. 111–185). Cambridge: M.I.T. Press. (Original work published 1964)

Elkonin, D. B. (1973). USSR. In J. Downing (Ed.), *Comparative reading: Cross-national studies of behavior and processes in reading and writing* (pp. 551–579). New York: Macmillan.

Elliott, J. (1991). *Action research for educational change.* Philadelphia: Open University Press.

Emerson, C. (1986). The outer word and inner speech: Bakhtin, Vygotsky, and the internalization of language. In G. S. Morson (Ed.), *Bakhtin: Essays and dialogues on his work* (pp. 21–40). Chicago: University of Chicago Press.

Emig, J. (1981). Non-magical thinking: Presenting writing developmentally in schools. In C. H. Fredericksen, M. F. Whiteman, & J. F. Dominic (Eds.), *Writing, 2: Process, development and communication.* Hillsdale, NJ: Erlbaum

Erikson, E. H. (1963). *Childhood and society* (2nd ed.). New York: Norton.

Fiering, S. (1981). Unofficial writing. In D. Hymes et al. *Ethnographic monitoring of children's acquisition of reading/language arts skills in and out of the classroom* (pp. H 1–161). [Ed 208 096]. *Final report to the National Institute of Education.* Philadelphia: University of Pennsylvania, Graduate School of Education.

Fish, S. (1980). *Is there a text in this class? The authority of interpretive communities.* Cambridge, MA: Harvard University Press.

Forman, E. A., & Cazden, C. B. (1985). Exploring Vygotskian perspectives in education: The cognitive value of peer interaction. In J. V. Wertsch (Ed.), *Culture, communication and cognition: Vygotskian perspectives* (pp. 323–347). New York: Cambridge University Press.

Forman, E. A., Minick, N., & Stone, C. A. (Eds.) (in press). *Contexts for learning: Sociocultural dynamics in children's development.* New York: Oxford University Press.

Gahagan, D. M., & Gahagan, G. A. (1970). *Talk reform: Explorations in language for infant school children.* Beverly Hills, CA: Sage.

Gaite, A. J. H. (1975). Review approaches to educational psychology—some recent textbooks. *Educational Psychologist, 11,* 197-204.

Gattegno, C. (1985). *The common sense of teaching reading and writing.* New York: Educational Solutions.

Garvey, C. (1990). *Play* (enl. ed.). Cambridge, MA: Harvard University Press.

Gee, J. P. (1989). What is literacy? *Journal of Education, 171,* 18-25.

Giacobbe, M. E. (1982). Who says children can't write the first weeks? In R. D. Walshe (Ed.), *Donald Graves in Australia: Children want to write.* Portsmouth, NH: Heinemann.

Giddens, A. (1979). *Central problems in social theory: Action, structure and contradiction in social analysis.* London: Macmillan.

Gilmore, P. (1983). Spelling "Mississippi": Recontextualizing a literacy-related speech event. *Anthropological and Education Quarterly, 14,* 235-255.

Gleason, J. B., & Weintraub, S. (1976). The acquisition of routines in child language: Trick or treat. *Language in Society, 5,* 129-136.

Gleitman, L. R., Gleitman, H., & Shipley, E. F. (1972). The emergence of the child as grammarian. *Cognition, 1,* 137-164.

Glucksberg, S., Kraus, R., & Higgins, E. T. (1975). The development of referential communication skills. In F. D. Horowitz (Ed.), *Review of child development research* (Vol. 4) (pp. 305-345). Chicago: University of Chicago Press.

Glynn, T. (1982). Antecedent control of behavior in educational contexts. *Educational Psychology, 2*(3-4), 215-229.

Goelman, H., Oberg, A., & Smith, F. (Eds.). (1984). *Awakening to literacy.* Portsmouth, NH: Heinemann.

Goldman-Eisler, F. (1964). In E. H. Lenneberg (Ed.), *New directions in the study of language* (pp. 109-130). Cambridge: M.I.T. Press.

Golick, M. (1986). *Reading, writing, and rummy.* Markham, Ontario: Pembroke.

Golick, M. (1987). *Playing with words.* Markham, Ontario: Pembroke.

Goody, E. N. (1978). *Questions and politeness: strategies in social interaction.* Cambridge, UK: Cambridge University Press.

Gouldner, A. W. (1975-76). Prologue to a theory of revolutionary intellectuals. *Telos, 26,* 3-36.

Grace, P. (1987). *Electric city and other stories.* Auckland: Penguin. (Reprinted in P. Grace, *Selected stories,* Penguin, 1991, pp. 171-172.)

Graves, D. H. (1983). *Writing: Teachers and children at work.* Portsmouth, NH: Heinemann.

Graves, N. B., & Graves, T. D. (1974). *Inclusive versus exclusive behavior in New Zealand school settings: Polynesian-Pakeha contrasts in learning styles* (Research Report No. 5). Auckland, New Zealand: South Pacific Research Institute.

Gray, B. (1985). Helping children to become language learners in the class-room. In M. Christie (Ed.), *Aboriginal perspectives on experience and learning: The role of language in Aboriginal education* (pp. 87-104). Geelong, Australia: Deakin University Press. (Distributed by Oxford University Press)

Greene, M. (1973). *Teacher as stranger: Educational philosophy for the modern age.* Belmont, CA: Wadsworth.

Greif, E. B., & Gleason, J. B. (1980). Hi, thanks, and goodbye: More routine information. *Language in Society, 9,* 159-166.

Griffin, P., & Cole, M. (1987). New technologies, basic skills, and the underside of education: What's to be done? In J. Langer (Ed.), *Language, literacy, and culture: Issues of society and schooling* (pp. 199-231). Norwood, NJ: Ablex.

Gumperz, J. J., & Herasimchuk, E. (1973). In R. W. Shuy (Ed.), *Sociolinguistics: Current trends and prospects* (pp. 99-134). Washington, DC: Georgetown University Press.

Halverson, J. (1991). Olson on literacy. *Language in Society, 20,* 619-640.

Hamilton, B. (1989). Giving effect to The Treaty in schools: A guide for teachers. *National Education, 71*(4), 129-131.

Hardcastle, J. (1985). Classrooms as sites for cultural making. *English in Education, 19,* 8-22.

Hawkins, D. (1978). Critical barriers to science learning. *Outlook, 29,* 3-25.

Heath, S. B. (1982). Questioning at home and at school. In G. Spindler (Ed.), *Doing the ethnography of schooling: Educational anthropology in action* (pp. 102-131). New York: Holt, Rinehart & Winston.

Heath, S. B., & Branscombe, A. (1985). "Intelligent writing" in an audience community: Teacher, students, and researcher. In S. W. Freedman (Ed.), *The acquisition of written language: Response and revision* (pp. 16-34). Norwood, NJ: Ablex.

Heider, E. R., Cazden, C. B., & Brown, R. (1969). Social class differences in the effectiveness and style of children's coding ability. *Project Literacy Reports, 9,* 1-10.

Hess, R. D., Dickson, W. P., Price, G. G., & Leong, D. J. (n.d.). The different functions of parenting and child care: Some mother-teacher comparisons. Standford University, mimeo.

Hill, C. (1972). *The world turned upside down: Radical ideas during the English revolution.* New York: Penguin.

Hoetker, J., & Ahlbrand, W. P., Jr. (1969). The persistence of the recitation. *American Educational Research Journal, 6,* 145-167.

Holdaway, D. (1979). *The foundations of literacy.* Portsmouth, NH: Heinemann.

Holden, M. H., & MacGinitie, W. H. (n.d.). *Children's conceptions of word boundaries in speech and print.* Unpublished manuscript, Teacher's College, Columbia University, New York. [Shortened version in *Journal of Educational Psychology* (1972), 551-557.)

Holm, A., & Holm, W. (1990). Rock Point, a Navajo way to go to school: A valediction. In C. B. Cazden & C. Snow (Eds.), *English plus: Issues in bilingual education. The ANNALS of the American Academy of Political and Social Science, 508,* 170–184.

Holmes, N. (1980). *Kid Stuff* (film). New York City: Central Park East School.

Hull, G., & Rose, M. (1989). Rethinking remediation: Towards a social-cognitive understanding of problematic reading and writing. *Written Communication, 6,* 139–154.

Hymes, D. (1962). The ethnography of speaking. In *Anthropology and Human Behavior* (pp. 13–53). Washington, DC: Anthropological Society of Washington.

Hymes, D. (1966, June). *On communicative competence.* Paper presented at the Research Planning Conference on Language Development in Disadvantaged Children, New York.

Hymes, D. (1973). Toward linguistic competence. In *Texas working papers in sociolinguistics.* Austin: University of Texas.

Hymes, D. (1981). *"In vain I tried to tell you."* Philadelphia: University of Pennsylvania Press.

Hymes, D. (1982). Narrative form as a "grammar" of experience: Native Americans and a glimpse of English. *Journal of Education, 164,* 121–142.

Hymes, D. (1984). *Vers la competence de communication.* Paris. (Page citations are to English ms.)

Hymes, D. (1987). Communicative competence. In H. von U. Ammon, N. Dittmar, & K. J. Mattheier (Eds.), *Sociolinguistics: An international handbook of the science of language and society* (pp. 219–229). New York: de Gruyter.

Ihimaera, W. (1977). Catching up. In *The new net goes fishing* (pp. 43–62). Auckland, New Zealand: Heinemann.

Irwin, K. (1989). Multicultural education: The New Zealand response. *New Zealand Journal of Educational Studies, 24*(1), 3–18.

Isler, I. (1981). *Teacher's modeling of specific verbal behaviors and toddler's social interactions.* Unpublished term paper, Harvard Graduate School of Education, Cambridge, MA.

Ivanic, R. (1990). Critical language awareness in action. In R. Carter (Ed.), *Knowledge about language and the curriculum* (pp. 122–132). London: Hodder & Stoughton.

Jakobson, R. (1960). Concluding statement: Linguistics and poetics. In T. A. Sebeok (Ed.), *Style in language* (pp. 350–377). Cambridge, MA: M.I.T. Press.

Johnson, H. M. (1972). Children in "The Nursery School." New York: Agathon. (Original work published 1928)

Kavanaugh, J. F., & Mattingly, I. G. (Eds.). (1972). *Language by ear and by eye: The relationships between speech and reading.* Cambridge, MA: M.I.T. Press.

Kelman, H. C. (1980). The role of action in attitude change. In *Nebrask a symposium on motivation 1979* (pp. 117-194). Lincoln: University of Nebraska Press.

Kerin, A. (1987). *One to one interaction in junior classes.* Unpublished master's thesis, University of Auckland, (New Zealand).

Kessel, F. S. (Ed.). (1988). *The development of language and language researchers: Essays in honor of Roger Brown.* Hillsdale, NJ: Erlbaum.

Kress, G. (1982). *Learning to write.* London: Routledge and Kegan Paul.

Kuhn, T. S. (1970). *The structure of scientific revolutions* (2nd ed.). Chicago: University of Chicago Press.

Laboratory of Comparative Human Cognition. (1985). *Non-cognitive factors in education* Subcommittee Report to National Research Council Commission on Behavioral Sciences and Social Sciences and Education. San Diego: University of San Diego.

Labov, W. (1969). Some sources of reading problems for Negro speakers on nonstandard English. In J. C. Baratz & R. W. Shuy (Eds.), *Teaching black children to read* (pp. 29-67). Washington, DC: Center for Applied Linguistics.

Labov, W. (1970). The logic of nonstandard English. In F. Williams (Ed.), *Language and poverty: Perspectives on a theme* (pp. 153-189). Chicago: Markham.

Labov, W. (1972). *Language in the inner city: Studies in the black English vernacular.* Philadelphia: University of Pennsylvania Press.

Lakoff, G., & Johnson, M. (1980). *Metaphors we live by.* Chicago: University of Chicago Press.

Lange, D. (1988). *The reform of educational administration in New Zealand.* Wellington, New Zealand: Government Printer.

Langer, J. A. (1984). Musings. *Research in the Teaching of English, 18,* 341-342.

Lemke, J. L. (1990). *Talking science: Language, learning and values.* Norwood, NJ: Ablex.

Leont'ev, A. N. (1981). The problem of activity in psychology. In J. V. Wertsch (Ed.), *The concept of activity in Soviet psychology* (pp. 37-71). Armonk, NY: Sharpe.

Levinson, S. (1983). *Pragmatics.* Cambridge, UK: Cambridge University Press.

Lyons, C. A. (1987). Reading Recovery: An effective intervention program for learning disabled first graders. (ED 284 170)

Lyons, J. (1963). *Structural semantics: An analysis of part of the vocabulary of Plato.* Oxford, UK: Blackwell.

MacLean, M., Bryant, P., & Bradley, L. (1987). Rhymes, nursery rhymes, and reading in early childhood. *Merrill-Palmer Quarterly, 33,* 255-281.

Malcolm, I. (1982). Speech events of the Aboriginal classroom. *International Journal of the Sociology of Language, 36,* 115-134.

Mattick, I. (1967). Description of the children. In E. Pavenstedt (Ed.), *The drifters: Children of disorganized lower-class families* (pp. 53-83). Boston: Little, Brown.

McDermott, R. P. (1977). The ethnography of speaking and reading. In R. Shuy (Ed.), *Linguistic theory: What can it say about reading?* (pp. 153–185). Newark, DE: International Reading Association.

McDermott, R. P. (1978). Pirandello in the classroom: On the possibility of equal educational opportunity in American culture. In M. C. Reynolds (Ed.), *Futures of exceptional children: Emerging structures* (pp. 41–64). Reston, VA: Council for Exceptional Children.

McDermott, R. P. (1988). Inarticulateness. In D. Tannen (Ed.), *Linguistics in context: Connecting observation and understanding* (pp. 37–68). Norwood, NJ: Ablex.

McHoul, A. (1978). The organization of turns at formal talk in the classroom. *Language in Society, 7,* 183–213.

McLane, J. B., & McNamee, G. D. (1990). *Early literacy.* Cambridge, MA: Harvard University Press.

McLeod, A. (1986). Critical literacy: Taking control of our own lives. *Language Arts, 63,* 37–50.

McNeill, D. (1974). How to resolve two paradoxes and escape a dilemma. In K. J. Connolly & J. Bruner (Eds.), *The growth of competence* (pp. 223–226). New York: Academic.

Medcalf, S. (1970). *The vanity of dogmatizing: The three versions by Joseph Glanvill.* Hove, UK: Harvester.

Mehan, H. (1979). *Learning lessons.* Cambridge, MA: Harvard University Press.

Mellix, B. (1989). From outside, in. In A. J. Butrym (Ed.), *Essays on the essay: Redefining the genre* (pp. 43–52). Athens: University of Georgia Press.

Metge, J. (1984). *He tikanga Maori: Learning and teaching.* Wellington, New Zealand: Department of Education, Maori and Pacific Island Division.

Michaels, S. (1981). "Sharing time": Children's narrative styles and differential access to literacy. *Language in Society, 10,* 423–442.

Middleton, S. (1991, April). *Towards a feminist pedagogy for the sociology of women's education in Aotearoa/New Zealand: A life-history approach.* Paper presented at the meeting of the American Educational Research Association, Chicago.

Miller, A. (1984). *Salesman in Beijing.* New York: Viking.

Miller, J. (1986). *Subsequent performances.* Boston: Faber & Faber.

Miller, P. J. (1982). *Amy, Wendy and Beth: Language learning in south Baltimore.* Austin: University of Texas Press.

Mills, C. W. (1959). *The sociological imagination.* New York: Oxford University Press.

Minick, N. (1986). The early history of the Vygotskian school: The relationship between mind and activity. *The Quarterly Newsletter of the Laboratory of Comparative Human Cognition, 8,* 119–125.

Ministry of Education (1989). *Syllabus for schools: English forms 6 and 7* (Draft). Wellington, New Zealand.

Mishler, E. G. (1975). Studies in dialogue and discourse: III. Utterance structure and utterance function in interrogative sequences. Harvard Medical School, mimeo.

Mitchell, L. S. (1948). *Here and now story book.* New York: Dutton.

Miyake, N. (1984). *Logo handbook* (in Japanese). Tokyo: CBS-Sony.

Moll, L. (Ed.) (1990). *Vygotsky and education.* New York: Cambridge University Press.

Morson, G. S. (Ed.) (1986). *Bakhtin: Essays and dialogues on his work.* Chicago: University of Chicago Press.

Moses, R. (1990, November 15). A folly of shallow thinking. *New Zealand Herald.*

Mueller, C. (1973). *The politics of communication: A study in the political sociology of language, socialization and legitimization.* New York: Oxford University Press.

Narogin, M. (1990). *Writing from the fringe: A study of modern Aboriginal literature.* Melbourne, Australia: Hyland House.

National Education: Journal of the New Zealand Educational Institute (1989), *71*(4).

Ninio, A., & Bruner, J. (1978). The achievement and antecedents of labeling. *Journal of Child Language, 5,* 1-15.

Nystrand, M., & Weimett, J. (1991). When is a text explicit? Formalist and dialogical conceptions. *Text, 11*(1), 25-41.

Oakes, J. (1985). *Keeping track.* New Haven, CT: Yale University Press.

Olson, D. R. (1977). From utterance to text: The bias of language in speech and writing. *Harvard Educational Review, 47,* 257-281.

Olson, D. R. (1990). Thinking about interpretation: A reply to Snyder. *Interchange, 21*(3), 56-60.

Otto, W. E., & McMenemy, R. (1966). *Corrective and remedial teaching: Principles and practice.* New York: Houghton Mifflin.

Paley, V. (1979). *White teacher.* Cambridge, MA: Harvard University Press.

Paley, V. (1988, January 24). [Review of *The learning mystique.*] *New York Times Book Review,* p. 8.

Palmer, C. (1947). Cartoon in the classroom. *Hollywood Quarterly, 3*(1), 26-33.

Parker, R. P., & Davis, F. A. (Eds.) (1983). *Developing literacy: young children's use of language.* Newark, DE: International Reading Association.

Penetito, W. T. (1989). *Integration or Maori control: A case for structural diversity* (Discussion paper prepared for the Officials Committee on the Implementation of Education Administrative Reform). Wellington, New Zealand.

Penny, M. et al. (1980). *Research area plan: Reading comprehension.* Reading and Language Studies Division, National Institute of Education, Washington, DC.

Perkins, D. N. (1985, August/September). The fingertip effect: How information-processing technology shapes thinking. *Educational Researcher,* pp. 11-17.

Philips, S. (1974). *The invisible culture: Communication in the classroom and community on the Warm Springs Indian Reservation.* Unpublished doctoral dissertation, University of Pennsylvania, Philadelphia.

Piaget, J., & Inhelder, B. (1969). *The psychology of the child.* New York: Basic Books.

Piestrup, A. M. (1973). *Black dialect interference and accommodation of reading instruction in first grade* (Monographs of the Language-Behavior Research Laboratory, No. 4). Berkeley: University of California.

Pinnell, G. S. (1985, Spring). Helping teachers help children at risk: Insight from the Reading Recovery program. *Peabody Journal of Education,* pp. 70–85.

Polanyi, M. (1964). *Personal knowledge: Towards a post-critical philosophy.* New York: Harper & Row.

Quirk, R., & Greenbaum, S. (1973). *A university grammar of English.* London: Longman.

Rathgen, E. (1991, June). Update on the sixth and seventh form English Syllabus. *English in Aotearoa,* pp. 31–34.

Rathgen, E. (n.d.). A response to Roger Moses: "A folly of shallow thinking" (Unpublished manuscript). Christchurch, New Zealand: Christchurch College of Education.

Ratner, N., & Bruner, J. (1978). Games, social exchange and the acquisition of language. *Journal of Child Language, 5,* 391–401.

Read, C. (1971). Preschool children's knowledge of English phonology. *Harvard Educational Review, 41,* 1–34.

Read, C., & Schreiber, P. (1982). Why short subjects are harder to find than long ones. In E. Wanner & L. R. Gleitman (Eds.), *Language acquisition* (pp. 78–101). Cambridge, UK: Cambridge University Press.

Reid, I. (1986). *The place of genre in learning: Current debates.* Deakin University, Australia. (Also distributed by Oxford University Press.)

Renwick, W. L. (1986a). *Moving targets: Six essays on educational policy.* Wellington, New Zealand: New Zealand Council for Educational Research.

Renwick, W. L. (1986b). *Forty years on in New Zealand education: A new net goes fishing.* Unpublished manuscript, UNESCO Regional Education Office for Asia and the Pacific, Wellington, New Zealand.

Resnick, D. P., & Resnick, L. B. (1977). The nature of literacy: An historical explanation. *Harvard Educational Review, 47,* 370–385.

Resnick, L. B. (1972). Teacher behavior in an informal British infant school. *School Review, 81,* 63–83.

Resnick, L. B. (1979). Theories and prescriptions for early reading instruction. In L. B. Resnick & P. A Weaver (Eds.), *Theory and practice in early reading* (Vol. 2) (pp. 321–338). Hillsdale, NJ: Erlbaum.

Resnick, L. B. (1987). *Education and learning to think.* Washington, DC: National Academy Press.

Reynolds, P. (1972). *Play and human evolution.* Paper presented at the annual meeting of the American Association for the Advancement of Science.

Richardson, E. S. (1964). *In the early world*. New York: Pantheon.

Rodriguez, R. (1981). *Hunger of memory: The education of Richard Rodriguez*. Boston: Godine.

Rommetveit, R. (1985). Language acquisition as increasing linguistic structuring of experience and symbolic behavior control. In J. V. Wertsch (Ed.), *Culture, communication and cognition* (pp. 183-204). New York: Cambridge University Press.

Rose, M. (1989). *Lives on the boundary*. New York: Free Press.

Rosen, C., & Rosen, H. (1973). The language of primary school children. Baltimore: Penguin.

Roskies, D. (1975). Kheyder food—for thought. Unpublished manuscript. New York: YIVO Institute for Jewish Research.

Rothery, J. (1989). Learning about language. In R. Hasan & J. R. Martin (Eds.), *Language development: Learning language, learning culture. Meaning and choice in language: Studies for Michael Halliday* (pp. 199-256). Norwood, NJ: Ablex.

Rowe, M. B. (1986). Wait time: Slowing down may be a way of speeding up! *Journal of Teacher Education, 37,* 43-50.

Scardamalia, M., Bereiter, C., & Goelman, H. (1982). The role of production factors in writing ability. In M. Nystrand (Ed.), *What writers know: The language, process and structure of written discourse* (pp. 173-210). New York: Academic Press.

Scheffler, I. (1968). University scholarship and education of teachers. *The Record-Teachers College, 70,* 1-12.

Schiller, P. H. (1952). Innate constituents of complex responses in primates. *Psychological Review, 59,* 177-191.

Scholes, R. (1982). *Semiotics and interpretation*. New Haven, CT: Yale University Press.

Schoolboys of Barbiana. (1970). *Letter to a teacher* (N. Rossi & T. Cole, Trans). New York: Random House.

Schudson, M. A. (1981). A history of the *Harvard Educational Review*. In J. R. Snarey, T. Epstein, C. Sienkiewicz, & P. Zodhiates (Eds.), *Conflict and continuity: A history of ideas on social equality and human development* (pp. 1-23). (*Harvard Educational Review* Reprint Series No. 15). Cambridge, MA: Harvard Graduate School of Education.

Shuman, A. (1986). *Storytelling rights: The uses of oral and written texts by urban adolescents*. New York: Cambridge University Press.

Scollon, R. (1976). *Conversations with a one year old: A case study of the developmental foundations of syntax*. Honolulu: University Press of Hawaii.

Scollon, R., & Scollon, S. B. K. (1981). *Narrative, literacy and face in interethnic communication*. Norwood, NJ: Ablex.

Shaughnessy, M. P. (1977). *Errors and expectations: A guide for the teacher of basic writing.* New York: Oxford University Press.

Shuy, R. W. (1973). The study of vernacular Black English as a factor in educational change. *Research in the teaching of English,* 297-311.

Shuy, R. (1981). Learning to talk like teachers. *Language Arts, 58,* 168-174.

Simon, J. (1986). *Ideology in the schooling of Maori children* (Delta Research Monograph No. 7). Palmerston North, New Zealand.

Sinclair, J. M., & Coulthard, R. M. (1975). *Toward an analysis of discourse.* New York: Oxford University Press.

Slaughter, M. M. (1982). *Universal languages and scientific taxonomy in the seventeenth century.* Cambridge, UK: Cambridge University Press.

Slobin, D. I. (1982). Universal and particular in the acquisition of language. In E. Wanner & L. R. Gleitman (Eds.), *Language acquisition: The state of the art* (pp. 128-170). Cambridge, UK: Cambridge University Press.

Slobin, D. I. (1985). Crosslinguistic evidence for the language-making capacity. In D. I. Slobin (Ed.), *The crosslinguistic study of language acquisition* (Vol. 2) (pp. 1157-1256). Hillsdale, NJ: Erlbaum.

Smith, F. (1982). *Writing and the writer.* New York: Holt, Rinehart & Winston.

Smith, F. (1983). Reading like a writer. *Language Arts, 60,* 558-567.

Smith, F. (1988). *Joining the literacy club: Further essays into education.* Portsmouth, NH: Heinemann.

Smith, L., & Smith, G. (1989). Which way? *National Education, 71*(4), 125-128.

Snow, C. E. (1977). The development of conversation between mothers and babies. *Journal of Child Language, 4,* 1-22.

Snow, C. E., Arlmann-Rupp, A., Hassing, Y., Jobse, J., Joosten, J., & Vorster, J. (1976). Mother's speech in three social classes. *Journal of Psycholinguistic Research, 5,* 1-20.

Snow, C. E., Dubber, C., & de Blauw, A. (1982). Routines in mother-child interaction. In L. Feagans & D. Farran (Eds.) *The language of children reared in poverty: Implications for evaluation and intervention* (pp. 53-72). New York: Academic.

Spiro, R. J., Bruce, B. C., & Brewer, W. F. (Eds.). (1981). *Theoretical issues in reading comprehension.* Hillsdale, NJ: Erlbaum.

Spolsky, B. (1989). Maori bilingual education and language revitalisation. *Journal of Multilingual and Multicultural Development, 10*(2), 89-106.

Sprat, T. (1966). *The history of the Royal Society of London for the Improving of Natural Knowledge.* St. Louis, MO: Washington University Press. (Original work published 1667)

Stanislavsky, K. (1948). *An actor prepares.* New York: Theater Arts Books.

Stanislavsky, K. (1963). *An actor's handbook.* New York: Theater Arts Books.

Stanovich, K. E. (1986). Matthew effects in reading: Some consequences of individual differences in the acquisition of literacy. *Reading Research Quarterly, 21,* 360–406.

Staton, J., Shuy, R. W., Peyton, J. K., & Reed, L. (1988). *Dialogue journal communication: Classroom, linguistic, social and cognitive views.* Norwood, NJ: Ablex.

Stoel-Gammon, C., & Cabral, L. S. (1977). Learning how to tell it like it is: The development of the reportative function in children's speech. *Papers and Reports of Child Language Development, 13,* 64–71.

Stokes, E. (1985). *Maori research and development: A discussion paper.* Wellington, New Zealand: National Research Advisory Council.

Stubbs, M. (1980). *Language and literacy: The sociolinguistics of reading and writing.* Boston: Routledge and Kegan Paul.

Thomas, D. R. (1975). Cooperation and competition among Polynesian and European children. *Child Development, 46,* 948–953.

Tillich, P. (1966). *On the boundary: An autobiographical sketch.* New York: Scribner's.

Tobin, K. (1986). Effects of teacher wait time on discourse characteristics in mathematics and language arts classes. *American Educational Research Journal, 23,* 191–200.

Tobin, K. (1987). The role of wait time in higher cognitive level learning. *Review of Educational Research, 57,* 89–95.

Todorov, T. (1984). *Mikhail Bakhtin: The dialogical principle.* Minneapolis: University of Minnesota Press.

University of the State of New York (1987, July). *Increasing high school completion rates: A framework for local action* (A working paper of the Board of Regents). Albany: The State Education Department.

Van de Ven, Susan K. (1991). *State adoption policies, publishing practices, and authorship: The production of Middle East chapters in world history textbooks.* Harvard Graduate School of Education: Doctoral dissertation.

Vygotsky, L. S. (1962). *Thought and language.* Cambridge, MA: M.I.T. Press.

Vygotsky, L. S. (1981). The genesis of higher mental functions. In J. V. Wertsch (Ed.), *The concept of activity in Soviet psychology* (pp. 144–188). Armonk, New York: M. E. Sharpe.

Waller, W. (1961). *The sociology of teaching.* New York: Russell & Russell.

Watson, J. (1968). *The double helix.* New York: Norton.

Watson, J. D., & Crick, F. H. C. (1953, April 25). Molecular structure of nucleic acids. *Nature, 171*(4356), pp. 737–738.

Weaver, C. (1982). Welcoming errors as signs of growth. *Language Arts, 59,* 438–444.

Webb, N., & Kenderski, C. M. (1984). Student interaction and learning in small group and whole-class settings. In P. L. Petersen, L. C. Wilkerson, & M. Hallinan (Eds.), *The social context of instruction: Group organization and group processes* (pp. 153–170). Orlando, FL: Academic Press.

Weeks, L. (1991, May 26). Brave new library. *Washington Post Magazine*, pp. 11-17, 27-31.

Weir, R. H. (1962). *Language in the crib*. The Hague: Mouton.

Weiss, C. H. (1977). Survey researchers and minority communities. *Journal of Social Issues, 33*(4), 20-35.

Weizenbaum, J. (1976). *Computer power and human reason: From judgment to calculation*. San Francisco: Freeman.

Wells, G., & Nichols, J. (Eds.) (1985). *Language and learning: An international perspective*. Philadelphia: Falmer.

Wertsch, J. (1985). *Vygotsky and the social formation of mind*. Cambridge, MA: Harvard University Press.

Wertsch, J. (1991). *Voices of the mind*. Cambridge, MA: Harvard University Press.

Williams, P. (1991). *The alchemy of race and rights*. Cambridge, MA: Harvard University Press.

Williams, R. (1961). *The long revolution*. London: Chatto & Windus.

Williams, R. (1977). *Marxism and literature*. New York: Oxford University Press.

Winograd, T., & Flores, F. (1986). *Understanding computers and cognition: A new foundation for design*. Norwood, NJ: Ablex.

Wolf, D. (1988). *Reading reconsidered: Literature and literacy in high school*. New York: College Entrance Examination Board.

Wolfson, N. (1978). A feature of performed narrative: The conversational historical present. *Language in Society, 7*, 215-237.

Wood, D., Bruner, J. S., & Ross, G. (1976). The role of tutoring in problem solving. *Journal of Child Psychology and Psychiatry, 17*, 89-100.

Woolf, V. (1942). Craftsmanship. In *The death of the moth and other essays*. New York: Harcourt Brace.

Zinser, W. (1985). *On writing well* (3rd ed.). New York: Harper & Row.

Subject Index

Assessment
- dynamic assessment, 133
- writing folders in first grade, 84
- running records, 117, 257-59

Attention. *See also* Awareness
- calling attention, as teaching strategy, 12, 117, 166
- cultural development of, 8, 15-16, 133
- focal and subsidiary, 4, 14, 60
- in activity theory, 43
- in beginning reading, 45-48, 65
- inner vs. outer, 233
- in writing, 83, 128-29
- to "The Electric Company" in classrooms, 57-58

Audience
- dual, 189, 200
- sense of, for writers, 149, 152-53, 155

Autonomous texts, 139-41, 153, 155, 206.
- *See also* Explicitness
- analysed in scientific article, 146-48
- as myth, 151
- textbooks as examples of, 167-68
- vs. contexts in the mind, 157-58, 188-89
- vs. intertextuality, 148

Awareness, 63. *See also* Attention
- critical awareness/understanding, 151-52, 154, 161-64, 167
- development of, 63-64
- in Reading Recovery, 130
- levels of, 4, 14
- metalinguistic, 22, 60-67
- of language as transparent vs. opaque, 26-27, 61-62, 66
- of language phrase structure, 90-94
- related to school instruction, 66, 74
- vs. automaticity, 132-33

Basic skills, ix
- taught in context, 3, 83-84, 152
- vs. high literacy goals, 31, 131-2

Bilingual education, 5, 21-22, 41
- code-switching in peer teaching, 31
- writing in, 93
- See also Richmond Road Primary School, Rock Point Community School, Second language learning

Bread Loaf School of English (Vermont), 234-41

Central Park East School (New York City), 48

Coach, teacher as, 167

Communicative competence, 190-91, 193, 196-8
- in peer teaching, 30-32
- in language acquisition, 28-29
- in referential communication, 31
- vs. inarticulateness, 200

Computer
- default option as metaphor, 227
- program for language play, 75
- programs and data bases, 161-63, 168-69

Concentrated encounters, 30-31, 112-13

Concepts, spontaneous vs. scientific, 14, 82, 92

Conferences, See under Writing

Context(s), 42, 165, 192
- as influence on tasks, 164-66
- internal and external, 56-57
- in the mind, x, 11, 42-48, 158-60, 188-89, 288
- in the classroom, 49-56

Critical language awareness. *See* Awareness

307

Author Index

About the Author

Courtney B. Cazden is professor of education at Harvard University. An international specialist in child language and education, she is known professionally as a psychologist, educational anthropologist, and applied linguist. In her teaching and research, she integrates these scholarly perspectives with her experience as a former primary school teacher. She also has taught expository writing to adults returning to college, and often teaches during the summer at the Bread Loaf School of English in Middlebury, Vermont.

Dr. Cazden is a past president of the Council on Anthropology and Education and of the American Association for Applied Linguistics, and is currently president-elect of the National Conference on Research in English. The current focus of her research is on the teaching of writing, both in the U.S. and internationally.